The Church: readings in
theology

THE CHURCH

readings in theology

Hugo Rahner	Hermann Zeller
Romano Guardini	Hans Küng
Josef Jungmann	Stanislas Lyonnet
Karl Rahner	Piet Fransen
Heinrich Schlier	Josef Ratzinger
Josef Neuner	Felix Malmberg

Foreword by Gustave Weigel

Compiled at THE Canisianum, Innsbruck

P. J. Kenedy & Sons   ·   New York

Nihil obstat: GAIL HIGGINS, O.F.M. Cap.
          Censor Librorum
Imprimatur: ✠ FRANCIS CARDINAL SPELLMAN
          Archbishop of New York
New York, September 4, 1963

The nihil obstat and imprimatur are official declarations
that a book or pamphlet is free of doctrinal or moral error.
No implication is contained therein that those who have
granted the nihil obstat and imprimatur agree with the
contents, opinions or statements expressed.

DEDICATED TO

HUGO RAHNER, S.J.

EDITORS

Albert LaPierre   Edward Wetterer
Bernard Verkamp   John Zeitler

TRANSLATORS

Hugo Rahner: C. E. Gavin
Romano Guardini: Albert LaPierre
Josef Jungmann: John Zeitler ("The Holy Church")
Robert Gloudeman ("The Council and Liturgical Reform")
Karl Rahner: Bernard Verkamp ("Leadership in the Church")
Louis Roberts, S.J. ("Christianity and Non-Christian Religions")
Heinrich Schlier: Lawrence E. Brandt
Josef Neuner: Author
Hermann Zeller: John Charlot / Peter Ahr
Hans Küng: L. E. Brandt / A. LaPierre
Stanislas Lyonnet: James Finley
Piet Fransen: Sisters of Regina Laudis Convent, Bethlehem, Connecticut
Josef Ratzinger: John Chang / Justin Clements
Felix Malmberg: Brother Henry Wansbrough, O.S.B.

Contents

| | Editors' Preface | vii |
| GUSTAVE WEIGEL | Foreword | ix |

PART ONE — *ECCLESIA AD INTRA*

HUGO RAHNER	The Church, God's Strength in Human Weakness
ROMANO GUARDINI	The Church, Encounter with Christ
JOSEF JUNGMANN	The Holy Church
KARL RAHNER	Leadership in the Church
HEINRICH SCHLIER	The Pauline Body-Concept

PART TWO — *ECCLESIA AD EXTRA*

JOSEF NEUNER	The Idea of Catholicity— Concept and History
HERMANN ZELLER	The Church—God's Party?
HANS KÜNG	Reunion and Doctrine on Justification
KARL RAHNER	Christianity and Non-Christian Religions
STANISLAS LYONNET	The Redemption of the Universe

PART THREE —
THE CHURCH IN COUNCIL

JOSEF JUNGMANN   The Council and Liturgical Reform

PIET FRANSEN   Theological Implications of
                    Liturgical Discussions at the
                    Council

JOSEF RATZINGER   Free Expression and Obedience
                    in the Church

Appendix

FELIX MALMBERG   The Human Existence of Christ:
                    Basis for a Christocentric
                    Ecclesiology

Editors' Preface

THERE CAN BE no doubt that the Second Vatican Council has increased men's awareness of the Church. The central place given in its program to the schema on the Church represents a challenge of the Spirit to all Christians to grow in their own concept of the Church.

The late Pope John's stirring Epiphany message of 1963 outlined the primary concerns of the Council's work. They center on the renewal of her inner life and structure and the adoption of a positive response to the needs of the modern world.

In our general outline we attempt to follow the late Holy Father's intentions. First we consider some fundamental truths about the Church in her essence and structure and then, secondly, we take up the openness of the Church to the problems and expectations of mankind. Our third section is devoted to reflections centering directly on the Church in Council. Finally, by way of an appendix, a speculative study of the Hypostatic Union is presented as background for an Incarnational understanding of the Church.

Needless to say, the present collection of essays does not claim to be an exhaustive or strictly theological development of themes connected with the Church. Rather we have combined theological speculation with articles which are more properly intended as vehicles for prayerful interior reflection. The present volume is, we hope, the first in a series which will attempt to communicate to an English-speaking audience some of the best of European theological thought in those fields where progress is most evident.

We are especially grateful to our former Rector, Father Josef Jungmann, S.J., and our Regens, Father Franz Braunshofer, S.J., for their kind encouragement and permission to carry out this task. Likewise, we wish to thank Father Hans-Bernhard Meyer, S.J., for his guidance, and the many students here in Innsbruck who have, in one way or another, given us their assistance.

Innsbruck, 1963

Foreword

"OF THE MAKING of many books there is no end . . ." (Eccles. 12:12). The Hebrew wise man certainly underlined a truth when he made that assertion. The plethora of books presents us with a problem. We cannot read all that is written, and yet some books should be assimilated. Which ones shall we go through? Much depends on a man's interests. For an English language reader to whom the Church is highly meaningful, the present volume should prove worth while.

In our time some books are being called non-books. Just how the phrase should be defined is not clear. Yet the term is applied to those publications which are the products not of thought, but of paste. Things are taken haphazardly from here and there to form a grab bag. Our present book is not a non-book. It does not indeed have a single, personal author nor is any one individual responsible for it, other than the publisher. Yet the authorship is one; one *Zeitgeist* fathered the whole endeavor.

Students of theology at the University of Innsbruck live together in a common international residence called the Canisianum. The American contingent now living there wish while abroad to be of service to their own country. They have conceived the project of annually publishing theological lectures and essays concentrating on one theological theme. For this purpose they approach the masters of theology in books and in the flesh. Most of the original matter selected will be German, for the Innsbruckers live and study in a German environment. For American readers the works must be translated, and this the men of the Canisianum are equipped and willing to do.

The first volume to make its appearance deals with the Church of God. In current theology the consideration of the Church is called ecclesiology. It is attracting much attention at present, and one of its most intriguing facets is that ecclesiologists today go about their work in a way differing from that of fifty years ago. The men of 1910 were more abstract; they looked for a tight, logical, skeletal blueprint of the Church considered as an organization. The bones came together but never lived. Scripture as the living Word of God was shelved in favor of a catena of text proofs serving as majors and minors of syllogisms. History was not lovingly pursued in order to see what the Church actually was in time. Some manuals of theology cited history only when it was used by adversaries against theses the manualists were proposing. These theses themselves were logical derivatives from a priori postulates and did not stem from a study of history. Since the wide inner life of the Church was scarcely touched, nothing was said about liturgy, proclamation, prayer, and lay action. Yet these factors were the average Catholic's immediate experience of the Church. The books and the theologians spent most of their time dealing with the ecclesiastical hierarchy, concentrating on it almost exclusively—and legalistically to boot.

From the 1920's on, a change in procedure was gradually introduced. Although many of the older ecclesiologists fought against the theological use of the Mystical Body symbol of Pauline literature, they had to accept it when the encyclical of Pius XII, *Mystici Corporis,* appeared in 1943. The Second World War and its aftermath ushered in the ecumenical dimension of Church life. Ecclesiology became theologically deeper, wider and more relevant to the believer as a living person in a living world.

In the centers of theology ecclesiology was tackled with fresh vigor. But the professors did not produce summaries and manuals. They wrote monographs on ecclesiological themes and numerous articles in theological journals. This very embarrassment of riches dismayed the older theologians, and those Catholics who wanted to find out more about the movement were overwhelmed by the quantity of reading demanded in order to follow the new current intelligently. Even now many a man, theologian or not, asks beseechingly: "What is it all about?"

The main drive in our ecclesiologists is their search for the *living* Church. They do not like logically constructed abstractions that neglect the churning, effervescent existence of the Church. Manual summaries, therefore, are not congenial to contemporary ecclesiology. In addition to this methodological opposition to merely logical synthesis, there is another factor militating against summary presentations of the work done. This is the fact that heuristic work is being industriously pursued. Theologians, with deep searching, are applying the best modern methods to the study of Scripture. The citation of an isolated text is not enough. This work is slow and requires the collaboration of all scriptural ecclesiologists.

Ecumenism is a large field demanding much historical and theological examination. In our day the liturgy is being subjected to the scrutiny of thousands of scholars. We are yet far from the achievement of a thesaurus earmarked by a wide consensus. The theology of the lay state is only beginning to be uncovered. The charismatic heart of hierarchic power is a relatively new topic for dialogue. It is too early to expect a nicely dovetailed outline of all the interests which belong to current ecclesiology.

Because of this situation, the Innsbruck offering to us should be helpful. The men whose thought is reproduced here in English are all stars in the theological sky. The table of contributors sounds like a selection made exclusively from the top echelon of distinguished scholars, an excerpt from a kind of theological Burke's *Peerage*. This selectivity assures us of a valid substance in the essays. These men are theologians, but their work as presented here is written so that non-theologians can understand it. (Perhaps, however, the essay of Felix Malmberg, S.J., is too technical for most non-theologians.)

A unified ecclesiological scheme is not given, though the editors did put some unity of themes into their book. No one man's theory is dominant for the whole tome. Yet it is remarkable how many ideas all of the authors share.

To the question, what is modern ecclesiology? an answer is given by this anthology. The answer is not explicit or formal. The theologians answer the question not by verbal statement, but by engaging in ecclesiology in the way which is proper to our time.

A word of caution must be addressed to the non-theological reader. New things are said about the Church; older expressions are given new formulations. But no new Church is being depicted. A theologian seeks an understanding of the abiding faith, ever old and ever new. Today's ecclesiologist scrutinizes divine revelation for its proclamation about the Church. The revelation is always there and always enlightens the living People of God. The theologian does more than simply repeat it. That is the work of the preacher and bishop. Employing concepts, rational principles, and inference, the theologian works with revelation in order to give it a structure pleasing to the intellect. His product is a superstructure on the Word of God as it is vitally preached by the Church. Such superstructures come and go. They are made to help the man of faith, but they are not the faith itself. A theology which attaches us more closely and more satisfactorily to the Church, has achieved its ambition.

GUSTAVE WEIGEL, S.J.
Professor of Ecclesiology,
Woodstock College

THE CHURCH

readings in theology

PART ONE

Ecclesia ad Intra

The Church, God's Strength in Human Weakness

by HUGO RAHNER

THE CATHOLIC CHURCH is a house full of glory extending far and wide into every land of this our terrestrial world. We sing her praises because we love her. For she is the hidden queen of human history. Even during her infancy her hymn echoed forth in the lands of the Germans: "Blessed be the Church in the strength of the Lord, for through her has God destroyed the power of the evil one. Blessed be she for her faith and her liturgy dominate the earth like kings. And never should hymns to the honor of the Church fall silent on the lips of men." [1] So they sang a thousand years ago in the reign of the Carolingians. So sing we today.

All this would be, however, only "boasting according to the flesh" (2 Cor. 11:18; 1 Cor. 1:29; Eph. 2:9) and not "glory in the cross of Christ" (Gal. 6:14)—all would be counterfeit, falsified, and therefore filled with that furtive disappointment that we so often experience after ecclesiastical ceremonies, if we did not also speak of the incomprehensible mystery of Christian existence which Paul describes with the words: "If I must boast, I will boast of the things that concern my weakness." The Apostle is speaking here of his own wretchedness. However, one of the principal truths of the revelation of the New Testament, as sketched by Paul, is that the strength of God reveals itself in human weakness. The salvific work of the Father, which was contained in love before the very foundation of the universe, reveals itself to men in the Word which became flesh, and will be completed through the instrument of the Church in the power of grace victorious up to its blessed conclusion in weakness. For as Scripture tells us: "The power of God reaches its perfection in weakness" (2 Cor. 12:9). Let us leave these words as they stand. Indeed let us keep the expression in the shocking bluntness of the Greek words: "The *dynamis* of God reaches perfection in *asthenia*."

The force of these words can be vaguely perceived from what technology has to say today about dynamics, and from what medicine has to say about asthenia. So, let us read: the power of God reaches its goal in asthenia, in stunted asthenic growth, in frailty, therefore in all that is in contrast to what is big, strong, healthy, well formed, humane, rational. So, and only so, does the explosive power of the eternal Father's salvific love reveal itself, passionately driving onward to victory in the mystical Christ. "For the foolishness of God is wiser than men, and the weakness of God is stronger than men . . . and the base things of the world and the despised has God chosen . . . lest any flesh should pride itself before him. So that, just as it is written: 'Let him who takes pride, take pride in the Lord' " (1 Cor. 1:25-31).

Let us therefore attempt to see the mystery of the frail and wretched Church against the background of biblical theology and the history of her existence on earth up to now. Then this hour of celebration may become an hour of consolation, and the hard bread that we must break may still satisfy us when the feasts of lofty thoughts are over.

Three fundamental notions should guide us in our quest: The Church of weakness is for us a fact of faith, a test of faith, and a joy in faith.

I. The holy Church of God in her role as the reproduction of the body of Our Lord here below on earth is always both strength and weakness, glory and wretchedness. She is lady and handmaid, the queen enthroned and the poor pilgrimess. This is a fact of faith. However, the people in the Church have always attempted to look upon the representation here below of the glory, the dominion, and the victory already assured in Christ, as the true essence of the Church—to such an extent that they note and regret her weakness and stupidity as an unavoidable toll exacted by the laws of her pilgrimage through history. This is a correct view. The glory of the Church must exist already here on earth; the weakness of the Church must be tolerated, cured, even fought. However, such a coexistence, the simple existence side by side of *dynamis* and *asthenia*, cannot be the final answer to the questions raised by the weakness of the Church.

Paul goes further, venturing the bold words: "When I am weak, then I am strong" (2 Cor. 12:10). Weakness itself was his strength. This is true of the Church as a whole. Exactly because she is weak, precisely in her *asthenia*, it should be apparent that we may take pride in the course of her existence on earth always and only in the *dynamis* of God.

He who does not realize this about the Church has not understood the essence of faith nor the mystery of the cross from which the Church was born. We understand the Church only under the aspect of the fact of salvation, surpassing all earthly rational measures: The divine Word died the disgraceful human death of the cross so that a murder-victim could say, "I have overcome the world" (John 16:33).

Further, he left behind him an explanation which summarizes the insoluble tension of his life between weakness and strength, between death and glory. "And I, if I be lifted up from the earth, will draw all things to myself" (John 12:32). And, "When you have lifted up the Son of man, then you will know that I am he" (John 8:28). Lifted up from the earth—this does not mean that he will be raised in the splendor of his glory with the Father, but rather that he will be lifted up on the beam of the cross, hanged as the image of the snake Moses raised in the desert. Thus Our Lord tells us himself (John 3:14); and so that we will not weaken the incomprehensible hardness of this saying the Apostle adds: "By this he indicated the sort of death he would die" (John 12:33). There he hangs, the Son of man, the snake, he who was spat out by his people, dying between heaven and earth. He is the hanged man in the desert of world history, who draws all men up to him. The hanged and the elevated. Both are one and the same. The death of the cross is glorification, weakness is power.

The Church must now follow him in this fate, for she is his body. Not only is she the symbol of victory and coming glory raised up among the nations; she is also hanged upon the gallows of her history on earth. In the midst of serpents and deserts, only the man who ventures with unflinching glance to look believingly upon the Church, and to confess her weaknesses, will find salvation and home. Christ has driven the Church, his people of God, out of the Egypt of human fleshpots. The promised land is assured her, but the path she must roam passes through the desolate land of her breakdowns in world history, through the crumbling of the late Roman empire, through the power struggles of the Middle Ages, to the failures of her modern missionary history, into the tragedies of Russia and China, to the rotting away of our culture, and into the explosive atomic future which we do not yet know. Everywhere on her path lie the ruins of her rusted weapons, stand the crumbling tombs of her great men who have become so small in death.

She has always had a Moses and an Aaron, but always also a grumbling people, always defection, complaints and denial. Often she has made compromises too early with a temporary situation, often she has understood the signs of the time too late. Always there have been small, narrow-minded, sinful men at work within her, leading but hindering, planning but foolishly. The Church is the tired, dusty pilgrimess through the desert.

This is, however, but one side of the mystery of her weakness. If we make our confession to her in faith, then we also think upon the other mystery of her insignificance. Her true greatness, the eternal, glorious holiness of this queen of the history of souls, prefers to envelop itself in weakness. It is hidden in the reliquaries of the hearts of unimportant people, for whom the Father alone has revealed the inward beauty of the kingdom. This Church lives among the unschooled, the little nuns, the silent sick; it lives in the concentration camps and prisons, in the misery of our brothers in the East.

So this is the Church of him who in her midst is hung, and in this Church will draw all men up to himself. "Come to me, you weary of soul and burdened," he says. This is the Church of Peter the fisherman who was crazily crucified upside down. This is the Church of our adventurous faith. Christian antiquity sang about the Church in a Preface for the feasts of Sts. Peter and Paul: "Therefore it should be proclaimed that it depends not upon the resources of man but on the gifts of God. It should be comprehended how all the apparent greatness of this world is but foolishness without you, O God. It should be taught how all folly will be lifted up through you, for so has your regal Will ordained." [2]

II. This talk of the asthenia of the Church is hard. Who can listen to it? However, we must formulate it in still harder terms. The Church of weakness is not only a fact of faith, but also a test of faith. It is true that the Church is queen even here below, and when our eyes are not stupid and blind we see in hours of grace the golden splendor of her nature shining through the rents in her miserable pilgrim's mantle. However, perhaps, precisely because of the consolation of such hours, we make our faith in the Church too easy and too cheap. We listen with joy to the immortal words of the First Vatican Council: "The Church is in herself an irrefutable testimony to her divine mission. By the strength of her outstanding holiness and her inexhaustible fertility of every virtue she is the sign raised up among the peoples that invites all those who do not yet believe." [3] This is true. This is eternal truth.

But when someone comes from outside and says: "Show me the *Una Sancta*, here and now, in your family, in your city, in Germany, in Rome, in South America, on the surface of the globe," let us be honest in our answer. Let us today put beside the sublime words of the Council another word, one which Augustine put into the mouth of the Church—Augustine, the passionate lover of the *Mater Catholica:* "Those who were already standing near me ready to believe were frightened away by the life of wicked and false Christians. How many, my brothers, do you think would wish fervently to be Christians, but would be insulted by their terrible morals." [4] "O yes, one praises the Church of God! Great men, those Christians, great is the *Catholica!* How they love one another! How they suffer for one another! Someone hears this and does not know that no mention is made of bad Christians. He comes, drawn on by this praise, and is repelled by the false Christians. Then come the others and say: Who are these Christians? What sort of people are these? Misers and swindlers! Are they not the same Christians who throng the theater and the circus who fill the Church on feast days?" [5]

These words must plunge like a sword into the bleeding heart of our conscience. Do not we ourselves become confused and weary with the Church because her earthly image is so miserable? More honestly: Is it not we miserable Sunday Catholics with the guarantee of our baptismal certificates, with our occasional piety, shepherds who have become well off, who distort and obscure the picture of the *Catholica?* Because we do, the Church is for many who stand outside a test of faith, perhaps often an obstacle to faith; and for many who are inside, the Church is a cheap excuse for our secretly doing precisely those things which we criticize so sharply in the Church. Only one thing can console us here, and it is the sweet mystery of the grace of him who was elevated, who draws all men to himself: that precisely this weakness will be the deepest source of faith for him who, in a moment of beatific enlightenment, has recognized the pilgrim Church as the hidden queen. This, however, is a consolation, not an excuse.

No, we must in this hour dare to test the genuineness of our belief with a steady gaze upon the Church, hung upon the wood of shame, in the desert of world history. We must learn to endure the Church. Our relationship to the Church is often that of children who have become knowledgeable and who discover the weaknesses of their parents. For this we do not need the *Keys of Peter*, with which the French writer Peyrefitte has recently attempted to open the dusty chambers of the Church. We need no immature criticism from those persons who have never outgrown their religious puberty. We ourselves know and are sad. However, if our naïve and childish faith is to become mature this burden must be borne.

The Church, as she actually lives, suffers, and in many of her parts rots, is and remains also for us a test of faith—a trying, discouraging, a burning anxiety. She can become a danger to faith, because we all are tempted to wish that she would become more spiritual, more attractive, more impressive, more overwhelming— and then we begin again, even today, to play the ancient ghost game of a Church of pure spirit, the game which drags on through all the centuries, from Montanus to Jansen and into the chambers of our hearts. This is the diabolical temptation to bring about the kingdom of God here on earth, to become enthusiastic only over a glorious Messiah, and thus to veil willful denial with the praise of a Church of intellectuals, of a Church of success in the interior life, of statistically provable progress, of a Church able to compete with other religious organizations. No, you who are out-side the Church, and you who are inside, no, seek not here the Church of him who still hangs on the gallows of shame today, and for the sole purpose of drawing all men to himself!

Only in the divine adventure of a Church of deniers, of the mediocre, of those delivered up to history and to their own miser-able hearts, can one discover what faith means, the darkness of faith, the torture of faith—the force of faith. We challenge all the spiritualists of the pure spirit and all realists of mere statistics, with the challenge that Tertullian in the antiquity of the Church hurled in the face of the Gnostics who were disturbed by the God in human form, born of woman, and hanged on the gallows of the cross: "For what reason do you destroy this necessary disgrace of our faith? What was unworthy of God is that which helps me. I find my salvation when I am not ashamed of my Lord. Cruci-fied was the Son of God: I am not ashamed of this, precisely be-cause it is dishonorable!" [6]

Let us in this hour of celebration cry out of the depths of our hearts: No, you poor *Catholica*, we are not ashamed of your weaknesses. We confess this weakness in the words of Pius XII: "We give you our energetic love, even in the appearance of your mortal flesh, in your weak human existence, even when your members do not correspond to the position they should hold in your holy mystical body." [7] Holy Church, you are the necessary shame of our faith. Mine will be salvation, and the whole world's will be salvation, so long as we are not ashamed of you.

III. Only now do the bitter words concerning the asthenia of the Church become sweet upon our lips again. For precisely in this weakness the Church of the crucified is the very essence of God's force of grace, the sacramentally humble symbol of the irresistibly victorious love of the Father of Our Lord Jesus Christ. This weak Church is the joy of our faith. Not only despite her weakness, but rather because she is weak. This is no theological dialectic that would release us from the responsibility of constantly attempting anew to perfect the power of the Church's witness, her holiness, even her glory that can be dramatized here on earth. However, our faith in the Church remains pure, resilient, filled with unshatterable joy in the victory of Our Lord, only if we perceive that the power and dominion of God, which is totally different in nature from anything else in our experience, chooses to show itself most often in earthly impotence and despicability—as long as we in the midst of the Church celebrate the death of Our Lord, until Christ returns as the Messiah of glory. Christ, once and for all, died beyond the barricades of human comprehensibility, and therefore the Church must bear his disgrace (Heb. 13:13).

This disgrace can already be for us the source of the most profound joy, but it is possible for us to have a presentiment of this fact only through grace. We shall first grasp this fact when, at the end of all earthly days, the hymn of exultation bursts forth from all peoples: "High above us shines the symbol of the cross sublime." At that moment when Christ will separate the spirits of world history with the words: "He who is ashamed of me and my words in this adulterous and sinful generation, of him will the Son of man also be ashamed when he comes with the holy angels in the glory of the Father" (Mark 8:38; Luke 9:26).

Alas, this is so difficult for us here below to comprehend. Our eyes are veiled, and our hearts are still as dull as those of the journeying disciples of Emmaus. They recognized the Lord only after the breaking of bread. Then, however, their hearts burned. It is the same with us. *Praestet fides supplementum sensuum defectui.* May faith assist the failure of the senses. This also holds true for the mystery of the Church. It is the same for her as it was for Our Lord: In sacrifice has he conquered, in the breaking of bread he inflames joy, in the fact that he was killed has he driven out the prince of this world. Therefore, we recognize him and his Church only in the breaking of bread, in the breaking of our believing hearts.

And from his broken Church we discover with the quiet delight of tested, suffered, disappointed and wise faith: Here is the Lord. Here is his Church, the holy, the catholic. Then our hearts also burn. Then we know: She is still on the desert path, but this leads into the promised land. She is still on the way of the cross to death's place of skulls, but only so will the Pasch come, and this means the transition to the eternal.

"Therefore, my brothers, let us sing the hymn of the death of the Church," once cried Cyril of Alexandria, "of her death that leads us home to the fountainhead of life, of the life which there is holy and in Jesus Christ. When you hear the word 'Church,' know that one is speaking to you about the holy community of the faithful. This Church is dying: But her death leads us into another life, from weakness into strength, from misery into glory, from decay into permanence, from the limits of time into the divinely immutable life." [8]

Therefore, let us love the Church of weakness. We know that in her, and therefore in us, the day of the coming world has begun and the star of the morning already stands over our darkened hearts. We are not ashamed of her because there are so many shameful things about her. We take it for one of the most overwhelming proofs of her unity and holiness that she has always had to suffer from the disdain of human refinement, which men have continually made use of to dismiss the Catholic things, or else to analyze them with shameless interest. We tremble for her when we see her excessively honored by the world. Rather we prefer to carry with her her shame outside the walls of the city, and wherever in the world it is a disgrace or a ridiculously old-fashioned thing to be a Catholic, there we know in the pure joy of our faith: the kingdom is near.

We love the Church of weakness, because she can prove only in her wretchedness the firmly grounded strength of our love for Christ. She still has stains and rents. But Christ "draws her up to him and fills her tenderly with warm life," as the Apostle says (Eph. 5:29). Therefore our love for the Church is not smallish, not pharisaical; it does not see the splinter in the eye nor count the wrinkles in the mother's face. That which is written in the Canticle of Charity is true also for the joyous love of the Church: She "bears all things, believes all things, hopes all things, endures all things" (1 Cor. 13:7).

There is again a saying of Pius XII, which we wish to inscribe in our hearts: "Probably there is much in the Church that betrays the weaknesses of our human nature. Her divine founder, however, endures these weaknesses. He endures them even in the higher members of his mystical body, for this reason, so that in this way the strength of the virtuousness of the flock and the shepherds will be tested, and that the merits of faith should grow in each of them. Christ would wish to know that even sinners are not shut out of this community. Therefore, the fact that many members suffer from spiritual infirmity is no reason for us to lessen our love for the Church, rather it is an occasion for us to feel deeper sympathy with her members." [9]

Thus it is with the weaknesses of the Church, just as it is with the *felix culpa,* the happy guilt without which we would not possess the superabundance of grace of such a saviour, just as with the disgraceful death of the crucified, without which we would have no life. Without weakness, the sinful wretchedness of the Church, there would not exist here below that love which in joy and sorrow, anger and zeal, patience and silence, fulfills the words of the Apostle: We must cherish the Church as Christ does. We must fill her with warm love. We must console her and embrace her. We must intercede for her with the jealousy of God. In a word, we must love her in her totality and without conditions. And behold, precisely in this love, the transformation of the Church from weakness to power, from crippled ugliness to immortal beauty, is taking place, silently and irresistibly until the end of time. Where this love is alive the Church grows up to the healthy maturity of the Lord. Already here below she will become the victorious, the eternal, the living Church. This is the mystery of the weak Church.

So, and only so, is the Church for us a fact of faith, a test of faith, and a joy in faith. Look about in this world—everywhere there is desert, aimless wandering, thirst that cannot be quenched, strangers who no longer know home. But in this desert you see a thornbush burst into flames, and you hear the divine words: "The place where you stand is holy ground" (Exod. 3:5). This is a type, a model of the holy Church. She is a wretched, prickly shrub in the desert, but even now she bursts into flames with heavenly fire. Here we stand: we believe in this Church of weak brambles and tremendous fire. She is our trial of faith and our love's joy.

This Church, says St. Ambrose, is "the holy land whereon we firmly stand. Where the Church is, there should be the fixed dwelling place of your heart. In the Church should rest the foundations of your soul. For so speaks Our Lord: In this Church I appear to you as once I appeared in a thornbush. You are the thornbush, I am the fire. I am the fire in the thornbush in your flesh. I am fire to illuminate you, to burn away the thorns of your sinfulness, to give you the favor of my grace." [10]

This is the Church of our weakness and our strength. Flames in the desert of our life, home on our wandering way, promised land already here before our happy arrival. A house full of glory, with the bulwark of strong towers—but all this, only when we in the midst of our need keep our gaze upon the day on which the symbol of the Lord appears gloriously in heaven. And therefore, let us sing now, unflinching and full of joy: "High above us shines the symbol of the cross sublime."

NOTES

[1] Hrabanus Maurus, *Commentary on the Book of Judith*, 13 (PL 109, 576).

[2] *Sacramentarium Leonianum* (Muratori ɪ, 333; PL 55, 51 BC). H. Rahner, *Mater Ecclesia, Lobpreis der Kirche aus dem ersten Jahrtausend christlicher Literatur* (Einsiedeln-Köln, 1944), p. 91.

[3] Denziger, 1794.

[4] *Enarrationes in Ps.* 30, Sermo 2, 6 (PL 36, 243).

[5] *Enarrationes in Ps.* 99, 11 (PL 37, 1278).

[6] *De carne Christi*, 5, 34 (Corpus Christianorum ɪɪ, 881).

[7] *Mystici Corporis* (Acta Ap. Sedis 35 [1943], 238).

[8] *Glaphyrorum in Genesim 6 and 4* (PG 69, 329 C 224 D).

[9] *Mystici Corporis* (Acta Ap. Sedis 35 [1943], 225.

[10] *Epistola* 63, 41, 42 (PL 16, 1200 CD). H. Rahner, *Mater Ecclesia* (Einsiedeln-Köln, 1944), p. 64.

The Church, Encounter with Christ

by ROMANO GUARDINI

I. OBVIOUSLY, A FRANK STATEMENT of Catholic impressions of present-day Protestantism is no simple task. For, try as one may, interdenominational exchanges on religious matters usually founder in controversy and partiality—a state of affairs beneficial to no one. Nonetheless, invited to do so, I felt obliged to attempt a Catholic appraisal of Protestantism, especially since over the years I have enjoyed close contact with Protestants and their work.

Thus I scanned more than fifty years of theoretical study and personal exchange, and the fact of Protestantism's vital relationship to Sacred Scripture was once again emphatically clear to me. Yet, equally clear was the fact that Protestantism's relationship to "Church" was very indefinite. As a matter of fact, as often as I have heard the word Church employed in a Protestant context, I have never been able to determine its precise connotation.

At the turn of the century (I recall the period well, since I was a student at the time), Protestants refrained whenever possible from all allusion to the concept of Church. Change occurred, however, particularly during the years of the struggle against National Socialism. The Protestant concept of Church took on new meaning. It became the battle cry against a totalitarian state which had appropriated to itself the title of sole society among men. Protestants objected by an assertion of the Church's right to exist. And there I found a living communal spirit. However, when considered, Protestantism's manifold groups and diversity in dogma raised the question: What precisely is meant by "Church"? So I formed the conclusion that the Protestant had no fundamental "Church" relationship.

Naturally, such an assumption may be unjust, but rather than spend the time debating the point, I prefer to explain what the Church means to me, how my relationship to her was formed, and the role of the Church in my own religious life.

But rest assured that you are dealing with a theologian who is accustomed to examine matters objectively through critical reflection. My exposition will not be merely an account of personal experiences. Nor will it be purely theoretical. In the end it should be evident why the Protestant concept of Church has always struck me as elusive and inadequate.

Before we continue, let me add that the following is in no way intended as a general, or even Catholic, theory for pointing out the necessary way to faith. Rather it applies to a particular case only—mine. But since I wish to avoid a mere biography, I have ordered the various phases and processes within their fundamental, ultimately spiritual context.

II. It is natural for a young man about to embrace the academic life to examine his stand in regard to faith (especially if he wishes to major in a field other than theology, as in my own case). He passes through various phases, questioning whether he can still believe those truths imbibed at home, at school, and in the parish: in a word, whether in the light of truth he may, or even should, believe, and to what extent his faith will shape his existence and give direction to his life and work.

At first he may feel, for the sake of honesty, that he must discard faith. Yet the desire for some religious affiliation almost always revives, and he finds himself once again grappling with Christian truths.

In this matter, a passage from the New Testament had always struck me with such immediacy that it offered direction and guidance. "He who finds his life" (that is, who wishes to save it) "will lose it, and he who loses his life for my sake, will find it" (Matt. 10:39). This text primarily refers to martyrdom, yet as occurs when such a passage touches the depths of one's being, it acquired for me a particular urgency. The Greek word *psyche* has two meanings. And when it is taken in the sense of "soul," rather than "life," the passage reads: "He who finds his soul will lose it, and he who loses his soul for my sake will find it."

This passage threw into relief for me that fundamental mystery of spiritual life: To find his true self, man must abandon himself, his immediate ego; to possess himself he must surrender himself. The cardinal question then was: "Abandonment and surrender to whom?" Who could call upon me and lay claim to my soul in such a way that this would actually occur? Who was sufficiently powerful to insure that one's self-surrender would be genuine and not mere delusion?

The answer rang out: God alone! Yet who was God? How was one to arrive at a correct understanding of him? And one must remember that at the time, prior to World War I, the intellectual factor in such problems played a far greater role than it does today, which in my opinion was not wholly disadvantageous for clarity and responsibility of faith.

At this time I was totally taken up with the problem of the reasoning process of the mind: the problem, that is, as to what degree the specific modes of knowing and the results of the effort to know were conditioned by psychological factors. This problem, once linked with the religious question, brought to the fore a most disturbing fact: If a man, in expounding on God, relied upon subjective criteria and experience, his conception of God showed a suspicious similarity to his own personality. Consequently, one man would find God to be the First Efficient Cause;

another, Pure Being or the Idea of the Good, and yet others, the
World Foundation, the Mystery of Life, the Racial Soul, the
Guiding Spirit of history, etc. Each man would stress the one
facet of the divine reality which best conformed to his own temperament, thereby losing sight of the living whole. At times the
similarity would be so great that the God proclaimed by the various parties was an exact idealization of their own nature, indeed
to such an extent that from a man's concept of the divine, one
could trace his temperament.

Therefore the way to truth was not that of "seeking after God"
through personal experience and subjective reasoning, as people
maintained. For if the inquirer thus conceived of God and bound
himself to such a God, then he actually remained imprisoned
within himself, clung to himself in a way far more restricting
and subtle than if he openly declared: "I am not in the least
interested in any God. I am sufficient in myself."

Who, then, in truth was God? How was one to think of him
in order to reach a true conception, in order to be able to come
to him and bind oneself to him and in him find freedom?

Clearly, there was something missing here. It was the ultimate
instance which guaranteed that when you said "God" you were
not in reality saying "me." Yet where was such finality to be
found?

In answer to this question arose the figure of Jesus Christ. The
more one considered the matter, the more convincing it became
that Christ stood justified in his claim to be the messenger of the
living God. His was a proximity to God that invested him with
a pre-eminent understanding of the divine will, a unity so intimate that his words were the words of God.

The fundamental Christian truth concerning the mediator and
saviour unfolded before me. It became evident why for Paul and
John "to speak about God" was "to speak about God out of the
power of Christ." The meaning of the words spoken by Christ,

according to St. John, were now clear: "I am the truth . . ."
(John 14:6).

In relation to that fundamental experience of religious life, of
which we spoke earlier, the above meant: The God who was
capable of laying claim to the soul and regenerating it, was guaranteed, not through subjective experience and autonomous
reason, but only when this God himself, in his reality and sovereignty, confronted one in the word and being of Jesus Christ,
as Christ himself said: ". . . and no one knows who the Father
is, except the Son, and him to whom the Son chooses to reveal
him" (Luke 10:22). And with Johannine concreteness: "He who
sees me sees also the Father" (John 14:9).

Christ was not only he who alone guaranteed recognition of
the true God, but also he through whom living progression
toward God must pass if it was to reach its end, as he himself
affirmed with such precision: "I am the way . . . No one comes
to the Father but through me" (John 14:6). The inference was
plain. There was no such thing as a freely accessible God. God,
the Imperceptible, who ". . . dwells in light inaccessible" (1
Tim. 6:16), stood in clear contradiction to the claim of autonomous search, experience and conception of God. Man reached
God only through the imitation of Christ, who revealed the way
and set the standard.

My pursuit was not yet at an end. My study involved the
Leben-Jesu Forschung, and my investigation the various theories
surrounding Jesus. The number of these was astounding. And
one could hardly contend that the differences separating them
were insignificant—comparable, say, to the variations between a
mosaic portrait of Christ and a Gothic portrait. They were not
differences stemming only from varying historical presuppositions, thus preserving the essential fact concerning Christ: He
was the living Son of God become man. Rather, these differences
struck at his very essence.

That central truth which Paul and John had proclaimed with such urgency was continually lost sight of: the eternal Son of God, who in time became man, remains man, sitting at the right hand of the Father. At times Christ was portrayed as mere man, at times as myth. He was a sage like Socrates or a Greek mystic, a philanthropist or a social reformer; a religious luminary or a spiritual revolutionary; one from the ranks of the prophets; a psychopath, schizophrene, megalomaniac—the list rattled on. But once again it was disturbingly clear that these individual theories concerning Christ were tailored to the personalities of their authors, at times to such a degree that they were simply idealized self-portraits of their proponents.

In the face of such conceptions of Christ and their origin, how could one rely upon the words of Our Lord: "No one knows who the Father is except the Son" and "No one comes to the Father but through me"? In other words, where was that ultimate instance which guaranteed the true Christ?

III. At this stage of the experience of which I speak the Church entered the picture. Jesus was well aware that he and his message alone were of importance. Naturally, he desired that the message be passed on to "all nations . . . until the consummation of the world" (Matt. 28:19–20); yet never once did he express the desire that this transmission take place in book form. It is true that he often alluded to the written word of God, but always in reference to the Old Testament. The medium which Christ destined for the proclamation of his message, however, was living testimony, and indeed through those whom he selected (Acts 1:2). How they should fulfill this testimony was made clear to them: through spoken and written word, commemorative action, deeds of witness and exemplary life. In short, through a living continuity graced with the fullness of the pentecostal Spirit and persisting until the end of time.

This living continuity is the Church. Christ guarantees the truth concerning the living Father, but it is for the Church to guarantee the image of Christ, or rather the Holy Spirit speaking within the Church, so that Our Lord might say of her, "He who hears you, hears me; he who rejects you, rejects me; and he who rejects me, rejects him who sent me" (Luke 10:16). When the Church speaks, Christ speaks, and Christ's words are the Father's.

As for Sacred Scripture, it is a vital element of the Church, stemming from the Church, brought to completion in the course of the first century and collected into an official canon by the Church at the turn of the century. From this Church of Christ there proceeds the demand, ever renewed, that the individual surrender his own soul if he wishes to possess it in newness and truth. And the Church's demand is a command dictated by a reality, divorced from her subjects' likes or dislikes, a command which remains oblivious of the subjects' autonomous will. If one of her subjects misinterprets Christ's message, the Church corrects him. If he fashions himself a Christ along lines of his own, she upholds the proper portrait. If he erases from Christ's personality all that which irks his own, she accents the missing characteristics.

In this continual confrontation with the concrete and contemporaneous Church, the figure of Christ rises ever anew to its proper sovereignty and reveals the Father as he truly is.

IV. In a word, then—to return to the experience about which I have been speaking—the step which truly led me in the freedom of faith to the whole truth concerning Jesus Christ and, in turn, through Christ to the sovereignty of the living God was faith in the fact that Jesus Christ spoke through the Church, so that "he who hears you, hears me" (Luke 10:16).

Such an assertion seemed more than out of place at a time when allegiance to the Church was equated with forfeiture of that freedom promised in the gospels. Yet, for more than fifty years I have held this concept of the Church and for more than thirty-five of these, as a full-fledged professor, I have been coping with theological problems and never once have I had occasion to doubt the role of the Church as true educator in Christian freedom. Of course, by freedom I do not mean the psychological possibility that allows one to select the attractive, nor the philosophical autonomy of judging the right by subjective criteria. The freedom to which I allude is that freedom which liberates the prospective believer from the bonds of his psychological, sociological and historical conditioning, and lays bare to him the reality of the one God, the God who reveals himself in Jesus Christ.

Conversion to the Church is a step taken out of genuine faith, and living in the Church is a genuine relationship of faith. They entail the triumph and danger of faith—a fact which now must be more fully developed.

V. Strangely enough, I received an understanding of the true concept of Church from an author whose name one would hardly expect to hear in this connection. I refer to the renowned Protestant philosopher, Sören Kierkegaard.

Kierkegaard wrote an extraordinary book entitled *Philosophical Fragments* and a commentary to it entitled *Concluding Unscientific Postscript.* The work proposes what at first seems a most extraordinary thesis: Only the contemporary of Christ could become a Christian in the true sense of the word (the term "contemporary" is used not in the sense of a psychological synchronization with Christ's life but rather in its literal sense of historical coexistence with Jesus Christ). For only then, maintains Kierkegaard, did the decision of faith entail that frightening risk which goes hand in hand with such a step if it is to be genuine. In short, only that man could truly become a Christian who lived during the lifetime of Christ and enjoyed personal contact with him.

According to Kierkegaard, an encounter offering such immediate relationship to Christ might well have come about in the following manner: an ordinary enough fellow came along and on some pretext or other engaged himself in conversation, during the course of which he stated that he was the Son of God and went so far as to demand of his listeners belief in the fact as the condition of their salvation. Such an assertion, of course, would not only have sounded preposterous, but it would have aroused indignation if not out-and-out laughter. "You? You, who were born yesterday and will die tomorrow, who grew up within these city walls of ours, whose clothes were made in the shop across the way, and who eats bread baked in the home next door, you are the Son of God?" (cf. John 8:57).

Yet, the ironic thing (Kierkegaard labels such a situation with its exacting illogicality the "supreme paradox") is that there would have been truth to the claim, for this man actually was the Son of God. However, it is a fact obvious only in the light of eternity. If so, the objection might well be made, how could the other party, contemporary that he was (that is, one confronted by a situation shrouded with uncertainty), have been expected to determine for certain whether the speaker actually was what he contended to be? And the objection is all the more pertinent when we take into consideration that the listener must arrive at that particular type of certainty upon which salvation hangs, namely faith. A momentous decision, indeed. If what this man claimed, was true and the hearer lent him credence, then, through him he would discover the God of salvation. However, if the man in question had been but human (perhaps extraordinarily blessed with this or that gift or laboring under delusions of religious glory), and the hearer accepted him, then he would not only have erred but would have fallen victim to the ultimate of nonsense. He would have, as Kierkegaard expressed it, made himself look absolutely ridiculous, and in the face of eternal truth at that.

Of course, in this instance, one could list a dozen reasons why the hearer should have gambled the risk of faith: astounding wisdom sprang from the words of this Jesus of Nazareth, he performed startling deeds, his entire being bespoke a divine essence, and from him radiated a presence both mysterious and perceptible.

Still, one may rightfully question whether these "proofs" were of a quality to warrant the risk involved in faith in Jesus Christ, an immense step, though capable of summation in the single sentence, "I believe that you are the Son of God and in you I believe in the Father." The proofs offered, replies Kierkegaard, did not justify belief. For no matter how astounding a thing strikes one as being, that thing still has its content in the realm of the human; it remains framed in space and time, therefore, finite and debatable. As a result, every argument urging one toward assent is balanced by one as weighty warranting a refusal, a "No." For everything in the realm of human experience always remains out of proportion to the all-important Absolute.

Thus the step into faith at all times remains something frightful, the risk of the Absolute Paradox: the decision to expect the eternal Absolute on the basis of the present-finite, and confidence that this decision forges a unity with the inscrutable will of God, a unity which will lead the believer to salvation. In all probability he will indignantly reject this unreasonable demand—by it he will be enraged, even scandalized. To break through at this point —that, Kierkegaard says, is faith.

However, what of Christ's non-contemporaries, the men who come years, centuries after his life? What of those who come after countless have taken the step of conversion, pouring out their very blood in witness to the fact that salvation springs from

Christ; after knowledgeable, astute, judicious men have contemplated and commentated on Jesus Christ, demonstrating the magnitude of his doctrine? At such a point in history, a positive response to Christ could hardly be termed faith, because such response lacks the acid test of coexistence with Christ.

Then would faith be impossible to the late-comer? Not at all, answered Kierkegaard, but the late-comer must project himself out of his present situation. To do so, he must sweep away the preconceptions and prejudices of the later day and age and revert to the days of Our Lord. The task is formidable, and Kierkegaard does not shy from referring to it in the harshest possible terms, terms well calculated to break the back of all novice enthusiasm or sentimentality. "Training in Christianity" is what he calls it. In other words, the late-comer must undergo this training, for only then does he reach that situation essential to the decision of faith.

VI. Kierkegaard's words troubled me for a long time, for they were charged with profound Christian sincerity. Yet I was forced to conclude that this "training" was simply out of the question. It is impossible to overcome the fact that we live after Christ. Kierkegaard's theory was (to borrow his own word) "desperate" —evolved in defiance of a lukewarm Christianity, a Christianity whittled away to nothing but rationalization and moralization.

Nonetheless, Kierkegaard had a point. One truly arrives at sincerity of faith only through contemporaneity with the witness of revelation. But where?

Naturally, Jesus of Nazareth can never be contemporaneous to me in an immediate historical sense, but his witnesses can and are. And the very taproot of Christian witness is the Church, who, living in all ages, considers all ages as one. The cathechism instructor who taught me of Christ and his message, the pastor who baptized me and preached to me, my fellow parishioners

who gathered around our parish altar, the bishop and his ordained ministers—all of these are the Church. Through her I
come to the message.

She includes, as well, that family of mine in whose midst I
imbibed the spirit and tongue of Christianity, that parish community with which I stand at the altar and all the others throughout the world, united to me in the one Faith. All of these—the
teachers and the taught, the leaders and the led—all are my
immediate contemporaries. Their humanity, all of it, the worthwhile as well as the questionable, includes itself in the message
and demands to be accepted in the responsibility of faith, and to
be borne in the communion of the Christian "we."

In all of this stands Christ. He addresses me, and he does so
not as a lone individual, but as the Church. Yet what a dispro-
portion exists between his figure and that of his Church through
whom he speaks! The Church stands victim to every type of
human frailty, peopled as she is with run-of-the-mill, common,
yes, even wicked men. To what extent things have fossilized in
dogmas, regulations, rituals and prescriptions—how she has become encrusted during history's long years with the guilt for all
that has been said or left unsaid, done or left undone, in her
name.

No wonder that the question enters one's mind: This? This
Church is to be the witness of him whom I can, should, must
believe in? This is the form out of which the Holy Spirit is to
utter his message—the Holy Spirit who entered history on Pentecost and who is, as Jesus promised, to guide us into all truth
(John 16:13)?

The overwhelming difficulty of that dilemma, which Kierkegaard terms the "Absolute Paradox," sweeps over one. Yet the
path to faith is to be found in such paradox, for by means of it
one comes into contact with Christ. To assert that one can find
immediate contact with him on one's own is but illusion. Even

the New Testament, which one might assume of itself would bring its reader immediately to Christ, is, after all, the Church.

The magnitude of this problem is illustrated by all New Testament scholarship—as well as by all those men who deny that they can in these texts find any binding word of God. And yet God speaks here.

Therefore, the first step for me was not as common polemics would have it, the easy way out, the shifting of personal responsibility to pastor, bishop, and pope. (Undoubtedly, with a certain number this is the case, just as with some the desire to decide everything on their own is sheer pampering of whim.) The matter of the fact is that we can contact Jesus only through the Church. The decision of faith can take place within her alone, because she alone supplies us with that situation basic to faith, contemporaneity.

Moreover, the members of the Church must continually renew their faith. They make their first and fundamental decision, of course, when they choose to unite themselves to the Church. But the human frailty of that same Church scandalizes their faith almost daily. Again and again, one meets the objection not only from others, but from one's own self: "What here confronts me can not be the Church as Jesus Christ intended it." And one must always rise to the occasion, always demand of himself the fresh commitment: "She is. I believe." Then, and only then, does that liberating and reassuring perspective which emanates from the Church, return to the believer.

So, the Church had become for me something which the critics, ranged against her, not only refused to recognize but altogether distorted. She became that assurance willed by Christ himself in order that he, within his freedom, might contact me. This is the point which, above all, I hope to have made in this paper.

If I have, then I have answered as well the question put to

me: how we who are called upon, day in and day out, to renew our faith in the Church, feel when confronted by a situation in which the concept of Church is replaced by the lone individual, or parish, or by a Church concept, bereft of clarity and force. Yet at the same time we find inspiring the earnestness which men such as Asmussen and his colleagues have displayed in their study of the concept of Church. They have drawn us into a dialogue, the effects of which are indeed inestimable.

The Holy Church

by JOSEF JUNGMANN

IT IS OUR COMMON practice when referring to the Catholic
Church to employ the phrase "the holy Church." We say that
"the holy Church" teaches or that "the holy Church" celebrates
a certain feast, and so forth. Why do we use such an expression?
Is it simply a flourish of etiquette, as one would address an acquaintance as "Mr. Smith" instead of as merely "Smith"? Or
does the expression have a deeper significance?

It is significant that the term "holy" is the oldest attribute applied to the Church. As a matter of fact, the Church was called
holy long before she was referred to as catholic or apostolic.
Further, the fact of the Church's holiness is a truism we have all
learned from our catechism: her doctrine is holy, her sacraments
are holy, and finally, she has guided many men along the path to
holiness.

Yet whenever the holiness of the Church is mentioned today,
we are prone to imagine a vague entity divorced from the reality
of our everyday lives, a quality there but mysteriously hidden in
the real Church, at most visible in pope or hierarchy. Originally,
however, *the holy Church* implied the real, visible Church, the
Church on earth; she was a Church composed of fallible mortals,
of artisans and merchants, of men, women and children—precisely today what is still signified in the prayer of the Mass immediately after the Consecration, by the words: "We thy servants
but likewise thy holy people." In the present day, more than
ever before, just such an appreciation of the Church is demanded. Passive adherence to the Church and to her laws and

precepts, no longer suffices. We need once again to understand and cherish the Church in her essence, and thereby realize our participation in her life. Otherwise Catholic action remains merely superficial activity, the liturgical revival an empty word.

Rather than pursue a strictly theological investigation of the Church's holiness, we shall content ourselves with a study of its significance in early Christian times. We must, therefore, begin with a look at the terminology employed by the early Church, specifically that found in the classic profession of faith, the Apostle's Creed.

To begin with, it is necessary to recall that in the earliest sources of St. Paul, the word "Church" was not the solely or predominantly employed word indicating the reality in question. More precisely, a term had yet to be decided upon and adopted. During this process, in the various writings on the nature of the Church, it was the sign of holiness which most frequently occurred. For holiness was a character clearly essential to the make-up of the Church.

The word normally employed for "Church" in Greek (as well as in Latin and the other Romance languages), namely, *ekklesia,* signified convocation or gathering. St. Paul speaks of "the gathering of God," that is, the assembly of people convoked by God. The Church is therefore *the* holy assembly, the people of God. The faithful are the "called ones" (Eph. 4:1, 4), more exactly, they who are "holy by vocation" (Rom. 1:7; 1 Cor. 1:2). The people are an edifice erected by God (1 Cor. 3:9), a temple of his dwelling (2 Cor. 6:16). When handled by St. Peter this concept takes on new beauty. He depicts the faithful as living stones, components of a holy temple resting upon Christ the cornerstone; he also singles them out as the chosen race, the royal priesthood (1 Pet. 2:4, 9).

Equally enlightening is Irenaeus' (Bishop of Lyons) second century account of the Church's origin (*The Demonstration of the Apostolic Teaching,* chap. 89ff.). Here he portrays the pagan as an arid wasteland—neither watered by the Word nor saturated with the Spirit. But with the outpouring of the Holy Spirit upon the earth there occurred a renewal, that spiritual renewal which effected our calling. Irenaeus continues to describe this *calling* as one which resulted in a conversion of hardened hearts and a plentiful harvest manifest in the Church. (The reader must, of course, note Irenaeus' play on words. The Greek word *klesis,* calling, immediately evoked in the early reader's mind *ekklesia,* the word for Church.)

Ekklesia became, very soon, the accepted term for the community of the faithful. St. Paul even used the expression in the previous century. And what in reality was our first catechism, the Apostle's Creed, incorporated it in its second century standardized form: "I believe *in the Holy Spirit, the* holy *Church.*" Holiness, then—already implied in the very name *ekklesia* (those called by God to be saints)—was the characteristic most underlined and stressed.

Significant, as well, is the fact that mention of the Holy Spirit immediately precedes that of the Church. In the mind of the early Church the fruit of redemption was the outpouring of the Holy Spirit upon mankind—and from this the Church took its origin. For she rose from the flames of Pentecost to proceed out into the world. God's holiness, the Holy Spirit, made contact with man; the spark of holiness, as it were, leaped from the Spirit to inflame the Church. Thus the Greek and Latin texts of the Creed repeat the word "holy" twice in immediate succession: *in Spiritum Sanctum—sanctam Ecclesiam.*

The Church then is holy, through the Holy Spirit, sent to her by Christ as his Spirit. But there is more. Incorporated in the text of this early Christian catechism stands a phrase inserted to safeguard proper understanding of the innermost nature of the Church. That phrase? *Communio sanctorum.* And its meaning?

Most modern catechisms interpret it merely as the expression of the union between the faithful on earth, the saints in heaven and the souls in purgatory. This is true enough, but hardly the emphasis primarily intended at the time of the phrase's original insertion. The Roman Catechism of Pius V, published in 1566, retains the traditional interpretation, according to which the *communio sanctorum* was intended merely as the inevitable consequence of the *in Spiritum Sanctum–sanctam Ecclesiam.* It expresses the fact that in the Church is a holy community—a community created through the action of the Holy Spirit, who breathes a soul into the Church, and nourished through the sacraments, in particular the Eucharist. Therefore, the phrase *communio sanctorum* expresses a bond and communion among the members of the Church comparable to that among the members of a living body.

This interpretation of *communio sanctorum* corresponds to that of the Church Fathers at the time when the term arose. We can pinpoint the term's meaning with even more precision in the light of the patristic writings by analyzing its component parts, *communio* and *sanctorum.*

In patristic literature, the *communio sanctorum* indicated either a community of holy *persons* or the common possession, the community possession, of holy *things*—depending on whether *sanctorum* derived from *sancti,* the masculine plural, or *sancta,* the neuter plural. If the latter, the implication was: a community which was one in that it shared the same faith, the same hope, the same sacraments, the same pilgrimage and goal.

St. Augustine preferred to speak of the *communio sanctorum* in this latter sense while modern translations presuppose the former, namely, a community of holy persons, the sanctified. Actually the two interpretations express one and the same idea. All participate in the same goods of salvation; all have been sanctified through the holy waters of baptism and, therefore, all are holy. They are a community of sanctified people because they share in the divine goods through which they attain salvation.

As for *communio*, it can be understood either in an abstract or a concrete sense. Taken abstractly, within the context of the Creed, it denotes: I believe in the holy Church and in a brotherhood, a fellowship, a common bond uniting the sanctified, that is, the faithful. There is a Church, and all the members within this Church are united by the bond of holiness. Taken concretely, *communio* means: I believe in the holy Church, herself a community, a union, a nation of saints. Although the difference between the two is insignificant, the concrete interpretation is more consistent with the context of the Creed.

The Creed proclaims the Church as simply the exact fulfillment of the parables of Christ—the one flock in which all were to be gathered together, the one vine on which the branches live; or as St. Paul put it, the temple of God. This, then, is what we profess in the Creed: God has poured forth his Spirit into the world, and in this Spirit has called together men, who constitute a holy assembly, ever sanctified anew; a nation of saints, because it is born from the waters of baptism and nurtured by the Eucharistic bread into holy fellowship. This was the understanding of the early Christians and it ought to be ours, a concept of the Church which we modern-day Catholics must make our own.

Further, the phrase "the Holy Spirit" is not the only phrase which precedes and casts light upon "the holy Church"; rather the entire context of the Creed does so, a Creed in which, first of all, faith is professed in the Father Almighty, and then in Christ and his salvific work.

It has been noted that the Creed says: "I believe *in* God, the Father Almighty, and *in* Jesus Christ, his only-begotten Son . . . *in* the Holy Spirit." However, when the Church is spoken of, the Creed no longer continues to say, "(I believe) *in*"—"the holy Church," but simply, "the holy Church." In other words one could conclude that the authors have inserted a caesura, a dash, to suggest a break in thought between the phrases "the Holy Spirit" and "the holy Church." Upon mention of a divine person the Creed thus states: "I believe in," thereby indicating an act which signifies not only a believing acceptance of the truth, but also that total personal commitment in faith, hope and love which is due to God alone. Whereas, the *in* is omitted in the remaining phrases of the Creed, for these list items which one merely holds to be true but do not involve personal commitment: the Church, forgiveness of sin, the resurrection of the dead, eternal life.

Protestant authors in particular have stressed this distinction. It is not entirely to their liking that the Church is even mentioned in the Creed, for according to Luther, each individual is obliged to settle his affairs personally and immediately with God, and this he does by an assent to the word of the Bible and confidence in the merits of Christ, the so-called *Fiduzialglaube* (fiducial faith). In reality this person has no need of the Church. The Protestants, therefore, emphasize the caesura which appears to stand between the phrases "the Holy Spirit" and "the holy Church" and thus would separate the "I believe in" from "the holy Church."

As a matter of fact, the Protestant theologian Ernst Wolf makes the following remark in a recent work: "Belief in the Church is easier and more meaningful for the Catholic mind than for the Protestant" (*Peregrinatio* [Munich, 1954], p. 282).

Obviously our relationship to the persons of the Blessed Trinity is something entirely different from the relationship between ourselves and the Church. The Church is a created entity; it is the way to God, not the final goal of our endeavor. However, this distinction is not stressed in the Creed. Nor was it considered when the Creed was formulated. It is correct that the phrase "believe in" (*pisteuein eis; credere in*) attained common Christian usage in an attempt to strengthen our expression of religious faith. But, at least at the time of the Creed's origin, no distinction between the different articles of faith was made.

St. Augustine was the first to use this expression of the Creed to describe that special relationship of total surrender in which the Christian stands to God. And others were quick to adopt his interpretation, though in reality it had not been thus intended. Rather, the Church had simply been listed among the major objects of Christian faith, and it was purely by accident (or perhaps for literary style) that the preposition "in" did not preface the statements regarding the Church and other mysteries of the faith.

The latter part of the Creed pulsates with one grand theme: the Church. The divine decree to save and sanctify the world has become visibly realized in the holy Catholic Church—holy in the sense that she is a communion of sanctified persons, catholic in the sense that she is directed toward the whole of mankind. The Church receives the Christian through "baptism unto the remission of sins" (a fact explicitly stated in the *Credo* of the Mass), and embracing him, prepares him for glorious resurrection and eternal life.

Obviously, then, the Church is the central thought of the latter section of the Creed. In fact, the early Christians cherished the thought of the Church as the aggregate of all goods necessary for salvation (or, in modern terminology, "the primordial sacrament"). The other forms of the Creed circulating throughout Christendom corroborate this notion of the Church as the preserver of salvific goods. A North African version, for instance, reads: "I believe in the Holy Spirit, the forgiveness of sins and life everlasting *through* the holy Church"; one Greek papyrus discovered in Egypt contains the words: ". . . *in* the holy Church." That is to say, the goods of salvation, the forgiveness of sins, sanctification and fulfillment in eternal life, not only are procured *through* the Church but also are to be found *in* the Church.

The holy Church accordingly occupies a central position in the final section of the Creed. As God dominates its introduction and Christ the Redeemer the middle section, so the Church plays the central role in the conclusion, because everything that God made available through Jesus Christ for our salvation is contained *in* her.

Here another point comes to mind. Does our relationship to Christ also find expression in the Creed? Yes. The passage treating of the Holy Spirit and the holy Church is presented as the consequence of Christ's salvific work, which is narrated in the preceding section. This essential aspect of the Church, namely, that above all she is the Church of Christ, has become more evident to us since Pope Pius XII emphatically recalled to mind the doctrine of the Church as being the mystical body of Christ. The Church is the body of Christ, the continuation of Christ in history, the fulfillment and the perfection of Christ (cf. Eph. 2:23). In the work of the redemption, the framework, so to speak, was created; through the Church it is brought to completion.

This relationship of the Church to Christ is expressed basically in two separate languages: the German *Kirche* as well as the English *Church*. Both words spring from the Greek *kyriakon*, that is, something which belongs to the *Kyrios*, the Lord, in other words, to Jesus Christ. The word was used from the fourth century on to designate the material edifice as the property of the Lord. Shortly thereafter it came to be applied to the assembly of people within that edifice, an assembly which belongs to Christ the Lord in a far more profound sense than do material possessions. Thus in two principal languages of the Western World, we find two meanings of the word "church" which, though stemming from different points of view, splendidly complement one another.

The word in the Romance languages (*eglise, chiesa, iglesia,* and so forth) stems from the Greek root *ekklesia. Ekklesia* refers primarily to an assembly of Christians and then, by extension, to the material structure in which this gathering takes place. As seen already, the converse is true in the English and German languages, where the word *kyriakon* first and foremost brings to mind the material building and only secondarily the community of the faithful.

The community of the faithful and the material edifice are both: *ekklesia,* place of the divine summons to salvation, and *kyriakon,* property of the *Kyrios.* In either case "the holy Church" in the context of the Apostles' Creed signifies always a people, the people of God, the totality of the faithful. Of course this people is not to be thought of as merely *en masse,* a disorganized and shapeless multitude.

On the contrary, a more adequate portrayal of the Church reveals that she possesses various offices and powers: that there are administrative offices for dispensing the sacraments, authoritative offices for governing the Christian people, and a doctrinal authority endowed with the infallibility so necessary to the Church as pillar and foundation of truth; that finally she has received from her Founder characteristic signs which distinguish her from other communities not deputized as the Church of Christ. Details such as these receive no express mention in the Creed since they simply serve to amplify the Church's basic concept. This concept denotes the holy community summoned by God through Christ in the Holy Spirit, the community of those who have responded in faith and thus in hope can look forward to salvation.

Despite the Creed's unmistakable language, a shift of emphasis has occurred during the past several centuries. The points of primary importance, once originally accented, have been shunted into the background, and vice versa. The inevitable reaction to the errors of the Reformation (which denied all Church offices and authority), all too often resulted in an absolute identification of the Church with her administrative force—the hierarchy.

Many Catholics consider the faithful as those who go to Church and are led by the Church, but are apt to overlook the fact that they themselves *are* the Church. This misconception cries for correction, for it breeds that attitude of indifference shown by so many toward the life of the Church. It accounts, as well, for the fact that many have no appreciation of the worship of God as a living worship nor of the active participation in the liturgy so emphatically urged by recent popes.

Who, then, would deny our desperate need to return to a full understanding of the idea: "I believe in the holy Catholic Church, the communion of saints."

Leadership in the Church

by KARL RAHNER

THE WORD "BISHOP" is rooted in the Greek *episkopos,* meaning an overseer, a guardian. As a title, "bishop" indicates the office-holder, who by divine right and in virtue of his relationship to the college of bishops directs a local church, his diocese, which is representative of the whole Church. (He does this primarily by reason of his communion with the pope, with the See of Peter.)

The office and concept of bishop, and its characteristic—membership in a college of elders—appear to have been prefigured in the Judaistic milieu of the New Testament. Already in the New Testament (where, for example, in Phil. 1:1; 1 Thess. 5:12; 1 Tim. 3:2ff; Tit. 1:5ff the episcopacy is clearly perceptible) this office of overseer and leader is linked to the theological conception of the office of pastor (Acts 20:17–36).

The *magisterium* of the Church has defined the divine right of the episcopacy (D960, 966, 1821, 1828, 2287). Therefore the pope cannot abrogate the episcopacy, despite his primacy of jurisdiction over the whole Church and each of her members, including the individual bishops. Nor may the bishops be considered officials and deputies of the pope. On the contrary, the bishops have authority originating from Christ, and proper to themselves. They tend their flocks not in the name of the pope, but in the name of Christ and in their own name as real authorities. They are successors to the apostles by divine ordination.

The divine right and institution of the episcopacy are manifest, first of all, in the will of Christ toward his Church and her hierarchy, and secondly, in the fact that the episcopal college is the apostolic college continuing down through history.

It is precisely as a college that the episcopacy (whose head is the pope, and the latter, in turn, being pope because he is their head) has rights and duties in the Church which are radical, inalienable and divine. Therefore it is wrong to assert that the pope has the same rights over the collegiate episcopacy which he has over the individual bishops.

The individual bishop is not the successor of any one individual apostle. Rather, the individual bishop is in legitimate succession to an apostle in as much as he is a member of the collegiate episcopacy, which, as a single body, is successor to the college of the apostles.

As in the apostolic college, so in the episcopal college: the college as such is that which is willed by Christ. It is a structured whole, and not an assembly of individual authorities, who possess their own authority in advance, and are united, so to speak, only by a subsequent decree. The pope's primacy is *primacy in the college*. He does not stand apart from the college and then, as it were, gradually unite it with himself and grant it authority. Thus, the college of bishops is the primary entity which succeeds the apostolic college. The pope is its prescribed head, without whom the collegiate episcopacy would be inconceivable. However, he is and can be pope only as member and head of this college.

This elucidates the Church's teaching that the supreme authority of the Church rests in the council (CIC c.228). It does not, however, imply a curtailment of papal primacy, because the college of bishops always has the pope as its head. Without this head the college of bishops would have no existence, whether in council or outside of it. Indeed, the pope acts as pope precisely when and in so far as he does not act as a private person.

This also sheds light on the infallibility of the Church's *magisterium,* or better, on the one exercising it. When the pope, acting alone or in conjunction with a council, issues an infallible definition of doctrine, it is not a question of two acts of two different subjects, but rather of two different modes of acting in one and the same subject. These modes are distinguished only by their circumstance. On the one hand, the one moral subject is dispersed over the breadth of the earth, while on the other hand, it is assembled in a determined place, thus effecting a clearer manifestation of the participation on the part of the collegiate members with their head, the pope, by way of collaboration and support. The same may be said of the "ordinary *magisterium.*"

We can now see the import of the college of bishops: The Church should be constituted not only through *many* members, but also through *qualitatively* different members. This pluralism, which must be in the Church according to the will of God, should also find expression in the head of the Church. There it should secure its own justification and completion.

The individual bishop realizes his function in the episcopal college for the whole Church when he authoritatively represents a definite member of the whole Church—the diocese. In so doing, the differentiation of the members of the Church, willed by the Spirit, can and will be real. However, as an individual bishop, he receives his strictly defined territory and his pastoral power from the pope. The pope in a case of necessity can suspend these episcopal rights.

The power of orders, basically the same for the bishop as for the pope, is received by the bishop at his consecration. It gives the bishop full potentiality to realize this unique sacrament. It enables the bishop to confirm the members of his diocese and to ordain his priests. The consecration of the holy oils, and the blessing of abbots and abbesses, are reserved to the bishop as well. By reason of his pastoral power he leads his diocese as the supreme shepherd; in dogma, in the charitable and pastoral activity of the diocese, by his legislative and juridical authority, and by attending to his administrative duties.

The Pauline Body-Concept

Το σῶμα τοῦ χριστοῦ

by HEINRICH SCHLIER

THE CONCEPT σῶμα is already used by St. Paul with reference to the Church in 1 Cor. 10:17; 12:12–27; Rom. 12:4–5. In these texts he has the individual communities in mind. However, the express designation of the Church as the mystical body is not found. But in a comparison of the local community with the human body in 1 Cor. 12:12 we find the observation, "So also it is with Christ," and in Rom. 12:5, "So we, the many, are one body in Christ." Implicit is the equation of Christ with the body; that is, we in Christ are equal to one body. Cf. 1 Cor. 10:17: "We, though many, are one body." This statement means precisely that we, who are one body, are Christ (as one body). Thus Paul asks in 1 Cor. 1:13, "Has Christ been divided up?" in referring to the division within the community. The remarks in 1 Corinthians and Romans deal therefore with the relationship of the one body to the many members and of the many members to one another. The latter concept is elaborated upon in 1 Cor. 12:12–27 (and Rom. 12, 4–5): the many members of the one body are joined together for mutual assistance, have need of one another, and are united in *sympatheia*. In all these statements charismata are considered to be inherent in the members.

We find another group of passages, prescinding from the passage at hand (Eph. 1:22f), in Eph. 3:6; 4:4, 12, 16; 5:23, 29; Col. 1:18, 24; 2:(10), 19; 3:15, in which the whole Church is always meant, being expressly characterized at this point as σῶμα or σῶμα τοῦ χριστοῦ. It is no longer just a matter of a comparison or an implied equation of the one with the other. With the term σῶμα τοῦ χριστοῦ the relationship of the Church to Christ is now explicitly stated. This is clarified in Eph. 1:22f; 4:15f; 5:23; Col. 1:18, (2:10); 2:19 by the relationship σῶμα-κεφαλή. Of course in Eph. 2:15 σῶμα is probably the σῶμα τῆς σαρκός of Col. 1:22. But here too the term σῶμα alludes to the relationship of the entire Church to Christ in as much as it is used perhaps deliberately in a twofold sense. As σῶμα and κεφαλή the Church is the "new man in Christ" (Eph. 2:15f). When the σῶμα is accorded the κεφαλή (= the Church, Christ) then the σῶμα τοῦ χριστοῦ which it is, is consummated in "perfect manhood" (Eph. 4:13f).

First of all, the essentially inseparable solidarity of the Church and Christ and their divinely prescribed co-ordination are indicated by the σῶμα-κεφαλή relationship (cf. Eph. 1:22f). Secondly, the subordination of the body to the head—that is, its submission to Christ, and consequently the supremacy of the head over the body, its sovereignty over the body—is stressed (cf. Eph. 1:22f; 5:23f). Thirdly, however, the κεφαλή characterizes Christ as him from whom the Church takes its growth, therefore as the efficacious fount and ultimate goal of this "growth" of the Church (cf. Eph. 4:15f; Col. 1:18 [Christ as ἀρχή]).

Fourthly, the primacy of Christ becomes the primacy of the beloved through the union of the concept of the κεφαλή of the Church with the idea of the syzygy of Christ with the Church (cf. Eph. 5:22, 25). On the other hand, the relationship of the κεφαλή to the σῶμα is tantamount to assistance in view of the equation σῶμα = σάρξ = γυνή (cf. Eph. 5:28–32). Fifthly, while the unity of the body is still emphasized, it is intended not only to stress the unity of the many members among one another (cf. Eph. 4:3f, 11–16; Col. 3:15) but also the unity of the two groups which constitute the human commonwealth, Jews and Gentiles (cf. Eph. 2:15f; 3:6).

And, finally, according to Col. 2:10, Christ is also the head of the powers of the world. The interpretation of Col. 2:19 is in dispute but in Col. 1:16f the same thought is alluded to in as much as Christ is the one in whom and for whom the universe is created, and in whom it has existence.

In general it is clear that according to Paul the Church as a whole or its local representation is conceived of as the body of Christ but in 1 Corinthians and Romans the equation ἐκκλησία = σῶμα is presumed rather than specifically stated. The import of these statements is based upon the comparison of this "body" with the human body, in view of the multiplicity of the members and the unity of the body as well as the relationship of the members to one another. In the epistles to the Ephesians and the Colossians, however, the equation ἐκκλησία = σῶμα is explicitly stated, and the relationship of σῶμα = ἐκκλησία to κεφαλή = χριστός is stressed on the basis of the equation σῶμα + κεφαλή = χριστός. Here too, σῶμα sometimes refers to the universe.

Thus it is evident that from a yet undetermined equation of Church to "body" and "body" to Christ in 1 Corinthians and Romans a more precise equivalence of Church to "body of Christ," the "head" of the "body," evolved in Ephesians and Colossians. The problem is whether this new equation, which of course includes that of Christ = body + head, linguistically— which in this case also means conceptually—represents merely a development of the old, or whether external moments did not influence the development of the new equation. In the enterprise of resolving this problem it is necessary to clarify the entire linguistic and conceptual context of Pauline statement.

In Greek and Roman antiquity the idea of the cosmos as an organic entity was widespread and enjoyed sundry variations. Most probably it is derived terminologically from Plato Tim. 30 B-34B where it is mentioned as a ξῷον and in this connection also as a σῶμα τοῦ παντός or τοῦ κόσμου. This idea was also adopted

especially by the Stoics (cf., e.g., Diog. Laert. 7, 138. 142. 143.
147; Cic. nat. deor. 1. 35; 3, 9; or Sext. Emp. adv. phys. 9, 79;
Sen. nat. qu. 6, 14, 1; *totum terrarum omnium corpus;* Corp.
Herm. 2, 2ff; 4, 2; 10, 12). In this cosmos, which is *one* σῶμα in
its essence and in the multiplicity of its parts, man is conscious
of being a part (μέρος) and a member (μέλος). Cf. Sen. ep. 95,
52: *omne hoc, quod vides, quo divina atque humana conclusa
sunt, unum est: membra sumus corporis magni. Natura nos
cognatos edidit, cum ex iisdem et in eadem gignerit.* Cf. Sen. ib.
92, 30; Mc. Aurel. 7, 13, 3; cf. 2, 1; 8, 34.

These parts or members are related to one another. A synthesis of sacred character embraces them; a solidarity affiliates
the whole. Thus the members ought to assist one another and
promote their mutual welfare. Cf. Sen. ep. 95, 52; Mc. Aurel.
2, 1, 3; Epict. diss. 2, 5, 24; 10, 3f. The head plays no part among
these members of the cosmos. The predominating principle is the
ψυχή. Of course the head can sometimes be distinguished from
the "subordinate parts" (of the body); cf. Sext. Emp. adv. astrol.
44.

The state also (and other human societies) is compared in
various respects to the human body: Plato rep. 5, 464 B; leg. 8,
828 D; Aristot. pol. 1, 1, 11, 1253 A; Cic. rep. 2, 3, etc. Not
merely is a comparison drawn, but under certain circumstances
an equation in which the concept σῶμα or *corpus* acquires a
juridical character, e.g., Cic. phil. 8, 5. 16; off. 1, 25. 85; Sen.
Clem. 2, 5, 1; Liv. 26, 16, 19, etc. With respect to the πόλις the
concept σῶμα accentuates the unity of the whole within the context of a multiplicity of members (cf. Liv. 1, 8, 1; Philo spec.
leg. 3, 131, etc.), and their obligation toward one another (cf.
Cic. off. 3, 22; Sen. ira dei 2, 31, 7; Plut. sol. 18).

Pertinent in this connection is the more ancient and well-
known fable of the stomach and the other parts of the body, which
was told by Menenius Agrippa to the Plebs who had wandered

out to the *Mons sacer* attempting to persuade them to return
(cf. Liv. 2, 32, 8–12; Plut. cor. 6). Where *corpus* or σῶμα is used
to characterize the state (or any other society), *caput* (or κεφαλή)
complements the corpus or the other members respectively. Cf.
Sen. clem. 1, 5, 1; 2, 2, 1; Tacit. Anal. 1, 12f; Cic. Mur. 51
(Plut. Cic. 14, 6); Plut. Galba 4, etc. *Caput* (κεφαλή) is in this
context the decisive and superior member, which represents the
concrete unity of the body and influences its well-being.

When one compares these passages with those of the Apostle
Paul, the following conclusions can be drawn: (1) In both cases
σῶμα (*corpus*) is used to characterize a human society and (in
Paul occasionally) the cosmos. (2) The concept is treated in both
instances under the aspect of the one body and the many members, and the integrity and solidarity of the members. In Paul
this occurs in 1 Corinthians and Romans almost exclusively, but
is used in Ephesians 4:25 with reference to the whole Church.
The statements in 1 Cor. 12:12ff reveal a peculiar affinity to the
fable of Menenius Agrippa and similar Stoic diatribes. The material discrepancies should of course not be overlooked. (3) In
both cases the κεφαλή as the complement of the σῶμα, according to
the Greco-Roman sense of the equation σῶμα = πόλις, occurs in
Paul only in the epistles to the Ephesians and Colossians. Κεφαλή
is used in both instances in terms of an entity which forms and
rules the σῶμα. (4) The Pauline statements differ formally, however, from the Greco-Roman in as much as they incorporate into
σῶμα and κεφαλή the concept of a specific "man" who himself is
his "body" and this "head" as well. Among the Greco-Roman
texts, there is no formal analogy to the equations: σῶμα (ἐκκλησία)
= Christus, κεφαλή = Christus, and σῶμα + κεφαλή = Christus.
This discrepancy is of signal moment not only materially—it de-
taches the Church from the sphere of human societies, among
which of course it still belongs—but also for the problem of the
historical origin of our conception of the σῶμα τοῦ χριστοῦ. This

poses the problem whether the Apostle did not conceive of the σῶμα τοῦ χριστοῦ with reference to the Church in terms of a linguistic usage other than the one cited.

As far as the influence of Judaeo-oriental antiquity in apostolic times is concerned, the concept σῶμα referring to a human society or to the cosmos occurs neither in the Septuagint nor elsewhere in Jewish literature. On the other hand, the concept κεφαλή pertaining to the ruler or head and the leader of the people occurs as a translation of ראש, which of course admits of various interpretations. Prescinding from the antithesis head-tail (= above and below) in Deut. 28:13, 44; Isa. 9:13f; Jub. 1:16; 1 Henoch 103:11; Ab. 4:15b; Philo praem. 124f, κεφαλή is employed in the sense of "ruler" (Jdc. 10:18; 11:8, 9, 11; 2 Reg. 22:44; 3 Reg. 20:12A; Isa. 7:8f; Philo. praem. 114). However, there is no amplification of this figure, which is suggested by Isa. 1:4–6, because in this text the comparison of Israel to a human body stands in the background (Vgl. Dan. 2:38). Only Test. XII Seb. develops the comparison somewhat along Greco-Roman lines.

Therefore, one cannot presume the Septuagint to be the origin of the specifically Pauline body-Christ conception. In the Septuagint the equations σῶμα = ἄνθρωπος, κεφαλή = ἄνθρωπος, and σῶμα + κεφαλή = ἄνθρωπος, are also missing—in other words, the correlation of the σῶμα-κεφαλή figure to an Anthropos conceived of as one who, on the one hand, embraces the human commonwealth or cosmos in such a way that they are his σῶμα, and who, on the other hand, complements them as their head.

A formal analogy of the Pauline conception or its presupposition is palpable, however, in the Jewish Adam-speculation influenced by the oriental-gnostic *Urmensch*-redeemer myth. The fact that Paul was acquainted with such Adam-speculation is evident from his juxtaposition Adam-Christ in Rom. 5:12–21; 1 Cor. 15:20–22; 44b–49. Here Adam is the first man, who

alludes to the second, and in terms of this relationship all who
bear their image and consummate their destiny are synonymous
with them. These statements are obviously to be understood in
the perspective of Judaeo-apocalyptic conceptions of the relationship between Adam and adamitic humanity.

But Philo also presumes such a relationship between the "one
man," the first-born logos, Adam, and the πνευματικοί (= ὁρατικοί).
Cf. Conf. ling. 41; qu. in Gen. 1:18; Plant. 32ff. Occasionally
Adam is termed "the apex" of the human race. Cf. Nu. R. 10
(158a). According to Mandaean tradition he is called with respect to his whole race, "the head of the race" or "the head of
the epoch." When he rises, his whole race—the "good souls"—
will follow him. Cf. RG 27, 17; 45, 36; 107, 26, 29, etc. Cosmic
dimensions are attributed to such an Adam under certain circumstances. Cf. Str. -B- Index; 2 Henoch 30:8f; Or. Sib. 3:24f;
Const. Ap. 8, 12, 17; but also Philo spec. leg. 1, 210f, etc.;
Hippol. El. 9, 13, 27; S.251, 14ff; Epiph. haer. 30, 17, 6f, S356,
18ff; 19, 4, 1, S. 221, 6ff.

As uncertain and late as such accounts often are, they portend
an Adam-speculation which evolves in the direction of the
Urmensch-redeemer myth, and which occasionally was even developed under its influence. The connection of this Adam-speculation with the conception of the son of man who is sometimes
the people of God (cf. Dan. 7:13 LXX) (and resides in their
midst, cf. 1 Henoch 45:3ff; 38:1; 53:6; 62:8; 7:71; 4 Esd. 7:28;
14:9) and sometimes the Messiah, is well known.

The cosmic man, in whose body the world reposes (that is,
whose body is the cosmos), is treated more clearly in the Orphic
fragment 168, where Zeus is depicted as the synthesis of the
cosmic god and cosmic man. His head, his torso (= his body) and
his feet embrace the heavens, the atmosphere, and the earth
down into the underworld. Indeed, these are precisely his head,
his body, and his feet. Cf. also Orph. Fragm. 167; περὶ Ἑβδομάδων

6, 1; Macrob. sat. 1, 20, 17; PGM XII 243. The κεφαλή is not accentuated in such conceptions.

The case is different in Philo qu. in Gen. 117. Here the logos, which is understood as διοικητής among the Stoics, is depicted as the head which rules the cosmos below it, imparts it life, and fulfills it. The cosmos is for its part the body (*membra*) which has need of this head. The two taken together constitute the *pleroma*. Thus the Judaeo-Christian Gnostics in Colossae might have conceived of Christ in approximately this way.

But in the process of coming to terms with them Paul developed his idea of the "new man" Christ, who incorporated the old one into himself, and who now has his body in the Church— that body of which he himself is the head. In my opinion, a trace of this can be found in Col. 1:24, whose juxtaposition to Eph. 1:22 is enlightening. Col. 1:24 reads: . . . καὶ ἀνταναπληρῶ τὰ ὑστερήματα τῶν θλίψεων τοῦ χριστοῦ . . . ὑπὲρ τοῦ σώματος αὐτοῦ, ὅ ἐστιν ἡ ἐκκλησία. The one who is the body of Christ is clarified in an explanatory relative clause. However, it is not self-evident that σῶμα is used with reference to the ἐκκλησία, as is also the case in 1:17 with τῆς ἐκκλησίας, which is used in apposition to τοῦ σώματος, regardless of whether Col. 1:12(15)–20 is a recast pre-Christian or Christian hymn.

Was another interpretation of σῶμα at all possible? Actually there was, because even though the interpretation of Col. 2:19 with respect to the body of the cosmos may be disputed, yet 2:10 in connection with 1:16f definitely shows that according to the Colossian Gnostics this body is the cosmos. The Apostle takes exception to this only in so far as he does not admit a cosmos grounded and fulfilled in itself. Christ as the εἰκὼν τοῦ θεοῦ and as πρωτότοκος πάσης κτίσεως (1:15), is the κεφαλή of the cosmos also. The σῶμα which is the Church is to be distinguished, however, from this σῶμα which is the cosmos of the powers and elements, the one which Christ once again has subjected to himself (2:15).

In order to secure this distinction, at variance with the view of the Colossians, ὅ ἐστιν ἡ ἐκκλησία is expressly added in 1:24. But when one compares this with Eph. 1:23, it is evident that here it is conversely formulated: τῇ ἐκκλησίᾳ, ἥτις ἐστὶν τὸ σῶμα αὐτοῦ. Here, therefore, it is presumed (in connection with evidence for the statement that Christ is the head of the Church, we may note that the relative in 1:23a is used as substantiating) that the Church is his body. In view of the established premise that the Church is his body and the established designation of the Church as the body of Christ, it becomes clear that God has given to the Church Christ as head. The identity of the Church with the body of Christ is also patently presupposed in Eph. 5:23.

It was possible for Paul to interpret the ἐκκλησία in the sense of "the whole Church" with the aid of this Colossian Anthropos-speculation, because in so doing he could hark back to earlier Adam-Christ analogies, originating probably in Jewish Adam-speculation, which already spoke of the body which Christ is, and of the faithful, who are "in Christ." In 1 Corinthians and in Romans such analogies were in the background, as we have seen.

In the foreground, only those features were emphasized which required a clarification, not of the relationship of the body to Christ, but that of the members of this body to the body itself and to one another. This was accomplished with the aid of the Stoic conceptions of the cosmos and the polis. In the epistles to Ephesians and the Colossians such Adam-Christ analogies come to the fore and are developed correspondingly in view of the relationship of Christ to the whole Church and of it to him. This development occurs under the impulse of questions arising from a disparate viewpoint and demanding an answer. The exposition takes this peculiar form because its substance could be expressed accurately to the members of the respective communities in these terms already at hand in the language, in conceptual categories, and in the particular outlook of the adversaries within the communities.

Just exactly how dominant a role these two components, which one finds in Paul's development of the body-Christ analogy, played in providing a substratum and background for early Christian thought is evident from the fact that for a long time they occurred in ancient Christian literature independently of Paul's treatment of the subject. For the development of the Pauline body-Christ relationship with reference to Greco-Roman antiquity, cf. 1 Clem 37, 5; (38, 1); 46, 7; Polyc. Phil. 11, 4; Tert. bapt. 6; the Agraphon of A. Resch, Agrapha no. 75. Judaeo-oriental Anthropos conceptions show their influence especially in Ignatius of Antioch, Eph. 4:2; 20:1; Trall. 11, 2; Smyrn. 1, 2; 4, 2; 11, 2; 2 Clem 14; P. Herm. v. 3, 3, 3; s. 18, 3f; 17, 5; 13, 5; 9, 12. Irenaeus writes along similar lines. The most liberal and intensive use of these ideas can be found in the Gnosis; cf. Ode Sal. 17, 14, cf. 23, 16.18; 24, 1; Act. Thom. 6 (Syr. Text); Act. Joh. 97–101, the so-called Naassen sermon, Hippol. El. 5, 7–11; the speculations of the Valentinians, e.g., Iren. 1, 5, 3; Exc. ex Theod. 42, 1–3; cf. 33, 2; 26, 1; 36; 58; 43, 2.

When we consider the aggregate of Pauline statement on the body of Christ and its background, it is obvious that the following relationships are suggested by the concept σῶμα τοῦ χριστοῦ:

1. A definite relationship of the Church to Christ such that: (a) The indissoluble solidarity of the Church as the "body" with Christ as the "head" is stressed. The two are necessarily correlative, because together they constitute "man." (b) Thus the supremacy of Christ over the Church is indicated. (c) Emphasized also is the fact that Christ is the fount and goal of the Church's life and growth. (d) There is also the notion that the

"body" as the body of this head is also the visible form and representation of the "head" in the cosmos.

2. As far as the concept σῶμα τοῦ χριστοῦ is concerned, *per se:*
(a) The universal and unifying character of the Church is suggested by its Judaeo-gnostic background, because σῶμα is to be
understood in this linguistic context as an enveloping spatial
reality. In the epistles cited, this aspect becomes apparent from
such passages as Eph. 2:16; Col. 1:16f as well as in the concept
of the ἕν σῶμα which expresses the receptive and unifying function of this one body. The concept parallel to σῶμα, that is,
πλήρωμα, also indicates the character of the body as a spatial reality.
Cf. Eph. 1:23; Col. 2:9; 1:19; Eph. 4:13. Above all, in the context of the aforementioned images, σῶμα τοῦ χριστοῦ expresses the
all-embracing character of the body of Christ, the Church. (b)
The "cosmic" character of the Church is implied in the concept
of the σῶμα as it is used in the epistles to the Ephesians and the
Colossians. The Church as the body of Christ (of the Adam-
Anthropos!) is a "world." Therefore in principle and in view of
its ultimate goal it is commensurate with the cosmos, i.e., the
universe. Everything is subject to its claims and its salvific agency,
and is renewed in it by Christ. Lastly, (c) the personal character
of the Church is adduced from the concept σῶμα τοῦ χριστοῦ. This
body of Christ is Christ in his body. Christ is present in it; it in
turn is his temple. In view of the σῶμα concept, the Church is
fundamentally a personal milieu and not a sphere of objectivities.
Its temporal character does not preclude the aforesaid, but adds
an institutional aspect to it, which, however, remains the institutional component of a personal reality. Consequently it can
invite all to find their personal fulfillment in it.

3. The fact that the Church is called σῶμα in this context
reveals something about its relationship to each of the faithful.
As the body of Christ it enjoys a collective primacy "over" them.
They do not primarily constitute the body, but the body con-

stitutes them as "members" in as much as they are incorporated into it. Thus this body is the *raison d'être* for interdependence, which is an essential characteristic of the "member."

As we have already seen, the Apostle was familiar with yet another body-concept of different orientation with respect to the Church. This is evident in 1 Corinthians and Romans. When the Church as an individual community is called here "body," this includes of course that it is "the Christ" and thus implicitly his body. However, this conception is superseded by another derived from popular Stoicism: namely, that it is a social entity. Here the Church is considered as a corporate body of men, united in number through Christ by virtue of the *Pneuma*: consequently *communio sanctorum*. It is the sum total of the faithful. In terms of this viewpoint the individuals exist anterior to the Church, and are the very ones who constitute it. Presupposing this particular concept of σῶμα, the Church is then a realm separated and necessarily distinct from the world. As a corporate body of those baptized in one body, and as a unity of many faithful bound together in solidarity through the *Pneuma*, this body assumes dimensions not synonymous with those of the cosmos. In this interpretation, it is not without qualification the representative of Christ, although it is the "image" of Christ and having been elevated to his magnitude is "body in Christ."

There are definite reasons why the Apostle does not develop aspects inchoate in the Adam-Christ speculation when he considers the Church as the sum of its members and with respect to the relationship of its members to one another. He eschews this influence by introducing in this case features of the popular Stoic conception, and admits it at most only in such formulations as οἱ πολλοὶ ἓν σῶμά ἐσμεν ἐν χριστῷ (so we, the many, are one body in Christ) in Romans 12:5. This is of course only a nuance of the formulation; however, it is not fortuitous.

If these observations are correct, the question spontaneously arises whether contradictory statements are not made about the Church when a conception of body is used which, on the one hand in Ephesians and Colossians, is oriented toward the cosmic "man" and, on the other hand in 1 Corinthians and Romans, toward a social "organism." Prescinding from the fact that both facets of this conception are derived from the notion of an Adam-Christ relationship, they not only are not contradictory, but they also complement each other.

According to the Apostle, the Church is always a synthesis of the two: it is a body of many faithful unified through and in Christ, and it is the body of Christ himself. Further, it is always Christ himself in his body, which he unites in himself into one body. *We* are "in Christ," in his body. Implied in this is that the Church is always the body of Christ, which has a primacy over the individual members and constitutes the individual faithful as "members"; that is, it accords them the possibility of being "members." But the Church is always the body which consists of the individual members, who assume their membership in terms of it. The former concept characterizes the Church more properly with reference to its origin or its principle (its ἀρχή!). Concretely, it proceeds from the one body of Christ on the cross (as 2:13ff shows) which embraces Jew and Gentile and which receives them into his sanctum of reconciliation.

Therefore the Church is always anterior to the individual, always more than the individual and the sum total of individuals. But at the same time it is constituted and unified by the individual faithful, who are "in Christ." The Church as the body of Christ and a communion of individual faithful has a primacy over each individual and is more than each member—individually and collectively. This communion of saints is even more than itself, but always a communion of the faithful.

However, in this sense too, the Church is both: it is always the all-embracing cosmos, and it is always an entity separated from the world. It is the encompassing cosmos within the compass of a limited entity. Precisely because it is the (new) world-body in an elevated and distinct social organism, it lays claim to all the world and consequently as the *Corpus Christi* attempts to draw it within its own and, therefore, Christ's body. From the very beginning of its history it has been in principle a world-church, and as such a concrete body of those baptized and believing in Christ. Only in this perspective does the history of the Church make sense, beginning with the infant community in Jerusalem, which did not remain long in its cradle without becoming aware of its essential character as the world-body of Christ. The Apostle Paul was the first to herald this, above all in his epistle to the Ephesians.

The Church is always both: "temporal reality" and "structure"; "body" and "organism" of individuals in whom the *Pneuma* is operative. Its sacramental character is connected with the former, and on this depends, always united with its sacramental character and partly as an outgrowth of it, its juridical character (1 Cor. 10:17). Here too the "personal" character of the body of Christ must not be forgotten. Inherent in the "organism" conception is the existential and charismatic character of the body of Christ. The organic unity and mutual implementation of both body-concepts is the key to an understanding of the entire phenomenon of the Church, in which sacraments and charisma are found in a juridical and concrete structure.

To ignore either of the two principal σῶμα concepts or any of their concomitant aspects would be to misrepresent the Pauline concept of the Church. Neither can be pitted against the other or made the norm for the other. Nor can they simply be placed alongside one another, as if the Apostle had a collection of notions on the Church at odds with one another.

On the contrary, one must first consider them in terms of their origin and content, respectively, and then explain their mutual relationship and actual congruity. Precisely the concept σῶμα for ἐκκλησία is a case in point, illustrating the rich historical background upon which the Apostle drew in formulating his thought, enabling him to present various aspects of ultimately the same phenomenon.

PART TWO

Ecclesia ad Extra

The Idea of Catholicity—
Concept and History

by JOSEF NEUNER

The Eschatological Idea of Catholicity

THE ULTIMATE MEANING of Catholicity must be derived from
the eschatological prophecies. Two series of biblical symbols are
brought to their conclusion in the last chapters of the Apocalypse—the idea of the spouse and the symbol of the Holy City.
First the Church appears as the spouse brought home, adorned
for her husband (Apoc. 21). She stands in contrast to the whore
who is bedecked as a harlot and offers the cup of seduction
(17:1). The Church is adorned for the husband, preserved as
virgin from corruption, with God's sanctifying love bestowed
upon her. None of the other biblical metaphors expresses the
personal character of the sanctity of the Church as forcefully as
that of the spouse. God has called the Church as spouse, has
sanctified and perfected her; he is the center of her life. This
loving faith and expectation remain the basic fact of the life of
the Church without which she would turn into an earthly institution.

In the metaphor of the Holy City the universality of salvation
and its transforming power is expressed. No trace of earthliness
is left in the Holy City, nothing profane. God is no longer distant,
God and world are inseparably united. The cubiform shape of
the city with equal length, breadth and height comprises all—a
unity in which there is no longer the heaven above the earth,

but instead the one heavenly world, or heaven enfolding the earth.

Nor are there any longer the segregated confines of the temple, "because its temple is the Lord God Almighty and the Lamb" (21:22); and as all beings are permeated by the uncreated light, the borrowed light of the sun has lost its meaning, because "the glory of the Lord shone there, and the Lamb gave it light" (21:23). The city is made of gold, transparent like glass (21:18). Gold stands for the high value of created things; but they have become transparent for God's light. There is neither death nor pain in the new world (21:4s), nor curse nor night any more, "but the throne of God and the Lamb will be there" (22:3).

Salvation had started with the first call of the chosen people to the pilgrimage through the desert during which God was with them; now the consummation has come: "Here is God's tabernacle pitched among men; he will dwell with them, and they will be his own people, and he will be among them, their own God" (21:3).

The measures of the walls express universality: the number twelve and its multiple "a hundred and forty-four," and its expansion into the thousandfold. Narrow national boundaries are no more. The nations and their kings have entered, and the doors stand ajar since there is no hostile world outside any more (21:24s). The stream of salvation that flows from the throne of God and the Lamb nourishes the trees of life on both banks, and they bear fruit every month, bringing health to all the nations (22:1ss). There is not just a single tree of life as in the middle of the paradise, but the life flowing from God has become the life of the world.

The promises for the end of time do not concern man merely as an individual. They are contained in the vision of the city, of the people of God, of the followers of the Lamb. In his final state man also remains embedded in the world in which he lived, incorporated into the community to which he has belonged. He would not be his true self were he not to remain united with his world. Hence the visions of the Apocalypse are widened into cosmic dimensions comprising man, his communities, the universe.

The other eschatological pronouncements of the New Testament also testify to this catholicity. The theme of Christ as head of the Church expresses the ultimate meaning of the universe, "recapitulating everything in him" (Eph. 1:10). Nor is the Church conceived as set apart from the universe, as a segregated realm, but rather the universe finds its fulfillment through the Church. Schlier says about Eph. 1:10: "The summing up of the universe takes place in its subordination under the head. And in its turn, this subordination of the universe under its head comes from the relation of the head to the Church. The fact that the Church receives her head implies that the universe receives its *kephalaion*, its summit which concludes, comprises and sums up her whole being. In Christ as the head of the universe it is held together as in its sum total."[1]

Thus the universality of God's kingship is verified in the created world. The history of the world ends with Christ's victory over all enemies, "when Christ places his kingship into the hands of God, his Father, having first dispossessed every other sort of rule, authority and power." Having also conquered death, "the Son himself will become subject to the power which made all things his subjects, so that God may be all in all" (1 Cor. 15:24–28).

God's sovereignty also means renewal in God, the universal restoration which is more than the return of things past. It means the fulfillment of all that God has pronounced through his holy prophets; it is final salvation in which man and the world are taken into the glory of God, become Christ's body, "the fullness of the one who fulfills all" (Eph. 1:23).

All these pronouncements are primarily eschatological and hence not directly applicable to the Church in her temporal existence. Still, there is no other way to determine the idea of catholicity in the visible Church but through eschatological perspective. The essence and the notes of the Church cannot be derived from her historical conditions, nor only from her institutional organization, in which they are embodied, but from her *mysterium,* from the transcendent, heavenly, eschatological reality which reveals itself in the terrestrial Church and in its history.

The Concept of Catholicity

Three elements rooted in the eschatological pronouncements of the New Testament are contained in the idea of catholicity: the unity of everything created in God; the universality of salvation, and the fulfillment of the destiny of the world.

The first of these elements is the transcendent union in God into which the created is called, beyond the limitations of its created existence. The world is destined for a unity which is not yet traced out in its natural structure, and hence cannot be achieved through its own efforts. It is the gift offered to the world if it allows itself to be called by God beyond its limits. The world reaches this destiny only if it becomes the spouse, called by God, only if it ceases to look at itself or at anything created, and is devoted only to the one who called it.

It seems that with this statement we touch the most important question of catholicity. Too often when speaking about the universality of the Church one has in mind only the earthly dimensions in which the Church is meant to spread. Perhaps we are no longer able to reach the breadth and depth of the earth because we do not know enough about God. The width of the horizon can grow only if we begin to see the world with the eyes of the transcendent God. The Church will not be able to transform the world unless the energies come from the world beyond. As long as she remains within the realm of this world, her work will be confined to reorganizing human life, perhaps according to better principles, but not integrating the world into a true catholic unity.

It is the constant temptation of the Church to give up the attitude of faith and to begin to be at home in the world, and as a consequence to lose her true catholicity. What an effort was needed for her in her early history to tear herself away from the self-centeredness of Jewish nationalism, to find the one God who is equally close to Jews and Gentiles.

Time and again Christianity discovers that, without intending to, it has drifted into a situation in which it is practically identical with a certain culture, for example the culture of the West, or with a certain social stratum. How difficult it is to set out again from the security of such a home and to return to the desert, to the loneliness and freedom in which God has established his covenant. Sometimes the connections of the Church are even more petty and narrow, embracing a caste or a group of similar economic interests with no urge to open the narrow circle for others. How difficult it is at times in the missions for a new convert to make contact with the closely-knit and exclusive social groups of Christian communities.

One might argue that all these people even in their narrowness firmly believe in God, and that in fact the deep faith of these Christians is their most precious asset. Therefore, the argument continues, it is not right to attribute their lack of catholic openness and responsibility to a defect in their attitude of faith. We answer: no doubt we are right in feeling true joy at the deep faith of many Christians in mission countries—but for all that this faith has its deficiencies. Sometimes it seems rather like a seed that has outlived the winter. It lives its own little life; it is protected, wary of being exposed to the dangers of frost. Its real purpose, however, is fulfilled only when it begins to grow, when it takes its own place in the gigantic enterprise of spring and is prepared to die in order to live.

Similarly the faith of many Christians is shut in and protected. It has become a well-guarded possession making our lives bright and secure, consoling and gladdening us. But it has ceased to be a living answer to God who has called us, a setting forth, a loss of life to find it. Its center is not the living transcendent God. On the contrary, it has turned itself back into our own world. The faith of these Christians no longer has the ring of expectant hope.

In the concrete experience of many Christians the Church is not so much the spouse searching for her bridegroom as the housewife with her hands full of work, who is no longer waiting for anything. With this well-intentioned zeal in a limited sphere, the strength of her catholicity, her "citizenship in heaven" (Phil. 3:2) dwindles. She becomes one of the many agents who are concerned about the betterment of the world and only dimly remembers the invitation to eschatological salvation.

It seems most important to stress this first and basic aspect in the idea of Catholicity: the eschatological union through Christ with the Father.[2] All the questions of spirituality, liturgy, catechetics, and the formation of priests found their relevancy to the Church's catholicity on this element. Catholicity is first of all the integration of the world into God's kingdom, and therefore cannot be limited to organizational and juridical schemes. It belongs to the inner life of the Church, to Christ's mystery which, through the Church, must be present in our world.

The second element of catholicity is the multiplicity of the universe which is united and transformed in Christ. Seen from the side of God, this element is based on the universality of salvation to which all are called in Christ. Seen from the side of the world, it expresses the stratified universe and the multiform life of man in culture and history which must find in Christ its ultimate and unifying meaning.

Hence Congar defines catholicity as "the quality of the Church through which its actual multiplicity enters into harmony with its actual unity." [3] It is the law that controls in her the relation between oneness and multiplicity. "This multiplicity is rooted in human nature itself: it includes the richness, the unlimited variations of human nature, the infinite possibilities of the first Adam which express themselves in many forms. They represent on the one hand the capacity for supernatural faith (theology calls it a *potentia oboedientialis*) and thus for a unifying bond through which all can be made one; on the other hand they comprise an infinity of nations and languages, of cultures, situations and conditions, of spiritual experiences and attitudes toward reality. Viewed from this angle, catholicity is the totality of all that is connected with man in so far as he is able to become one, to exist in a universal totality and to be led to a transcendent unity."

Thus catholicity means that man and his universe are to be integrated into oneness. It comprises first of all the whole man. If we speak of the whole man, we mean not only and not primarily the breadth of the geographic and cultural expansion of man in the course of history, but man's personal self. The Church is truly catholic only if man lives in it with the fullness of his freedom. This seems, at first glance, very obvious, for no one is forced to be a member of the Church.

However, it is highly questionable whether all members of the Church are personally committed to her. This was normally the case in the first Christian generation when the single believer had to accept salvation in Jesus Christ in a personal and sometimes dangerous commitment. It is one of the reasons why early Christianity was more catholic than later periods, though it was so much smaller in numbers and geographical extension. The whole man, his entire freedom, was committed to God in the Church. However, already during the intervals between the persecutions it became clear that many Christians belonged to the Church due to inherited habit rather than personal conviction.

In the Middle Ages practically no other alternative remained available: those who were not Christians had no place in that well-structured society. Yet, Christianity still continued to be the principal formative power of people's lives, whereas today it has become unreal and ineffective among many who still bear the Christian name. Their lives are linked with the Church only by means of certain dates in the calendar; their values and orientations are no longer determined by God. When such shallowness extends throughout entire nations, the term "Catholic countries" becomes rather questionable. We can speak truly of catholicity only where man is personally committed to the guidance and renewal that comes from God.

Man is further a collective being. It is not as an individual that he is redeemed into the communion of the Church, but as a member of the human race. The eschatological visions do not portray single souls as having been saved, but the people of God, the countless fellowship of the Lamb, the net filled with fish and the harvest gathered into the barns. Man's relation to the community must be primarily expressed in the consciousness of communion with others, in experienced solidarity, in the responsibility which he freely accepts towards his neighbor and towards the world. The Church is catholic when she inspires her members with a sincere and universal love which effectively breaks through the ring of self-related and group-related exclusiveness.

But catholicity must also be connected with concrete social structures: first of all as the new people of God, constituted as the visible Church, with its own community structure established by Jesus Christ. Still, to be truly catholic, the Church must penetrate the closely meshed network of our earthly communities. She is present first in the natural community of the family, which from apostolic times appears as the first pastoral unit. But she must permeate also the ever more complicated organism of modern life. Her members remain men of this world, committed to their earthly tasks. If the whole man belongs to the Church, the entire texture of modern life is drawn into the sphere of the Church.

The Church does not live alongside the world, but in it. In fact, she realizes more and more that in most cases she is no longer in a position to develop her own institutions parallel to the gigantic organizations of the modern state and society. She renounces the attempt to do so, not out of dire necessity, but in order to be catholic. She may not retire into the ghetto of ineffective isolation, and she cannot allow real life to go on outside her sphere of influence and hence remain unredeemed. The Church is catholic if she includes people as fully engaged members of modern society, not only during a weary hour or so of their occasional days off, but in their active responsibility in public life.

Ultimately, the whole man is the creative man who, according to God's will, explores, dominates and animates the universe and leads it to its destiny. Along with man, his work also must enter the Church, as in the vision of the Apocalypse the kings enter the Holy City with their treasures. In this way the Church becomes the safeguard and sanctification of the cultures not only of the West and not only of the past. If the Church were not able to overcome the present crisis of her estrangement from modern scientific and technical culture, her catholicity would be narrowed.

The third aspect of catholicity remains to be shown: the fulfillment of the world's destiny. Catholicity finds its full expression where the real world is unified and transformed in God. The Church is the place where God meets and sanctifies the world, and where the world is to be united and renewed. For the Church, to be catholic means to be the place of encounter and of consecration where the living God and the real world meet. The Church does not live for herself, nor is her pastoral care to be confined to the esoteric circle of her faithful. She seems to be absorbed by the world and yet becomes its renewing force.

When reflecting on the mystery of the presence of the Church in the world we must read once again the lines of the unknown author of the epistle to Diognetus: "Christians are not different from the rest of men in nationality, speech or customs. They do not live in cities of their own, nor do they use a special language, nor adopt a peculiar way of life. Whether fortune has given them a home in a Greek or foreign city, they follow local manners in the matter of dress, food, and way of life. Yet the character of culture they reveal is marvelous, and, it must be admitted, unique." The writer goes on to compare the life of Christians in the world with the influence of the soul on the body, in that the soul too leads a life in no way visibly segregated from the body and yet becomes the unifying and determining principle of bodily life.

The comparison must not be overstressed. Obviously the Church has her own life bestowed on her from God. She has her life, however, in order to give it. She is entrusted with God's word not to repeat it in a sterile monologue with herself, but to offer it in ever new ways to men of changing ages; she is salt that salts in being dissolved; light that gives itself up in radiation. She is not concerned about herself, she can never lose her life, for she does not belong to herself. She is nothing else but God's salvation and truth in the midst of the world.

Catholicity in the Old Testament, and the Segregation of Israel

We turn to the history of catholicity in the stages of biblical revelation and in the phases of the history of the Church. In them, both the meaning and the problems of catholicity are unfolded. We can focus our attention only on a few aspects of this history; the selection may seem arbitrary. We select those points of view which have special significance for the understanding of the modern missionary task.

We presume the universality of salvation as taught in the Old Testament.[4] The segregation of Israel, however, seems to contradict this universalism. Only Israel was called into the special covenant with Yahweh, whereas the other nations seem to have been omitted. This exclusiveness, stressed by Israel's isolation from other nations, was pushed to such extremes that subjected tribes had to be uprooted in order not to entice Israel out of its segregation. Was not such isolation an expression of fear which must lead to poverty and narrowness?

The seclusion from the religious cultures of the surrounding nations and, in particular, the prohibition against representing God in sculptures deprived artistic activity of its most sublime object. The exclusion of "pagan" mythologies kept religious literature on a primitive level, for creative forces express themselves primarily in mythological figures. The seclusion was bound to become a real danger at the very moment when the narrowness of the Jewish world was broken open from outside. The danger was present already in the infiltration of the pagan cults of surrounding nations, but it had its full impact when the people were led away into captivity in the midst of the high cultures of Assyria and Babylonia, and became alarmingly aware of their own insignificance in the face of the powerful administrative machinery, the proud architecture and the complex economic system of the contemporary world powers. What precisely was the significance of this segregation for the education of the chosen people to catholicity?

The result of Israel's segregation was certainly the preservation of pure monotheism in at least one nation where it could spread to other peoples. But apart from this pedagogical purpose, it seems that even the segregation itself was the first and decisive step towards catholicity. This we have to explain.

We have described catholicity as the unity in multiplicity, the fullness of human life under God's obedience. This theme of God's kingship over the universe is unfolded in history, and so we may expect at the beginning of this history God's unequivocal claim in which he demanded the totality of human life for himself, placing man under his law, taking him under his care. God must be revealed as the only principle of union, without which no universal union in this world was possible. Already the covenant of Noah linked all mankind to God, but its content must be defined more clearly. In the covenant of Abraham the central demand of salvation was contained, namely, man's total obedience in faith. Finally the covenant of Sinai expressed Yahweh's relation to Israel as a nation. Israel belonged to Yahweh not only like other nations, in that they were guided by his providence, but also because she was chosen as his own.

Israel's history begins—a history which is not like the calculable result of a natural balance of powers, but one which stems from God's free disposition. In every respect Israel must be conscious of her immediate dependence on Yahweh. Unlike Egypt, she did not receive her living from the annual irrigation, which could be rationally utilized. Rather, she received a land "that is watered by the rain of the sky of which the Lord thy God takes care" (Deut. 11:11).

The dependence on God became even more palpable because of her geographic position between the two power blocks, Egypt and Assyria, from both of whom she must, according to the direction of the prophets, remain equally independent in order to rely on God alone. One single nation had first to understand, live and suffer through what it meant to belong to God and to have a history which was not its own, but which God had reserved to himself to reveal his salvation.

Hence it was through her particular history that Israel became the witness to the true God, the universal Lord of all nations. Her exclusive election was not meant as a narrowing down of salvation, but as an exclusive tie with the living God. Only if Israel knew the true God could she begin to communicate him to others. This communication began early in single cases like that of Naaman; later on the exile had, in God's plans, the meaning of bringing the knowledge of the true God to the Gentiles (Tob. 13:6ff). Israel became the bearer of the mystery of salvation for which the nations were longing: "A time is coming when there is never a man of Jewish blood but shall have ten Gentiles at his heels, and not two of the same speech; clinging all at once to the skirts of him, and crying, your way is ours! The tale has reached us how God is there to protect you" (Zach. 8:23).

So it becomes clear why the universalism of the Old Testament is intimately connected with the idea and worship of God. As long as Yahweh was considered a tribal god who led his people and defended them against other peoples and their gods, there could be no true understanding of the universality of salvation. The more the idea of God was elevated and purified from its anthropomorphisms, the more was he also understood as the God of the universe and as Lord and saviour of the nations.

This progress was not a matter of merely intellectual clarifications, but of man's basic religious orientation. So long as he enclosed God in narrow human conceptions, gave him mythological names, represented him in images—which according to primitive thinking meant nothing else than keeping him within reach and being able to make use of the divine power for one's own service—just so long did the idea of God remain particularistic and unfit for redeeming man from his isolation. This is the very meaning of revelation: that God manifested himself as universal Lord and king, and that man was called out of his self-centered world to belong to God under his holy and free decrees. Hence, what primarily matters in revelation is not the conceptual idea of God, but whether God is to be subject to man (either as an individual or a self-interested tribe), or man to God, ready to take his place under God's universal kingship.

It follows that in the Old Testament not only was the cult of strange gods an abomination—as anti-national as it was anti-religious—but also the false cult of Yahweh, performed on the high places, was forbidden, because not only did strange gods lead man astray, but the true God too could be misinterpreted and his cult could become idolatrous. It is idolatrous when carried out according to human designs and with superstitious intentions, because in worshiping thus, man does not subject himself to God, but serves himself and tries to make God's majesty, power and even love subservient to his own interests.

All this remains valid also in the Church. In the New Testament the one living God remains the deepest mystery, and it remains the basic duty of every Christian to bow down under God's Lordship and to become truly obedient. Our self-examination for true catholicity must, therefore, begin with a scrutiny of the worship and spirituality of the Church, because here the innermost sources of catholicity are hidden, and they must not be kept buried.

From the Old Testament we also learn how in Israel the universalism of salvation was lost sight of: "The children of the kingdom will be put forth into the darkness outside" (Matt. 8:12). The reason for this failure was not a total loss of the substance of revelation but the perversion of Israel's relationship to God. Originally the covenant meant a relationship of service and submission under God's own Lordship, but it was turned by the Jews into an insurance to guarantee salvation independently of penance and obedience. The Jews considered it sufficient to have Abraham as their father (Matt. 3:9). Circumcision was the mark of faith. It became the symbol of their being preferred to the Gentiles. The temple was God's house, and center of his worship. It became, however, the rallying point of Jewish nationalism, embodying a national-religious sense of superiority, so that every hint of the relativity of its significance was considered a crime against the nation (Matt. 26:61; Acts 6:13).

Even the growing missionary activity of the post-exilic period became a means of self-glorification (Matt. 23:15). The books of the history of salvation, with their prophetic openness towards the messianic fulfillment, became for the Jews the chartered title of their own rights, to which they appealed even against God when he invited them to true salvation in Jesus: "We are disciples of Moses" (John 9:28). Thus Israel lost her mission. To be sure, she still went on dwelling among the nations, and was even more dispersed, not as a sign of redemption, but of lost grace.

Such considerations are of deep significance for the missionary catholicity of the Church. The task of the Church consists in doing God's work, in letting his light shine, in seeking his glory —not in building her own kingdom. Whether the Church has always expressed this attitude in her mission work may be checked against each of the points mentioned in connection with Israel. We certainly should be aware that, at least in the eyes of non-Christians, the Church appears to be far too much centered upon herself. Too often we come across the distinction between Christ, who is somehow accepted, and the Church, which is spurned. People who come from outside find it hard to see the connection between the simplicity of Christ with his message and the complex apparatus of modern ecclesiastical life with the strong emphasis on organizational and intellectual structures which seem to become an end in themselves. They are not an end. They are only the concrete presence of God's words in human signs. The reflections on the Old Testament should aid us in examining the extent to which the concrete human appearance of the Church reveals God or conceals him.

The Universality of God's Kingdom in the New Testament

In the New Testament the idea of catholicity is expressed not so much in the sphere of the visible Church as in the universality of God's kingship and of the world's salvation. Of course, the visible Church also received the universal mission through Christ's command to go and teach all nations (Matt. 28:18). These words contain a program of missionary universalism for proclaiming the gospel and establishing the Church. Yet, while on the one hand these words were only the concluding formula of a long initiation of the disciples into the meaning of catholicity, on the other hand, seen in the light of the early history of the missions, they are comparable to an anticipation of the universal missionary work which at first was not fully grasped and the complete understanding of which was the result of prolonged efforts. It seems therefore that the consideration of the universalism in the New Testament should not begin with these words of universal mission, but rather should inquire into Jesus' spirit of catholicity.

Jesus' earthly life still pertained to the framework of the old covenant. He considered himself sent only to the lost sheep of the house of Israel (Matt. 15:24); he did not send his disciples abroad (Matt. 10:5). But within the narrow Jewish frame of his life, a new world was in the making. The source of all salvation was God, whose love and kingdom were equally close to all men. There was no longer any prerogative of birth or covenant before God, which would allow an appeal to Moses or Abraham. It was precisely the confidence in their privileges that made the Jews blind to true salvation, with the result that they were cast out, while many came "from the east and from the west and will feast with Abraham and Isaac and Jacob in the kingdom of heaven" (Matt. 8:11). While the Jews remained without, the others entered from the streets and lanes, the highways and hedgerows; all were called, the poor and the blind, the crippled and the lame (Matt. 4:21ff).

The innermost reason for Jesus' universalism is found in his preaching of God's kingship. It was the core of Jesus' message against the self-centeredness of Jewish religious life. The ethics of the Sermon on the Mount contained the call to the people to dispose themselves for the kingdom of God. The whole sphere of religious life—prayer, fasting and alms—was gathered up under the ethics of God's kingdom, and therefore directed toward God alone.

Prayer was no longer a formula to which human anxiety clung in a superstitious craving for security, but became the trusting word of the heart before God the Father. It relied on no one but God, the only Lord, the sole refuge, the witness before whom the hidden intentions of the heart lay open. In Jesus' mission to take the world to his Father all the great figures of the past lost their particular significance. Abraham, Moses, Elias, Jonas—all led to Jesus, but their task was preparatory only to his mission of proclaiming and establishing God's universal kingdom.

But Jesus was more than teacher. In him God's Lordship and love were translated into the solidarity of salvation for all mankind. He entered the world as one of ourselves and took his place in the rank of sinners to be baptized by John. He bore the curse of sin with us, and for us, unto death. For Jesus the universality of God's kingdom consisted not primarily in the expectation of the Church's expansion—though it was constantly present in his mind and appeared as an undercurrent in many of his sayings [5] —but most of all, and in a more personal sense, in his own communion with, and responsibility for, the world.

In him God showed how much he loves the world, and therefore Jesus' life became self-surrender for the salvation of the world. He saw himself as the light of the world, as the fountain of the waters of salvation, as the bread of life. The whole meaning of his coming was contained in the consciousness of his solidarity with mankind. He could not think of his own life without the desire to bear fruit in the branches of the vine, nor of his glory without speaking of the spirit whom he sends to strengthen, teach, and sanctify his own. When he was overwhelmed by the vision of the glory which he would share with his Father, he prayed that his own would also be there with him.

So Jesus' universalism consisted in his belonging to man through his love unto death and into glory, to all without limits and distinctions, so that his own life became the life of the world. The life and teaching of Jesus were catholic not because some general appeal to the human race was subsequently added to them, but because he himself belonged to the world.

Consequently, the missionary education of the disciples was also free from missionary slogans. They must learn first the true service of God and the sincere love of their neighbor, and be ready to do him service. Slowly they must understand that greatness in God's kingdom consists only in greater love, and that the discipleship of Jesus must be tested by the changing of their small, self-centered lives. Only after having learned to give themselves to God and to their neighbor, would the disciples be prepared to receive the missionary command of Jesus.

In our day the missionary enterprise of the Church is suspected of being a veiled policy of power, a last attempt of the

West to stabilize a spiritual hegemony over the world. The Church can escape such suspicions if, according to her master's example, she discards resounding slogans (one should know, for instance, of the allergic reaction of many non-Christians to words like "crusade" and other terms burdened with historic remembrances). Today more than ever the missionary spirit must grow at the springs of the mystery of salvation, as the consciousness of common solidarity and personal obligation for the salvation of many.

We omit further reflections on the universalism of the New Testament, particularly of St. Paul, and turn to the growth of the young Church in the early Christian centuries.

Catholicity in the Patristic Age

In the post-apostolic era the word was finally found that henceforth stood for the universality of salvation and the world-wide mission of the Church, namely the word "catholic." Ignatius of Antioch was the first to use it. From the beginning it has comprised the two aspects of universality in unity which mark the essence of catholicity. It stands for the Church in so far as she contains salvation for all, and therefore is spread over the world. But it stands equally well for the total adhesion to God in the obedience of faith, against schism and heresy.[6] The early Christian experience of universalism in cult [7] and doctrine [8] comprised both, the world-wide expansion to all nations together with the consciousness of being united to God in Christ.

However, we do not intend to enter into an analysis of the patristic concept of catholicity. Rather, we are concerned with two main questions: How did the catholic spirit of the early Church express itself in missionary work, and what was the attitude of the early Church toward the non-Christian world?

Both questions are of significance for the missionary theology of today.

It seems that the missionary achievement of the early Church is one of the movements of history that defies an adequate explanation. One should not, of course, imagine that in three centuries the entire Roman Empire converted into a Christian world. With cautious experts one may perhaps assume that one-eighth or one-tenth of the empire became Christian during this period [9] —which is close to the proportion of Christians in modern Africa. Nor should one presume that all these Christians excelled in their Christian life. The sermons of the great bishops of East and West give testimony of pastoral problems which exist at all times. Nevertheless, the Fathers rightly considered miraculous the expansion and consolidation of Christianity during this period.[10] A superior power manifested itself, entering into history and prevailing. The realistic politician Constantine clearly understood that the future belonged not to the greater number and the more powerful institutions of the pagans, but to the more dynamic minority of the Christians. If ever the mission work of the Church has attained its goal, to establish the Church, it was in these early centuries.

We know little about the concrete methods of the missionary enterprise. No blueprint existed for an extensive missionary propaganda. There were, to be sure, prophets and wandering preachers in the Church along with the official hierarchy.[11] But it would be wrong to attribute the main burden of the missionary work to these extraordinary agents, especially since their relationship to the hierarchy was unstable and at times the free life of these wandering apostles could hide pseudo-prophets.[12] Nor do we find any real missionary literature. L. Hertling remarks: "It is altogether striking that in the Christian sources into the fourth century and beyond we are little conscious of missionary purpose or even of missionary enthusiasm." [13]

The writings of the Apologists were not so much an invitation and initiation into Christianity as a defense, and for this reason they contain only fragments of real Christian doctrine. We must conclude that this decisive period of Christian expansion did not witness a specialized missionary enterprise. The real supporters of the work were not special organizations, not even outstanding missionary figures—the support came from the Church herself and, more precisely, the local community.[14]

We have no coherent description of the way in which the Church fulfilled this task, but we can reconstruct it to some extent from the documents. The center of all Christian propagation was the word of God, the good tidings and Christian instruction. St. Paul already considered preaching his main task, not organization, not even the administration of sacraments. The platform for preaching varied: first the synagogue, then the public lecture room, often the private household enlarged by neighbors and friends. One should not think of the sermons as the exposition of a doctrinal system. The attraction of Christianity was based not so much on a theoretical synthesis as on the genuineness and vigor of the message. Soon catechetical schools developed in which a systematic approach to the Christian message was worked out and reasoned answers were given to theological problems.

Yet the strength of Christianity continued to be the power of the spirit and the consciousness of having access in Jesus Christ to the true and living God. In our age, which relies so much on indirect missionary methods (which indeed often are indispensable), it is important to remember that early Christianity relied primarily on the force of its message. If today we concentrated more on the force of our message, our organizational means and methods would have better prospects of success.[15]

The center of the Christian message was the new idea of God or rather man's new relationship to God.[16] It was not only doctrine, it was life revealing itself, according to frequent testimonies, in the victory over all demonic powers. Unredeemed man experienced the sway of strange and hostile powers, either ruling his life from the stars, as he believed, or besieging him as evil spirits, or dwelling in his own breast. In many a mission country even today one can see how the fear of these evil powers can be an obsession with man. Hence the message of Jesus as the victor over demons, as the Lord of the cosmos and the ruler of human destinies, was a strong factor in the propagation of Christianity.

Also important were the moral values. The preaching and the example of virginity as the consecration of oneself to God gave new dignity to human life, especially to women. The witness of confessors and martyrs made a deep impression as they professed with their lives their faith in God's ascendancy over all created things. The testimony of charity was also significant. It became an impressive objective lesson in the Christian idea of God and the solidarity of men. Almsgiving developed into a universal and well-organized practice. The help for the sick and abandoned became the concern of Christians. Care was provided for prisoners and those sentenced to the mines. Christians were noted for their hospitality. They even took charge of burying the dead. There was mutual assistance among the Christian communities.

All this was not practiced as propaganda calculated to attract new members to the Christian communities by material advantages—the charge of "rice-Christians" was unknown in the early missionary work of the Church, even among the adversaries of Christianity—it was rather the spontaneous expression of Christian faith. The Christians felt that they were the new people of God, redeemed from sin and hostile powers, children of God the Father, united in the Holy Spirit. They lived this solidarity in a liturgy much more spontaneous and understandable than in later times, so that all could take part in the sacred mysteries without any artificial helps.

There were, moreover, factors which especially favored the expansion of Christianity. Some will be mentioned, for they have their striking parallels in our time. Early Christianity expanded in surroundings where fixed norms and orientations had been lost. The Apologists frequently referred to the stupidity of polytheism; even where the concept of the one supreme being was accepted, it remained abstract and without life.

Increasing the general uncertainty was the mixture of nations and religious traditions. None of the inherited philosophies or religions was in a position to offer orientation for the new cosmopolitan world which formed around the Mediterranean. Religion either remained the antiquated practice of traditional rituals which had long since lost their meaning, or it turned into magic or became a philosophical speculation. In addition, the traditional socio-religious ties of family and tribe were loosened, especially in the cities, with the result that the acceptance of a new religion became easier. With the new universalism, a new religion of cosmopolitan, "catholic" character was also necessary. Thus Christianity entered a world which not only offered the exterior means of speedy expansion (the easy routes of communications and a common tongue), but which also in a special way was open to and in need of the Christian message. The analogies to the present situation are obvious and need not be pointed out in detail.

Our second question is also important: What was the attitude of Christianity to the surrounding world? The real beginning of early missionary activity consisted in the break-through into the pagan world. There was, of course, a necessary minimum of consideration for the Jewish tradition, insisted upon by the Council of Jerusalem, but, generally speaking, it was the first and only time in history when the Church had full freedom to adapt herself to the new world into which she entered. Christian life and worship could develop in a creative way. They naturally took shape in the language and the customs of the time. Though Christians were intensely conscious of themselves as the people of God, they remained embedded in their milieu, so that exteriorly they could not be distinguished from non-Christians.

Yet one line was drawn very clearly: anything savoring of pagan rites or in any way connected with immoral customs was banned. Over a long period, for instance, no incense and no musical instruments were used in Christian worship because they had played such an important role in the pagan temples.[17] Christians kept away from anything connected with the *"pompa diaboli,"* especially from public spectacles, and Tertullian assures us (perhaps a little too optimistically): "The rejection of these amusements is the chief sign that a man has adopted the Christian faith." [18] For the rest, Christian life developed in the Syrian, Greek and Roman world without special problems.

The question of adaptation became difficult only in the encounter with contemporary intellectual life. Christianity could not but enter into the philosophical discussion of its time if it wished to present its doctrine scientifically, to compare it with other doctrines and to safeguard it against objections.

It was not surprising that different attitudes are taken in this encounter: the open and optimistic attitude, represented mainly in Alexandria where Greek philosophy was conceived as the pedagogical preparation for Christ, and the scornful rejection with which Tertullian spurned the wisdom of the world before the folly of the faith. The two attitudes were complementary, and both together were "catholic," that is, they embraced the entire world and referred it to God so that human wisdom was at once fulfilled and conquered in divine faith. As a result, the treasures of ancient thought were integrated into the tradition of the Church, and at the same time molded anew.

The Church borrowed from different sources. It is obvious that Epicurus was excluded. Aristotle was viewed very skeptically in the early centuries, while later on his thought strongly influenced John of Damascus and triumphed in the schools of the Middle Ages. The Stoics wielded an early and great influence through their doctrines of the logos and their noble ethical principles, and also probably because of their innate universalism. The greatest impact, however, was exercised by Plato in his Neoplatonic garb, through the sublime doctrine of God and stress on the world beyond.

However, in each of these encounters the content of the system was subjected to the criterion of Christian revelation. So it happened that in spite of errors which crept into the thinking of the Fathers—since errors cannot be avoided wherever man tackles problems earnestly and courageously—their doctrine remained clearly distinct from the philosophical systems because revelation was always its center of gravity. This is the delicate border between gnostic systems and Christian theology: Gnosticism takes possession of revelation and subjects it to the categories of man-made systems of thought, while Christian theology makes use of religious and philosophical systems in order to reach a deeper and more comprehensive understanding of the word of God.[19]

The way in which this encounter with Greek philosophy takes place must be studied in a concrete example. Such a study is both instructive and important for a truly "catholic" theology. Gregory Thaumaturgus gives us a vivid account of Origen, his master.[20] He begins with the frank statement of his own total disregard for the pagan philosophers—a frequent phenomenon among neo-Christians—because "they bring upon the very name of philosophy extreme ridicule from the great mass of men." Origen, on the contrary, impressed him by his genuine soberness: he demanded of his disciples at once deeds and words, he "urged us to practice righteousness." Origen insisted not only on intellectual instruction but on the formation of the whole man.

Yet this training was not meant to lead into an intellectual ghetto: "He was the first and only man that urged me to study the philosophy of the Greeks." Apart from the atheistic systems, "all other systems had to be studied." It was Origen's intent to show to his disciples one partial aspect of truth through each system. This, of course, was meaningful only if he himself knew the goal toward which he moved, and if "as translator and interpreter" he was able to introduce his disciples to divine revelation and to direct them to center their minds "on God only and on his prophets."

And Gregory continues his description of Origen: "The greatest gift this man has received from God, and the noblest endowment God has bestowed on him from heaven is that he should be an interpreter of the oracles of God to man, and that he might understand the words of God even as if God spoke to him, and that he might recount them to men in such wise as they may hear them with intelligence."

For Origen, therefore, Christianity was not a doctrine side by side with others, but the recapitulation, interpretation and final judgment of all human wisdom. This truly catholic attitude gave the disciples the freedom "to go round the whole circle of knowledge." There were, to be sure, dangers in this method, but certainly these principles express the very essence of "catholic" theology as it must be pursued even today, namely as the science that gathers the totality of human knowledge into the oneness of God, thereby perfecting and transcending it.

Such was the way early Christianity lived its catholicity, clearly marked against the world, yet never segregated. It was, in principle at least, free from compromise with pagan surroundings, and yet did not hesitate to take over that way of life, language and way of thinking. So it became the powerful ferment of a new world, stronger than the existing pagan traditions.

Catholicity in the Modern Church

In our time as well, catholicity means the union of the world with God, the renewal and sanctification in God of the whole world as it is today and as it grows. Such a preliminary application of our concept of catholicity to modern conditions should make us understand already that the problem is not restricted to the mission field. Today, catholicity is not primarily a matter of numerical expansion, but a question of the life of the Church.

Undoubtedly the missions are among the most important tasks of the Church, and it is quite possible to use missionary progress as an indication of the catholic spirit of the Church herself, but it would be a dangerous mistake to consider it the only sphere in which the catholicity of the Church must manifest itself. In the growth of the missions the life of the Church reveals itself. The urge to spread and develop springs from the whole Church, while on the other hand slowness of growth is an indication of a lack of vitality.

To carry out her missionary task the Church must first of all live in close contact with the supernatural forces which give her life. They are more decisive than her organizations. But it is equally necessary that the Church take her place in the modern world. If the Church had no answer to the problems of our time, derived from the word of God; if she were not able to think out and interpret the happenings of our day in the context of the divine plan of salvation; if she could not meet modern man as he is, in his self-assurance and in his latent anxiety—if the Church were not able to do all this in the modern world, she would be doomed to failure also in the missions, because the young nations are in search of the true meaning of man and the world.

Some of the deficiencies of the Church are more clearly visible in the missions. For instance, it is all too evident that the Church has remained a stranger to the great nations of the East. It would seem, however, that the reason for this failure lies, to some extent, in the West, because the Church has been estranged from the Western nations as well—or at least from vast portions of them—and has neglected contact with forces that are at work in the modern world. It would not be right to attribute the slowness of missionary progress to the missionaries only or to the lack of financial and organizational aid. The missionary situation is ultimately a matter of responsibility for all Christians. The whole Church must examine itself. No one can redeem himself from this examination of conscience through gifts of money, not even by dispatching missionaries. The whole Church must give expression to its catholicity.

For this reason it is so important to investigate the concrete meaning of catholicity in the modern Church, not only in the mission field but also all over the world.

A word at least must be said about the hierarchical structure of the Church. We are living in a world which as never before has become one. In this situation it is hardly possible to overestimate the importance of the firm hierarchical structure of the Church. This unity of the Church is not the result of laborious efforts, but rather God's gift from above. Yet the Church must never cease to reflect on the concrete forms in which this unity should be expressed.

The hierarchical government of the Church must comprise the totality of ecclesiastical life and of the modern world. There is a deep-rooted prejudice in mission countries that the Church is Western, or even Italian. This prejudice cannot be effectively removed except through the picture of a truly world-wide representation in the actual government of the Church.

Such a supernatural universality must, moreover, be supplemented by the representation of experts in the various spheres of modern life. Admittedly it is not the task of the Church to prepare economic programs or to advise scientific research centers. But it is necessary for her, in the fast rhythm of our time, to be able to express her attitude on ever-new questions. She can do so only if there are men who, along with their theological formation, have an insight into the achievements and the problems of the modern world—experts in medicine and hygiene, population problems, international law, development programs, and so forth.

Finally, the variety of conditions and tasks in different regions must come into play if the richness and multiplicity of life is truly to be preserved in ecclesiastical unity. Much has been said about a more regional structure of the Church and a gradation of authority from the local bishop over an ecclesiastical region to the supreme authority of the Roman pontiff. These questions are of great significance and actuality today, bearing as they do on the Church's adaptation of herself to the modern world, by which she can present herself to all as truly catholic.

NOTES

[1] Kittel, *Theologisches Wörterbuch*, III, 682.

[2] Y. Congar describes the element of oneness in the concept of catholicity: "Seen from the angle of unity, catholicity is based on the fullness of the grace of Christ who is made by God, head of the new human race, and, even further, of the world. (s. Eph. 1:22ff; 3:19; Col. 2:9). Christ is constituted by God principle of a new existence of all things. His fullness consists in the power, indwelling in him, to redeem, to heal, to transform and to lead to God all that is truly human in man, the totality of his possibilities, and even the vastness of the universe that is destined for man in order that he may sing his praise. The catholicity of the head is the basis of the catholicity of the Church. The latter consists essen-

tially in the power to transform, to save, to fulfill, to lead to unity everything that is human in the world, i.e., all that can be animated by man." "Catholicité" in *Catholicisme, Hier, Aujourd'hui, Demain* II, 724.

3 Y. Congar, *op. cit.*, 723f.

4 Cf. H. H. Rowley, *The Missionary Message of the Old Testament* (London: 1945); Y. Raguin, *Theologie Missionaire de l'Ancien Testament* (Paris: 1947).

5 Cf. Meinertz, *Theologie des Neuen Testamentes* (Bonn: 1950), I, 53–56.

6 "Apart from the bishop, let no one perform any of the functions that pertain to the Church. Let that Eucharist be held valid which is offered by the bishop or by one to whom the bishop has entrusted this charge. Wherever the bishop appears, there let the people be, as wherever Christ is, there is the catholic Church" (to the Smyrnians 8).

7 The Eucharistic prayer of the Didache reads: "As the broken bread was scattered upon the mountain tops and being harvested was made one, so let the Church be gathered together from the ends of the earth into thy kingdom" (cp. 9). "Make thy Church perfect in thy love, and gather it from the four winds sanctified for thy kingdom which thou hast prepared for it" (cp. 10).

8 Irenaeus, *adv. haeres.*, 1, 10, 1.

9 The estimates vary from less than one-twentieth by Gibbon to one-half. Cf. Latourette, *A History of the Expansion of Christianity* (London: 1938), I, 108–12.

10 Latourette, *loc. cit.*, I, 112: "Never in the history of the race has this record ever quite been equaled. Never in so short a time has any other religious faith, or, for that matter, any other set of ideas, religious, political, or economic, without the aid of physical force or of social or cultural prestige, achieved so commanding a position in such an important culture."

11 Origen gives an impressive description: "Some of them made it their business to itinerate not only through cities, but even villages and country houses that they might make converts to God. And no one would maintain that they did this for the sake of gain, when sometimes they would not accept even necessary sustenance." Nor could vain glory be the motive: "At the present day the discredit attaching to it among the

rest of mankind is greater than any supposed honor enjoyed among those who hold the same belief." (*Contra Celsum* III, 9).

[12] Cf. Didache 11, 5.

[13] L. Hertling, *A History of the Catholic Church*, transl. (Newman Press, 1957), p. 10f.

[14] Cf. Schmidlin, *Missionsgeschichte*, 71, based on Harnack, *Ausbreitung des Christentums* (1909), I, 415.

[15] Jungmann sees the value of the reflection on conditions in early Christianity "especially in the spontaneity and simplicity of the Christian life, in the clarity of its ideals which were not split up and diluted, but lived in the conscience of the faithful with their original vigor, and gave them the assurance and the impetus which conquered a pagan world." *Die Frohbotschaft der Glaubensverkündigung* (1936), p. 29.

[16] It is the main concern of the Apologists to develop the Christian idea of God in contrast to the pagan errors. St. Gregory of Nyssa does the same where he gives a description of the method of instructing the pagans in the introduction to the great Catechesis: The entire course is centered around the idea of God, its foundations and clarifications. Similarly, St. Ambrose describes the stages of the instruction of the pagans in the following way (in the *Commentary to St. Luke*, VI, 104): The presentation of the doctrine of the one God; the true worship of God; the need of discarding superstition and idolatry; initiation into the salvation through Christ.

[17] Cf. Jungmann, *Missarum Sollemnia* (Freiburg: 1948), I, 393f.

[18] *De spectaculis*, 24.

[19] These questions have actual significance also today, not only in the clarification of the relation of mythological elements to Scripture and patristic thinking, but also in determining the catholic attitude towards the great religious systems of the world. They are borrowing—just as in hellenistic times—from Christian sources, and, in doing so, stiffen their defenses against the Christian message. Modernized world religions form a new type of gnostic system in which elements of all religions, and mainly Christian elements, are integrated into their own philosophical and spiritual context.

[20] *Oratio Panegyrica in Origenem*, M.G. 10, 1051ff.

The Church—God's Party?

by HERMANN ZELLER

AN HISTORICAL ERA is distinguished first and foremost by the profound changes it introduces into patterns of thought and life. The causes of these changes are both material and spiritual, coming from natural, physical laws and free, personal impulses; they work in gradual transformation of society or in sudden revolutions.

It is to be expected that the characteristics of a particular era will leave their mark on the religious forms of that era, for religion is an intimate part of human life, and cannot, if it is to remain vital, be immune to the forces of development inherent to human life. This involvement in human development, however, presents a searching problem to Christianity: the Church of Christ must develop with its members, and yet remain the unique, final, divinely guaranteed community of salvation for all; it must become all things to all men and yet remain itself.

It is beyond the scope of this article to examine all the individual impressions made on religion by modern attitudes; we should like, therefore, to pick out one prominent ideology of modern social life to illustrate the ambiguity of a church among temporal men. It is a dangerous ideology, which has unconsciously penetrated from secular into religious thought. We refer to the ideology of the Party, which has become an important form of life and thought of the modern masses.

The Church is never a Party! Not even the Party of God! She has her own rights and truths to represent, but not as a Party. We shall see later what this means.

The growth of the "Party mentality" is due to two factors: one secular-historical—a disintegration of democracy, and one religious-historical—the disintegration of Christianity into a number of unreconciled "denominations."

Let us first consider the rise of Party mentality in the secular world. With the coming to power of a new social order in the last century, an order based on the idea of popular sovereignty, came also the organization of men into groups which were to control society by winning as many adherents as possible to the program of the Party. But the ideas of the parties developed, in the struggle for adherents, into narrow-minded systems which lost sight of the rights and interests of others. The solicitation of the masses became demagogy whereby one group dragged the others along with ever more questionable methods. The power of numbers led these groups to the attempt to demand from their adherents a blind obedience, and unconditioned opposition to those outside the Party.

It is not our intention to judge these things politically: we are considering them only in relation to their effect on religious and ethical development. We are pointing a finger at a human danger, in order better to recognize this danger as it threatens religious life.

When this group egoism finds its way into religious life, it finds nourishment above all in the splitting of Christianity into hostile denominations. Thus we come to the consideration of the second, the religious-historical cause, of the Party mentality in the religious sphere.

There have been schisms in the Church from the very beginning; Christ predicted them, and in the letters of the apostles we can read warnings against those trying to divide the Christian community. A thousand years ago the Christian East went its own way, to be followed six hundred years later by Protestantism. Today, of the approximately nine hundred million Christians, only a little more than one-half are members of the Catholic Church; the others constitute a myriad of confessions.

The divisions among the many confessions are much deeper than political or cultural ones: the ecumenical meetings of the past few decades reveal, in addition to much good will, the impossibility of compromise in questions of faith and conscience. Only God's grace will be able to free us from the shameful state of affairs of this division of his Church.

It is, however, at least our duty to do away with this spirit of sectarianism, this modern religious form of the Party mentality. For, if we Catholics are not to blame for the separation itself, we can still be guilty of its growth and persistence.

A victory over sectarianism is not easy. Some have sought a brotherhood in the area of Christian practice alone, prescinding more and more from doctrinal differences. Such an attempt must fail, for it ignores the very heart of our dissension. Others undermine the doctrinal differences by pursuing a theoretical solution which on principle concedes all confessions freedom of opinion and an equal right in exercising the duties of Christ's successor, hoping all the same to bring them to one table under one roof. It is their belief that any human society claiming immutable truth and right would already be practicing sectarianism. But their efforts are in vain, because the majority of confessions have always held to the conviction that God's revelation, in its unequivocal binding force, remains the foundation of Christian hope for salvation and community.

Still others, falsely appealing to the truth that "outside the Church there is no salvation," assert their own absolute position, and demand from others total surrender. They set their own church against the others as the Party of God against the Party of Satan. They are frustrated, however, by the consciousness of others that they and all that lives in them are not simply in the wrong before God and their conscience.

We find ourselves, then, in a painful dilemma: on the one hand, our Christian conscience forbids disunity, while, on the other, it forces it on us. We can escape this dilemma it would seem, only through a reconsideration of the Catholic concept of the Church and of the relationship of the Catholic Church to the separated confessions and to non-Christians as well.

There is no road to salvation other than the Church, no way to unity other than a home-coming to this Church. But the journey to reconciliation will be much easier and will by-pass the party strife which so burdens our times, when we know and feel ourselves as Christ's Church, not building a self-sufficient, indolent ghetto, but rather sharing the Church's responsibility to the world.

It will not suffice to define Christ's Church by a mere enumeration of external characteristics. Of course, Christ meant his Church to be a visibly constituted society under a visible head, but the Church is more than just that. Just as every man has a visible form and yet can only be understood in his essence and activity when this form is seen as an expression and instrument of his soul, just as Jesus himself can only be understood when his divinity is seen shining through his humanity, so also the Church, continuing Jesus' humanity in the world and sanctifying man's humanity through her sacraments, is a sacramental reality herself, composed of corporeal and spiritual elements. neither of which can be understood without the other.

The ecclesial community in the New Testament is the divinely ordered sign of community with God. But because the signified is not simply identical with the sign, there is positive free play between the two, and a nuance of expression in the sign itself. There is even the case in which the sign and the signified completely dissociate themselves: in those sins which, while maintaining the sign of ecclesial life, destroy the signified life of grace, thus converting the sign into a lie.

The concept of the Church is thus not a simple one, like that of some material object. Her presence or absence, her members or non-members are realities impossible to determine finally and unequivocally by mere statistics.

The Church's visibility, as that of the sacraments, is balanced between matter and spirit, and is thus above exclusive regulation by the laws of the material world. The Church is visible enough to be found, but she is not imprisoned in the facile form of visibility to which we would like to bind her. We have no right to condition her members' internal and external relations on sociological and psychological contact alone, just because we ourselves have been fortunate enough to have found this contact. St. Augustine appositely said: "There are many outside who seem to be inside, and many inside who seem to be outside."

We must now explain the nature and work of the Church in the light of Christ's nature and work. We are entitled to do so inasmuch as the Church, according to unanimous testimony of Holy Scripture and tradition, is, as it were, Christ living on here and now: his "mystical body." In the Church, Christ continues his visible presence among us, a presence which, notwithstanding his intimate eucharistic presence, is no longer a presence in the physical body animated by his soul and withdrawn from us by his glorification, but a presence in an edifice which, animated by the Holy Spirit, fulfills his words: "When I am raised up, I will draw all things to myself." Graced humanity is to become one with its head, the first among many brothers, the new Adam. And just as this incorporation into Christ progresses by degrees toward full expression and fruitfulness, so too with incorporation into the Church.

1. First of all, every man has an indestructible relationship to Christ simply because he is a man, a natural brother of the God become man. Moreover, Christ expressly devoted his advent and teaching, his death and resurrection, to the redemption of the

whole world. Thus, the objective starting point for every human life is no longer only the estrangement from God through sin, the hopelessness coming from Adam; it is also the common call to salvation in Christ. Alongside the solidarity of sinful nature stands already the solidarity of a nature assumed by God in Christ: the *anima naturaliter christiana*, in Tertullian's expression.

2. Respecting our own dignity and happiness, God addresses us as men, as persons who act, know and will with individual responsibility. Consequently, the redemption is effective in us only when we also do our part. Theology and Scripture call this "faith" and know many degrees of it: from the interior affirmation of the Lord's revealing himself to the conscience, to the express acceptance of the gospel and the sealing of the faith in sacramental baptism. In this way, through these degrees, we become children of God, members of Christ and of his Church.

3. We must never forget that this growth has an inner dynamic in which God's order and our individual spiritual nature press to the last degree of open encounter; at no level can one stop. The salient motive for all convert and mission work is not, therefore, the "holy war," but rather the gradual manifestation of the children of God in the Church until her fulfillment in the second coming of Christ.

The Church does not, then, stand in any real opposition to men of good will outside the inmost circle of her visibility; she does not confront them as Party, but rather as a home and mother who gathers together her scattered members, her lost sons and daughters, because, seeing more deeply than they themselves do, she recognizes herself in them. She calls herself Catholic, not just to have some sort of name, as we might call ourselves Miller or Farmer without actually having anything to do with a mill or a farm, but because she *is* catholic, embracing by her very nature all human reality.

To see this relationship of the Church to the whole world, one must learn not to judge things only empirically or only with human opinion. For, considered only externally, the world has little to do with Christ or the Church: the two are seemingly disparate or even contradictory. But with the eyes of a faith taught by God, man can perceive the inner unity of the world over and above all contradictions.

We who are so much addicted to parties and quarreling have much more in common than we think! Our dissensions encourage parades and polls in support of "our side," but these dissensions are continually being absorbed by the unpretentious, peaceful, and yet greater reality of our human and Christian solidarity. It is significant that those men who have matured through painful experience of the truly great and universal questions of life have also attained a charitable, brotherly disposition; while others, seemingly more fortunate, find it very difficult to abandon their party spirit and bury their petty differences.

Finally, let us look at Christ himself, for the Church has no better example of how to conduct herself than his. The gospel pictures him as a man capable of making clear and difficult demands, a man who consciously set his word and work in contradiction to the world, and brooked no idle peace. But how respectfully and sympathetically, with what consideration and kindness, he encountered all men of good will. He did not adopt a Party mentality in gathering his flock; he saw all men as on the way to him, and he encouraged them on their way. He knew that we men are only "bent reeds and glimmering wicks" and would not break or extinguish us.

To a Pharisee, a member of the Party of his enemies, he spoke the encouraging words, "You are not far from the kingdom of God," when the Pharisee gave a wise answer in a conversation. He gave the opportunity of forgiveness to the despised tax collectors and sinners. The criminal who was crucified with

him had only to look to him with faith to be promised paradise.
Christ did not make his own the chauvinism of his people; he
found words of appreciation for the pagan centurion and the
Canaanite woman. He promised a more merciful judgment to
pagan cities than to those who heard his words, received his
good works, and still remained unchanged.

He tolerated no group egoism, though it be pious: to those who
prided themselves on their attachment to him and who would
make his word a Party platform, he directed this rebuke: "I tell
you, many will come from the East and from the West and sit
down at table with the patriarchs in the kingdom of heaven; but
the children of the kingdom will be thrown out into the darkness outside." He knew that he has "other sheep, who are not of
this fold." "I must also lead them," he said, "and they will hear
my voice, and there will be one flock and one shepherd."

By his birth and death, he has made himself one with every
man, although he had cause enough to set himself apart from
us. Now this great saving law is in effect: what happens to him
concerns us too, and what happens to us concerns him now as
well. And so he can allow faith in him to begin with a cup of
water handed mercifully to someone thirsty, with every kindness
shown wastefully to the humblest and least of men, with the
works of human love, about which he will ask us at the judgment. *In Christ, therefore, all men and all human values have
found an inner unity, which we, as Christians, should not break
up again.* His Church is the focal point of these values; she
gathers together rays of light coming from the most different
directions and greatest distances. She does God's work in the
world: God gathers, the devil scatters.

It is for us, then, to free ourselves from this attitude of group
egoism which weighs so heavily upon our age. We must determine, in the name of Christ, the saviour of the world, and in the
name of our catholic mother, the Church, to see all men as

brothers, even those in the ranks of our enemies. This is the greatest contribution we can make to the peace which the world cannot give itself, to the fulfillment of Christ's prayer, "that all may be one."

Reunion and Doctrine on Justification

by HANS KÜNG

THE ECUMENICAL DIALOGUE can be approached from a number of points. Yet no matter what the issue—be it Mariology, the papacy, the sacraments or the Church—it is soon apparent that the heart of the matter lies elsewhere: in the doctrine on grace and ultimately in Christology. "Jacente articulo justificationis jacent omnia. Necesse igitur est, ut quotidie acuamus . . . et inculcemus eum. Nam satis vel nimium non potest concipi et teneri." This principle, found in Luther's *Commentary on Galatians 1, 3* (1535), due to the reluctance of the age and its own limitations was ignored at times, and yet it was valid.

For how is one to reach accord concerning the Church (and *there* is where a genuine Mariology as well as a genuine sacramental theology terminate) if one cannot agree concerning Christ, the Lord and head of the Church; concerning the grace from which she derives her life; concerning the justification in which she is grounded; concerning the faith which bears her witness. The theology of the Reformers took as its focal point the doctrine on justification. Thus, as far as reconciliation is concerned, everything depends upon whether or not in this point agreement is to be found. Perhaps, then, a few ideas along this line will prove of use, ideas intended as guidance toward a solution and not as a solution in themselves.[1]

[1] However, in theology guidance toward a solution has little effect if the one giving it already has not carried out his own directions to the

1. The Need for Self-knowledge

Theology is not mathematics. The Catholic doctrine on justification cannot be worked out like the Pythagorean principle *more geometrico:* either one grasps it or one does not grasp it. Justification of the sinner is a revealed truth, a mystery of the faith, to be discerned only through humble, constantly renewed, deadly earnest, scientific effort on one's own part. Results will be forthcoming only after such an attempt. It all would be such child's play if one needed only to skim through Denziger or a dogmatic textbook.

Yet the definitions of the Church, those impregnable bastilles, are not there to create an enclosure of blank walls, but to secure a vantage point over the landscape, particularly in that direction from which danger threatens. For as anyone who has the slightest notion of the development of dogma realizes, Catholic dogmas are not hard-and-set formulas which exhaust or completely define a mystery, so as to render Holy Scripture superfluous; rather the definitions of the Church take into consideration the mystery and its inexhaustibility, since of their very nature they connote a necessary (and for the most part polemically determined) limitation. Thus upon closer inspection one cannot but realize that the Tridentine decree on justification, for all of its infallible objectivity, is characterized by a certain, historically necessary

---

full, or is not even in the process of doing so. Therefore we refer the reader to our study: *Rechtfertigung, Die Lehre Karl Barth und eine katholische Besinnung, mit einem Geleitbrief von Karl Barth;* published in conjunction with Johann Adam Möhler-Institut Paderborn (Einsiedeln: Johannes Verlag, 1957), 304 pages; published in English under the title: *Justification. The Doctrine of Karl Barth and a Catholic Reflection* (New York: Thomas Nelson and Sons, 1963). Many readers who consider the present article all too cursory and unsubstantiated will find in this larger work the necessary qualification, clarification and proofs.

anthropocentrism. Moreover, it need hardly be stressed that theological textbooks, being introductions to theology and hence naturally limited, do not attempt a full and complete presentation of the Catholic doctrine on justification.

In short, then, comprehension of the Church's doctrines is to be had only through an understanding of their historical and ambiguous background. The defensive character of the definitions in general, and of the Tridentine decree on justification in particular, leave many aspects of the doctrine, perhaps extremely important aspects at that, unaccentuated. It must be kept in mind therefore that Sacred Scripture, interpreted according to the binding force of Catholic tradition, is in the end the primary source of Catholic dogma, and is so not only because the entire content of Christian revelation is to be found there, but also, and above all, because Sacred Scripture alone represents the formal, immediate witness of God himself, in its original form and provenance. Thus Scripture alone is Word of God in the strictest sense.[2]

Obviously, if agreement concerning the doctrine on justification is to be reached, the theological method of procedure is a basic question. It should be remembered that the Catholic doctrine on justification is not something easily pinned down, that is, it is as difficult for the opposition to define and criticize it as for its proponents to summarize it into crystal-clear formulations. Protestant theology is liable mistakenly to maintain that this or that plays *no* role in the Catholic doctrine, while for Catholic theology to attain a realization of the full Catholic truth, the entirety of which is to be found only in Old and New Testament revelation *as a unit*, is most difficult.

Consequently when considering the development of the doctrine on justification during the past four hundred years, one should not be surprised (rather one may accept it *a priori*, and indeed, with a belief in a Spirit of Christ vitally working in the

[2] Cf. *Rechtfertigung*, pp. 105–27.

Church, must accept it) that certain facets of the mystery of justification stand out more perceptibly today than in previous generations, though of course the mystery as a whole has received affirmation at all times; in particular this is true of the Tridentine decree which today is capable of greater clarification than was previously possible under the existing circumstances. In theology, as with all else, self-knowledge is an acquirement which comes only with time.

2. Understanding Others

This as well is no easy task. In a situation such as we have here, snap judgments are of no value; the measures required are deliberation, patient listening, careful biding of one's time, and the dogged attempt to learn ever more.

Did we say, to learn? Even Catholics? And from others? From those without the Church? Yes, and why not? It is revealed truth that in Christ *all* men are created and that in him *all* are redeemed. Therefore *all* men—and that includes those beyond the walls—are united with Christ in one way or another, with Christ who is Truth itself. And why should this not be particularly true in the case of our fellow Christians, separated though they be? Why should one maintain that on their side exists *nothing* but error? With her belief in the universal mystery of Christ the Church would interpret *"Extra ecclesiam nulla veritas"* in similar fashion to *"Extra ecclesiam nulla gratia."*

Thus one may feel free to seek Catholic truth even outside the walls of the Church. We say *Catholic* truth because the Catholic Church would not be Catholic if she did not claim *all* truth as her own, wherever it was found. Thus one may act accordingly, indeed one is obliged to act accordingly, not only because of the obligation every Christian has to an apostolate of the Word (such a "retrieving of the Word" is all too easily misconstrued), but also for the sake of the theological knowledge of truth itself. Was it not the Church Fathers themselves who complained that to the deprivation of the ancient Church the schismatics were taking along with them the *"spolia Aegypti"*— and what precious, irreplaceable truths those *"spolia"* often included. Why should this Church property not be restored to her and thus receive the illumination once again of its only proper context?

The Catholic theologian will, therefore, look for truth also outside the walls: not in "free," anarchic inquiry, but in strict union with the Church; not with the naïve and optimistic enthusiasm characteristic of an emigrant, but rather in a spirit of total fidelity to his true home, a home unforgettable and priceless. If he so proceeds, he is bound to make genuine rediscoveries, to see truths in a completely new light. Indeed, precisely because he makes his investigations in unison with the Church and does not allow himself for a moment to lose sight of his true home, his rediscoveries will occur not only outside the walls but at the same time within them.

Nevertheless, in the world of theology, the discovery of buried treasure—both within and without—requires more than a superficial spading-about; it demands a real digging-in. One must force oneself to think beyond the mere terminology used by the other in order to get down to the essence of the issue itself: dogmatic formulations are not sufficient, one must penetrate the very heart of the matter. *What* a person means is quickly said, *how* he intends it is another matter altogether and the decisive factor involved. Just as one word can possess two meanings, so two can possess one, and this has often been the case with the doctrine on justification.

The history of this doctrine is a mysterious one, shot through as it is with questionable ambiguity: *ambiguity*, because what is one and the same truth has often been interpreted in two ways;

questionable, because the following question is valid: in reality are not these two interpretations but complements of one and the same truth? The term "grace" is employed, and one intends by it the favor, the good will of God, the other the gift of God; the term "justification," one meaning the declaration of justice, the other the actualization of justice; the term "sanctification," one intending ethical self-sanctification, the other ontic growth in holiness; the term "freedom," one intending divine filiation, the other human faculty of choice; the term "faith," one meaning *fides viva,* the other *fides mortua.* How often identical terminology has been used but with variant meaning, and how often variant terminology with identical meaning. Understanding the other here means understanding oneself, and vice versa.

3. *Four Key Questions*

The traditional and most important questions in the polemic surrounding the doctrine of justification can be grouped around the key words "grace," "justification," "the one justified" (*simul justus et peccator*), and "faith." What is their meaning? One cannot possibly doubt that in the exigency of the dispute these realities were very often given a sharply polemic character by both sides. Crude polemics belongs now, of course, to a bygone age. However, one should not overlook the fact that the terms in which many of the truths of faith are couched, though no longer patently polemic, still retain polemic undertones, often subconsciously in the one employing them. Should it not be possible today to give at once a truly Christian and balanced answer to the question of what these four words mean—free of all veiled polemics, if one considers Scripture, read in the context of Catholic tradition, and also Protestant theology, which shares too in the Christian tradition? Could one not find an answer which would enjoy the agreement of Protestant theologians as well?

One should not, however, minimize the difficulties involved. These questions cannot be resolved in a few sentences. An approach to solving the question is of more concern here than a definitive answer. And in this context it seems possible to ground the following solutions in terms of Catholic theology which would also be acceptable for Protestant theologians.

"Grace" is the favor of God, at once personal [3] and efficacious, granted in Christ Jesus, radiating through the Church [4] into the world and working the sanctity of man. "Justification" is the personal judgment of God on the sinner, effected—once and for all with respect to the Church—by the death and resurrection of Jesus Christ. It is simultaneously God's declaration of justice and the actualization of justice in man.[5] "*Simul justus et peccator*," [6]

[3] Grace is not primarily a physical entity in the human subject. Rather it is thoroughly *personal*, a mode of being of the living God himself. "Received grace," then, is first and foremost "his" grace and not simply "the" grace. This highlights as well the *theocentric* aspect of grace: grace is directly centered in God. It is not a floating "third" reality between God and man. It is the gracious God himself. Grace concerns *his* gracious *being*, and not *my possession* of grace: I do not "have" God, God "has" me!

[4] The grace of the Father in Jesus Christ, effected through the Holy Spirit, is not a private grace: it builds a community, the community of Jesus Christ, his mystical body. Grace is, then, essentially ecclesiological.

[5] *Despite* the sin, God declares the sinner just. Precisely because it is *God*, and not man, who makes this declaration, an *inner* renewal is effected in the sinner. The declaration is God's Word, the *vox Domini potens in virtute!* And the Word of God *effects* what it says: God says: "Let there be light!" And there was light. He says: "This is my body," and it is his body. "Arise!" and the dead rose. So it is with the sinner's justification: God makes the judgment: "You are just!" And the sinner *is* just, really and truly, externally and internally, wholly and completely; his sins *are* forgiven. "'Are not my words as a fire?' said the Lord, 'and as a hammer that breaks the rock in pieces?'" (Jer. 23:29). God's declaration of justice is therefore at once the actualization of justice.

[6] It is presumed that our discussion of the "*simul justus et peccator*"

rooted in Scripture and Catholic tradition and practice, can serve as a good expression for the imperfection and continuous potential of the justified man for sinning, and for the continuous "estrangedness" of the justification truly within him. "Faith" as acceptance of the kerygma at once insight and trust excludes, as far as justification itself is concerned, all works and merits.[7] It tends, however, once justified, to participate actively in sanctification through works of love.

One need not elaborate upon the fact that the minimal treatment given here is highly open to misunderstanding. How it can be grounded and explained within the pale of Catholic teaching is the decisive factor.[8]

---

cannot be in the same vein as that of the Reformers: it cannot question the genuineness of divine justification. The justified man is *really* justified, inwardly in his heart. His justification is not only a bandaged "as-if"; the man is not only called justified, he *is* justified, and this justification is not only external, but internal, not only in part, but wholly, not only negatively, but positively: a new man! So much is beyond discussion. Our question is much more: Can the man, inwardly and fully justified, rightfully and meaningfully be called a sinner? Can such a man be a sinner? Is there a Catholic *"simul justus et peccator"*? If correctly understood, no Catholic can deny the same. The reader is referred to *Rechtfertigung*, pp. 232–42.

[7] *"Sola fide"* can be understood in an orthodox sense. One can understand the Lutheran "alone" as a meaningful elucidation of Rom. 3:28. It is certain that the "alone" in the translation is not Luther's discovery. Already *before* the Reformation such translations existed: According to Lyonnet, one can read in the German Bible (Nürnberg: 1483) for Gal. 2:16: *"gerechtfertigt . . . nur durch den Glauben"* (justified . . . only through faith); the same also (according to Oltramare) in three Italian translations (Genoa: 1476, Venice: 1538 and 1546): *"ma solo per la fede"* or *"per la sola fede."* More important than these translations is the fact that *"sola fide"* belongs absolutely to Catholic tradition: Cf. Belarmine, *De Justificatione* II, 25; and Thomas Aquinas' commentary on 1 Tim. 1:8. The reader is referred to *Rechtfertigung*, pp. 243–56.

[8] Cf. *Rechtfertigung*, pp. 194–276.

4. The Fundamental Problem

When one gives these key questions (and the many others which are connected with them) serious consideration, one gets the impression again and again that a basic difficulty lies at the root of all these problems and their solutions: a fundamental difficulty which exerts a negative influence on the solutions alluded to above and which highlights their insufficiency. All these statements show the complete incapacity of man to justify himself in any way whatsoever. Nevertheless, it has always appeared to the Protestant that the Catholic position did not sufficiently exclude every possibility of a self-justification. Why? Because, although man sins he remains what he is, a free, good man, and if this is so it is difficult to understand why he is not ultimately capable of self-justification, and why he is not ultimately independent of the grace of Jesus Christ. Is Catholic teaching, in spite of all its talk of sin and grace, not then a veiled—and therefore especially pernicious—unchristian humanism? A covert and therefore all the more sophisticated self-encomium of man?

Who has not experienced the gravity of the accusation and the difficulty in finding an answer? Provided one does not wish to state in sheer repetition what has already been said time and again, and thus contribute nothing toward ameliorating the dissatisfaction of those questioning the Catholic position, one must go to great lengths. One must go beyond the doctrine of justification to the teaching on sin, and from there to the doctrine of creation, in order to derive ultimately at the center of Christology the force for a solution. Herein lies the center of gravity of the doctrine on justification.

One must consider, therefore, not only *the fact that* the sinner does actually continue to exist (that too is not at all self-evident), not only *how* he continues to exist (that is with his whole nature and with his free will), but also and most especially *why* he continues to exist. Scripture comments on this question to a greater extent than one might suppose at first sight. But one must take the trouble to see the various statements (especially those in the Old Testament) on sin and death in their relationship to one another and on the basis of this to consider the mystery of creation in Jesus Christ. In this perspective the mystery of faith concerning a Christocentric creation can truly be interpreted as *saving* truth and can elucidate the mystery of the sinner's justification. Precisely this mystery of Christocentric creation is given paltry consideration in our secularized age, and even then it is unconvincingly platonic.

Here is not the place to delve into details.[9] But the solution of the fundamental problem involved in the doctrine of justification can certainly be anticipated along the path already blazed, a solution which is in the main satisfactory. One could perhaps formulate it approximately thus: Why, then, is the sinner radically incapable of any kind of self-justification? Because in the eyes of God the man in sin has merited immediate death and the full measure of corruption, from which he did not preserve himself by means of the power of his nature and his will, but from which the solicitous mercy of God has saved him through the grace already won in our redemption by Jesus Christ. From all eternity God foresaw the fall of man, and from all eternity he irrevocably determined the redemptive incarnation of his Son and established his intimate communion with all humanity. And further, from all eternity God let the corruption and destruction which man actuates in his sin come to naught, inasmuch as he created all in Christ, inasmuch as he constituted all in its incorruptible repose in him.

A creation in Christ is the presupposition for a justification in Christ. A creation in Christ is the reason why man in his sin

---

[9] For a more complete treatment cf. *Rechtfertigung*, pp. 127–93.

remains upon this earth and remains a man. Here we encounter the final power of sin with its ultimate impotence, and here too truth of freedom with its folly. The sinner owes his entire existence therefore to the prevenient and embracing grace of Jesus Christ, his Redeemer in whom he was created and in whom he has repose. Consequently that is the reason for his radical inability to justify himself in any way, and the reason for his total dependence upon the grace of Jesus Christ.

These allusions must also be thoroughly grounded, elaborated upon, and defined if they are not to be misunderstood. However, within the framework of an introduction they may perhaps suffice.

Is then, when one considers the whole, a reunion of our separated brothers possible in the fundamental question involved in the controversy over the doctrine of justification? We have good reason to suppose so. It is not as if *all* differences of opinion with reference to the doctrine of justification could possibly be prescinded from immediately—that is not necessary. It is only necessary that the differences which cause the *separation of the churches* should be eradicated, and this should very well be possible along the lines already indicated.

There have always been differences in theological opinion *within* the one true faith and there will always be such in the Church of God. The possible solution indicated here lays claim to no more, but also to no less, than just this. It is of decisive importance to view the mystery of the sinner's justification from the center of faith: Jesus Christ, in whom God and man are revealed, in whom creation and the redemption have their ultimate meaning. If this is achieved in the right spirit, reconciliation in the doctrine of justification is not only a possibility but a reality, and over and above this one may hope that in meaningful dialogue on the basis of our common ground, Jesus Christ, other controversial questions will also approach a solution.

Christianity and Non-Christian Religions

by KARL RAHNER

"Open Catholicism" implies that historical forces confronting the Church possess a meaning for her, even though they are not related to her by ties of peace and mutual acceptance. It means that the Church cannot ignore them as purely secular and devoid of any significance for her.

"Open Catholicism" further entails the task of establishing a relationship with these forces which acknowledges their existence (to the extent that simple approval of their existence is not possible)—a relationship that endures the scandal of their opposition and that molds the Church so that she is capable of surmounting this pluralism (at least in so far as it should not exist) by an appreciation of herself as the higher unity of this opposition. Thus "open Catholicism" means the taking of a definite stand toward the contemporary pluralism of ideological forces.

Obviously, such pluralism is not a fact which we can simply ignore as incomprehensible. Rather it is a fact which simply requires reflection and which—despite its inherent and undesirable elements—must be reordered by a broader vision within the integrity of a Christian understanding of existence.

Among the elements of this pluralism with which we live belongs the pluralism of religions. It is one of those elements whose correlation is extremely difficult and yet one with which we as Christians must come to terms. Here we are not referring to the pluralism of the Christian confessions, which also constitutes a reality, a problem and a challenge for the Christian. That is not our present concern. Rather, we are concerned with the basically more difficult problem of the persistent plurality of religions in the Christian era, and this after a two-thousand-year history of the Christian mission.

Today all religions, Christianity included, possess a common enemy—a complete lack of religion, a total denial of religion, a denial which displays the religious fervor of an absolute and holy system paradoxically presenting itself with its official organization as *the* religion of the future, the crystallized, absolute secularization and final formula of human existence. Yet it remains true that precisely this denial which threatens religion as a whole, possesses one of its most potent weapons in the lack of union within the religious world today.

Aside from this, religious pluralism poses for Christianity a greater threat and grounds for greater anxiety than for all other religions. For no other religion, not even Islam, proclaims itself so absolutely as *the* religion, as the one and only valid revelation of the one, living God. Therefore, after a two-thousand-year history this very real, abiding, ever new and virulent pluralism of religions proves the greatest scandal and danger for Christianity.

And today this danger even more ominously threatens the individual Christian. Formerly, another religion was for all practical purposes the religion of another culture, of a history peripheral to one's own; it was a foreign religion in every other respect as well. No wonder, then, that no one questioned the fact that an alien and strange people had a different religion; no wonder that it was impossible to seriously consider the other religion as a challenge or even an alternative. Today it is different. An isolated Europe no longer exists, a Europe which could simply look upon itself as the center of world history and culture, and whose religion, therefore, could appear as the obvious and only form of divine worship for a European (this point is made within the purview of fact, and abstracts from the question of a believing assent).

Today every man is neighbor to every other man in the world, and is therefore influenced by communication with every existential, global situation: every existing religion has become, in a way similar to all cultural realities of the "other," a challenge and a prospect for every "I." Just as the culture of the other is experienced as a relativization of one's own, demanding a real and existential response, so too with the alien religion: it has become —and no longer in theory alone, but concretely—an element of the individual, existential situation. Accordingly, it is experienced as a challenge to the absolute claim of one's own Christianity.

The question of the composition and understanding of religious pluralism is then an especially urgent aspect of the challenge to come to terms with contemporary pluralism in general. This question could be approached from different sides. Here we will attempt only to reiterate some fundamental elements of a Catholic dogmatic interpretation of the non-Christian religions in the hope that these will help us to solve the problem of the Christian disposition toward the contemporary pluralism of religions.

Unfortunately, since modern Catholic theology has not sufficiently studied these questions, we cannot claim that our conclusions are commonly held by Catholic theologians. Therefore, what is said carries only as much weight as its arguments—which again can only be indicated. Where a somewhat greater theological weight is given to the principles developed, this will be for the theologically educated a consequence of what is said. If we say it is a question of a *Catholic* dogmatic interpretation, this should not be construed to mean exclusively a matter of an inner-Christian theory of polemical theology. Rather it is simply said that we cannot concretely explore the acceptability of our theses within Protestant theology. Further, we say that it is a question of a *dogmatic* interpretation, for we posit the question not as empirical historians of religion, but from the autoconsciousness of Christianity itself—thus as dogmatic theologians.

Thesis 1. The first thesis (first, because it is basic for rendering the other religions theologically intelligible within Christian belief) reads: Christianity conceives of itself as the absolute religion determined for all mankind, as a religion which can recognize no other as having equal rights alongside itself. This sentence is obvious and basic for an understanding of Christianity. Here there is no need either to prove it or to develop its meaning.

If for Christians a valid and legitimate religion is first and foremost not the relation of man to God which man autonomously establishes himself, not the self-interpretation of human existence by man, not the reflection and objectivization of the man's experience through himself and with himself, but rather God's act upon him, the free self-revelation in the self-sharing of God with mankind, that relationship which God himself establishes with man and in so doing reveals himself—and if *this* relation of God to all men is basically one and the same, since it is rooted in the incarnation, death and resurrection of the Word of God become flesh, if Christianity is the divinely intended, incarnate expression of this relationship established in Christ for all man, then Christianity alone can recognize itself as the true and legitimate religion for all mankind there and then, where and when it invades another religion with existentially unavoidable force challenging this other religion by judging it in the light of itself. From the time of Christ, from the time that he came in flesh as the absolute Word of God and really and truly reconciled the world, making it one with God by his death and resurrection, this Christ and his abiding historical presence in the world, namely the Church, is *the religio* binding mankind to God.

We must, however, immediately make an observation on the first thesis. Though Christianity itself may have its own prehistory extending it back into the genesis of human history—to be sure, in an essentially graduated manner—and though this possession of a "prehistory" may be of much greater import for the theoretical and existential foundation of Christianity's absolute claim, made on the authority of the New Testament, than is generally recognized by modern Catholic fundamental theology, still the beginning of Christianity as such is a definite moment within history.

Christianity did not always exist; it began. It was not always and everywhere *the* way of salvation for mankind, at least in its historically tangible, ecclesial-sociological constitution, in the reflex state of self-realization of God's saving work in Christ and toward Christ. As an historical entity this Christianity had a spatio-temporal, punctiform beginning in Jesus of Nazareth and in the salvific event of the one and only cross and empty tomb in Jerusalem. As such, however, this religion of absolute claims, even at the moment it begins to be fundamentally absolute for all men, must meet those men to whom it presents itself as their legitimate and necessary religion in an historical manner.

The question (which, up to now, Catholic theology, for want of a honest confrontation with the duration and complexity of a genuinely human time and history, has not given sufficient reflection) is this: does that point of time at which the absolute religion in its historically palpable constitution becomes an existential force demanding a response, occur for all men simultaneously, or is the very entrance of this moment itself a history, and so not temporally simultaneous for all men, cultures and historical epochs?

Generally the beginning of the objective binding force of the

Christian message for all men (thus the removal of the validity of the Mosaic religion *and* that of all other religions which, as we shall see later, could also enjoy in themselves a moment of validity and divine approbation), is considered as having taken place in apostolic times. Consequently, the Christian message would also have been binding in the period of time between this beginning and the actual acceptance or personally responsible rejection of Christianity in a non-Judaic world and history: in a period of time spanning the accomplished promulgation of the law and the actual taking into cognizance of the law by those for whom the law was intended.

Whether such an understanding is correct, or whether, as we prefer to think, one might be of a different opinion and place the beginning of Christianity for concrete periods of history, cultures, and religions at that point of time in which this Christianity has become a real historical force within the individual history and culture, and thus a genuine historical moment within this determined culture, is not merely a stale academic question.

One conclusion usually drawn from the first opinion, for example, is that beginning with the first Pentecost the baptism of infants about to die has been necessary *everywhere* in the world for their supernatural salvation, though prior to Pentecost this was not the case. A proper and balanced solution could be of great importance for other questions as well: for the avoidance of premature conversions, for the justification and significance of "indirect" missionary activity, and so forth.

Is one not forced to question the possibility of holding to the first opinion in the face of a two-thousand-year history in which missionary activity still stands at the beginning, especially when, for example, a man like Suarez already saw that, at least regarding the *Jews*, the *promulgatio* and the *obligatio* of the Christian religion (and not just the *divulgatio* and the *notitia promulgationis*), take place in an historical evolution? Actually we cannot answer this question here. Yet it may be registered at least as an open question and the propriety of the second theory can be practically presupposed, since it alone accords with the genuine historicity of Christianity and of saving history.

Further, it affords us a more carefully nuanced understanding of our first thesis: we affirm positively that according to her constitution Christianity is the absolute and only religion determined for all mankind, but we leave open the question (at least fundamentally) in what precise moment this absolute responsibility of every man and culture toward Christianity is concretely present in the sense of an *objective* responsibility. Even so, this thesis remains exciting enough: wherever Christianity expressly encounters man in the genuine urgency and profundity of his concrete existence, Christianity consequent upon its autoconsciousness, presents itself as the only valid religion for this man and as a religion necessary for his salvation not only by a necessity of precept, but by a necessity of means.

It should be noted that it is a question of a social quantity as a necessity for salvation. If this is Christianity and not any other religion, it may still be said without hesitation, indeed it must be said, that the second opinion is implicitly contained in this thesis, namely, that in the concrete existence of man the social composition of religion belongs to the very essence of religion, and that only then does one have a religion—when one has it in a social form. Consequently, the man who is commanded to have a religion is also ordered to seek and accept a social form of religion. We shall soon observe what this consideration offers for judging the non-Christian religions.

Finally, a further point may be mentioned here: if the determining factor in the *concept* of *paganism,* and so of the non-Christian, pagan religions (this word is intended merely as a theological concept and not in a derogatory sense), is not the factual rejection of Christianity, but rather the lack of a sufficiently historical encounter with a Christianity of historical force adequate to allow her a vital presence among this pagan people and within their history, then paganism in this sense ceases to exist with the explosive evolution of the West into a global world history in which each people and each culture become an inner moment of every other people and every other culture. More precisely, perhaps, it is a gradual evolution into a wholly new phase: we have the *one* world history in which *one* history Christian and non-Christian (pagans old and new) live in the identical situation and encounter one another in dialogue. So the question of the theological meaning of the other religions now arises all the more forcefully.

Thesis 2. Until that moment when the gospel truly enters the historical situation of a given man, a non-Christian religion (even though other than the Mosaic religion) includes not only elements of a natural knowledge of God intermingling elements of depravation due to human frailty flowing from original sin, but also supernatural moments of that grace which is given man by God on Christ's account, and therefore it can be acknowledged as a *legitimate* religion, without forgetting that this legitimacy will vary, nor denying the existing error and depravation in it. Such a thesis will require much explanation.

First of all, the *terminus ad quem* must be considered—that point of time up to which this assessment of non-Christian religions is valid: the moment when Christianity becomes an historically real quantity for the men of these religions. Whether this point of time theologically coincides with the first Pentecost, or whether for individual peoples and religions it lies elsewhere, need not be definitively determined here. We have, however, worded our formulation so, because it indicates the earlier opinion which to us seems the more correct, whereby once again the more exact criteria for the entrance of this point of time remains undefined.

The thesis itself is divided into two parts. It first states that in the non-Christian religions wholly supernatural, grace-bearing moments can be assumed a priori. This statement in no way implies that all moments of a polytheistic conception of the divine or of all other religious, ethical, and metaphysical depravations, theoretical or practical, in non-Christian religions, should or may be made light of or overlooked. The entire history of Christianity and its interpretation of the non-Christian religions, beginning with the epistle to the Romans and flowing in the vein of the Old Testament polemic against the religion of the "heathen," resounds with protest against such moments of depravation. All this protest remains preserved in what is actually meant and said, and continues to be a part of the message which Christianity and the Church has to say to the people of such religions.

Our task here is not to pursue an a posteriori history of religion. So we cannot empirically describe this quality of what should not be and of what is opposed to God in these non-Christian religions, nor can we present its diverse kind, degree, and amount. Our pursuit is dogmatic and so we can only reiterate the universal and unrefined verdict of what should not be in the non-Christian religions at that moment in which they encounter Christianity with historical force (and at first in this way only!).

Yet it is clear that this in no way is to deny the quite essential differences within the non-Christian religions. The pious heathen who is pleasing to God is already a theme of the Old Testament, and this just heathen cannot be considered simply as living completely outside every concrete social religion, autonomously constructing his own religion. Similarly Paul in his speech at the Areopagus does not exclude a radically positive attitude toward pagan religions.

Central to the first part of our thesis is the basic theological notion: if we want to be Christians, we must profess the article of faith affirming the general and real salvific will of God embracing all men, even during that phase of salvation following paradise and original sin (we avoid here the more precise nuances). We know indeed that in this article of faith nothing more definite is said about the *individual* salvation of man as actually realized. Yet God does will the salvation of all. And salvation thus willed is the salvation of Christ, the salvation of supernatural, divinizing grace; it is the salvation of the *visio beatifica*, a salvation which is intended truly for all men who lived in perhaps the million years before Christ and who since Christ have lived in civilizations, cultures, and epochs of the greatest variety which were still beyond the purview of the men of the New Testament.

If, on the one hand, we comprehend the redemption as specifically *Christian,* if there is no salvation outside of Christ, if according to Catholic doctrine the supernatural divinization of man can never be replaced merely by man's good will, but rather is itself necessarily given during this earthly life, and if on the other hand this salvation is really intended by God truly and earnestly for all men, then both points cannot be reconciled except by saying that every man is really and truly exposed to the influence of divine, supernatural grace offering an interior community with God and a share in the life of God himself, however the individual may stand with respect to this grace in accepting or rejecting it.

In the face of the enormous magnitude of this history of salvation and damnation outside of Christianity, there is no sense in assuming cruelly and hopelessly that outside the pale of official and public Christianity modern man in general is all so evil and obdurate that the offer of supernatural grace must go for the most part unheeded, since previous to such an offer individual men have made themselves unworthy by subjectively grave offenses against the natural moral law.

If these things are considered with greater theological precision, then, one cannot view nature and grace as two temporally successive phases in the life of the individual. Further, it is inconceivable that this offer to all men of supernatural, divinizing grace due to the general salvific will of God, apart from relatively few exceptions, remains ineffective because of personal guilt on the part of individuals. For the gospel gives us no convincing reason for such pessimism.

On the contrary, despite all merely human experience, we have every reason to think optimistically about God and his salvific will—God who is far more powerful than the very limited stupidity and malice of men. Optimistically, that is, to hope and trust in God in a truly Christian manner. For God certainly has the last word. He has revealed to us that he has spoken his powerful word of reconciliation and forgiveness into the world, no matter how little we can judge with certainty the ultimate fate of any individual within or outside of officially constituted Christianity.

If it is true that the eternal word of God became flesh for sake of our salvation and despite our guilt died the death of sin, then the Christian has no right to assume that the fate of the world still travels its own way in the "no" of man, that the history of the world is just as it would have been if Christ had not come. Christ and his salvation is not simply one of two possibilities offered to man's freedom of choice, but rather the act of God which victoriously opens and redeems man's false choice. In Christ God gives not merely the *possibility* of salvation which still must be worked out by man himself, but the actual salvation itself, however much this includes a right decision—precisely as given by God—of human freedom.

Where once sin ruled, grace reigns in superabundance. So we

all have the right to assume not only that grace is offered outside the Christian Church—the denial of which would be jansenistic error—but also that, at least to a great extent, grace achieves a victory in man's free acceptance, an acceptance effected by grace itself. It must be more expressly shown than space here allows that the empirical image of man—his life, religion, personal and general history—proves that this optimism of faith, which recognizes the entire world as under Christ's redemption, is no impossibility.

Yet if we consider that the theoretical and ritual elements in good and evil are but a very inadequate expression of what man existentially and actually accomplishes; if we consider that the transcendence of man (also the transcendence elevated and set free by God's grace), as one and the same, can perfect itself under the most varied forms and names; if we bear in mind that the religious man, when he truly acts religiously, choosing and at the same time viewing reflectively and critically, makes use of the varied forms of institutional religion or unreflectively omits them; if we consider what an immeasurable difference most probably prevails even now in the Christian realm between what is objectively wrong in moral life and what is actually realized as true, subjectively grave sin—then we will not consider it impossible that grace is at work and even accepted in the intellectual-personal life of the individual man, even though his life may appear at first sight primitive, unenlightened, dull, and buried under earthly affairs.

We can say simply: where and to the extent that a moral decision is made in the life of an individual (and where could this be said to be entirely impossible—except in pathological cases?), such a moral decision can be so understood that it too fulfills the concept of what is supernaturally elevated, a believing and thus saving act, and so is actually much more than just a "natural morality." If one seriously believes in God's general salvific will

in Christ for all men, it is neither necessary nor possible to doubt
that, therefore, in the life of every man, if one considers him
primarily as an individual, the gracious influences of the specifically Christian supernatural grace are conceivable, and can even
occur as accepted despite man's sinful state and his apparent
distance from God.

Our second thesis goes even further, however, and states in
its second part that as a result of their supernatural moments the
concrete religions of "pre-Christian" mankind should be considered a priori not as simply illegitimate but as having a quite
positive meaning in God's saving providence. This legitimacy,
however, is predicated of the individual religions in a quite vari-
able sense. The various religions will be able to raise the claim to
legitimacy only in varying ways and degrees. However, as we
will have to demonstrate, the concept of a legitimate religion in
no way excludes this variability. By legitimate religion we mean:
an institutional religion whose "use" by men at a given time can
be considered on the whole as a positive medium of the proper
relation to God and thus of obtaining salvation, and as such is
positively taken into account in God's saving plan.

Theological analysis of the structure of the Old Covenant
shows the possibility of such a concept and the underlying
reality, even where such a religion in its concrete form manifests
myriad theoretical and practical errors. We must first of all consider that the concept of a religion, which, because in one way
or another founded by God already bears within itself the abiding norm, as a permanent institution and inner moment of itself,
for discerning between what is right (willed by God) and wrong
in religious matters, is a concept which is realized only in the
New Testament, in the Church of Christ, as in an eschatologically definitive and *therefore,* and only therefore, "indefectible"
and infallible quantity.

Although the Old Covenant lacked any such institutional element, it must certainly be acknowledged as a legitimate religion. The Old Covenant as a concrete, historical, religious manifestation contained elements of right—what was willed by God—*and* wrong—what was false, erroneous, and depraved. But in the Old Covenant there was no abiding, permanent, institutional instance which could authoritatively and infallibly decide for the individual conscience what was willed by God and what in the concrete religion sprang from depraved humanity.

Indeed, there were the prophets. But they were not a permanent institution; rather they were Israel's conscience necessarily aroused ever anew to protest corruption of the concrete religion, thereby confirming the fact of depravity. The official institutions of the monarchy and priesthood were so little proof against such ungodly degradation that the latter could work the destruction of the Israelitic religion itself.

Moreover, since there were also false prophets, and no infallible, "institutional" court for distinguishing genuine from false prophecy, it was ultimately left up to the conscience of the individual Israelite to determine what was truly God's covenant in the concrete expression of the Israelitic religion and what was a human, free exposition, and consequently, in certain cases, a debasing exposition and corruption of this divinely founded religion. Objective criteria with which to differentiate the good element from the bad could exist, but their application could not depend only on an "ecclesiastical" court, not even in essential questions, since in these too the official offices could break down, and ultimately did collapse.

This complex entity—with its discernment between the divinely willed and excessive human autonomy left to the individual's decision—was the concrete Israelitic religion. We have in Scripture the official and valid outcome of this diacritical discernment of spirits which stirred Old Testament religious history. But since the infallible canon of the Old Testament is given only in the New Testament, so also the precise and final discernment of legitimate and illegitimate elements in the Old Testament religion is possible only on the basis of the New Testament as the eschatologically definitive quantity.

Yet the unity of the concrete Old Testament religion, though resting (ultimately) on the individual's groping discernment of its various elements, was for the Israelites the providentially salvific and legitimate religion willed by God. In this respect it must be noted that this religion was intended for the Israelites alone, and no one else, since the ordinance allowing racially non-Jewish adherents, the proselytes, is a very late innovation. Thus it cannot belong to the concept of a legitimate religion in the above sense—that in its concrete, visible form it is free from depravation, error, and what is objectively immoral, or that an unequivocal, objective, and abiding last instance is found within it for the individual conscience, enabling the individual to distinguish infallibly between elements willed and established by God and merely human and degenerate elements.

We must abandon the preconception that in a non-Christian religion either everything must stem from God and thus accord with God's will and providence, or else the religion is to be considered as merely another human institution. Moreover, if the individual man in these religions receives divine grace—and to deny this is certainly preposterous—then the fact cannot be overlooked that the supernatural, grace-bearing character of this man makes itself visible also there (even if not there alone) and so becomes a constitutive moment of his concrete life, where this life thematically establishes a relationship to the Absolute, therefore, in the religion.

Perhaps one could theoretically maintain that when a certain religion not only possesses a false, humanly depraved element in its external concrete form, but, expressly and reflectively clinging to the element, consciously considers it as an explicit moment in itself constituting its essence, then this religion in its innermost and specific essence is false and so no longer comes into question as a legitimate religion, not even in the broadest sense of the word. This may be correct on the conceptual level.

Yet the question remains whether in any or in which non-Christian (specifically: non-Catholic) religion there exists a moment which elevates what is wrong to an actual constituent of the essence, thus presenting man with the alternative of accepting this essentially evil element or of completely rejecting this religion. Even if such a judgment could be made regarding Islam, still it would always have to be denied regarding the majority of religions. In each case the question would have to be asked as to what extent the "adherents" of such a religion really agree with such an interpretation of the religion in question.

If one considers further how easily one's real intention is always directed to the one and same Absolute in the concrete, radical, religious act, even when this Absolute presents itself under the most diverse names, then one can never say that theoretical polytheism, as blameworthy and despicable as it objectively is, must always and everywhere be an absolute obstacle to the accomplishment in one such religion of genuinely religious acts rooted in the one true God. This is especially true, since it is very difficult to prove that the practical religious life of the early Israelites, at least in its popular-theoretical expression, was always something more than mere henotheism.

Now there is a further point to consider: the individual should and must have during his lifetime the possibility of participating in a genuine, saving relationship with God, and this in all the ages and situations of human history. Otherwise there can be no discussion of a real and actually efficacious unfolding salvific will of God for all men at all times and places. In view of man's social nature and in view of the social bond among men which

in earlier times was still more radical, it is absolutely inconceivable that the individual man could have been able to maintain the relationship with God which he must have and which
God does and must make possible to him if he is to be saved,
within absolutely private interiority and apart from the actual
religion offered him by his milieu.

If man everywhere and always could and had to be *homo
religiosus,* so that as such he might save himself, then he was
this *homo religiosus* within that contemporary concrete religion
in which "one" lived and was forced to live, and from which
he could not totally disengage himself, however much he cared
to oppose and did oppose his religion by being critically selective
in certain points and by existentially accenting something other
than the official doctrine of this religion. If man can always have
a saving positive relationship with God, and if he has always
had to have it, then he has had it precisely within *the* religion
actually at his disposal as a moment of his existential milieu.

As we have already stated, the embodiment of individual religious practices in a socio-religious order is an essential trait of
a true, concrete religion. If one, therefore, demanded of the
non-Christian man that he consummate his genuine saving relationship with God wholly without the religion socially offered
him, one would make of religion a formless interiority, an accomplishment always and everywhere indirect, a purely tran-
scendental religion lacking all categorical tangibility. Thus the
aforementioned principle positing the necessary social character
of every concrete religion would be removed. As a result even
ecclesiastical Christianity would no longer possess the necessary
presupposition, a presupposition along universally human, natural law lines, required for establishing its necessity.

Moreover, since being willed simply and in all its elements by
God in no way belongs to the concept of a legitimate religion (a
religion intended by God as positively salvific for the individual

man), then the religion can be claimed as a completely legitimate religion for the man in question. The divinely intended
means to salvation for the individual meet him within the
concrete religion of his actual existential milieu and historical
contingency, according to God's will and forbearance (which so
intermingle that they are no longer clearly separable). This does
not abrogate his right and limited possibility of criticizing and
adverting to those impulses toward reform, which through God's
providence constantly arise within such a religion.

For a clearer understanding of this fact, one need only reflect
on the natural and socially constituted morality of a people and
a culture. This morality is never pure; it is always depraved, as
Jesus affirmed even of the Old Testament. Therefore, it can
always be contested and corrected even by the individual, following his conscience. Yet, taken as a whole, it is still *the* way in
which, according to God's will, the natural, divine, moral law encounters the individual and acquires concrete force in his life. In
other words, the individual cannot as self-appointed metaphysi-
cian construct anew the divine law on his own responsibility.

As a whole, therefore, the morality of a people and an age
(despite its capacity for and need of reform) is the legitimate
and concrete form of the divine law, so that the institution
guaranteeing the purity of this expressed form (with the necessary reservations) becomes a moment of this expression only in
the New Testament and not earlier. Accordingly, if *before* this
moment there is a legitimate presence of the divine moral law
and religion in the individual's life, then this is valid without
the need for making its absolute purity, its constitution by moments willed by God alone, the condition of legitimacy.

In fact: if every man who enters this world is pursued by
divine grace and if this grace as an elevation to supernatural salvation—according to the better theory within Catholic theology—
has effect, transforming consciousness, even if *in itself* this grace

cannot simply be a direct object of a certain immediate reflection, then it is impossible for the concrete religions not to bear in themselves some traces of this encounter with grace by all men. These traces may be difficult to discern, even for the enlightened vision of the Christian. Still they must be there.

And perhaps we have viewed the non-Christian religions too narrowly and with too little love, really to see them. At any rate, we can never consider the non-Christian religions as a mere conglomeration of natural, theistic metaphysics and a humanly perverted interpretation and institutionalization of this "natural religion." The concrete religions must bear in themselves supernatural, gracious moments, and by the practice of *these* religions the pre-Christian man (who most probably still exists in our day, even though his era *today* is slowly coming to an end) could attain to God's grace.

When we state that in the pre-Christian period there were legitimate religions outside of the Old Testament, this is not to say that these religions were legitimate in *every* respect. To affirm this would be absurd. Nor is it implied that *every* religion was legitimate, since within the concrete, historical situation of the people involved, of their culture and age, they were confronted by varying religious systems which demanded of them a choice—the choice of *which* way, according to the dictates of conscience, was *hic et nunc* the more correct and thus, *in concreto,* the only permissible way of finding God.

This thesis does not maintain that the legitimacy of the Old Testament was of exactly the same kind as that which we in some measure claim for non-Christian religions, since Old Testament legitimacy was in the charge of the prophets, even though this was not an institutional office. In the public, saving history of the Israelitic religion the prophets afforded the possibility of distinguishing the legitimate from the illegitimate. This cannot be said to the same degree of the religions outside the Old Testament. Yet this does not mean that we can in no way speak of a divinely guided history of salvation in the institutional and historical life of these religions. The chief difference between such saving history and that of the Old Testament most probably consists in the fact that the New Testament, as an historical event, has its immediate prehistory in the Old (a prehistory which is amazingly short when compared with the entire span of saving history before the redemption—perhaps a million years). Thus, this short span diacritically reveals saving history in its divine and ungodly elements by a distinction which we cannot so clearly trace in other religious histories.

Two things are positively contained in the second part of our second thesis: the extra-Christian and the extra-Old Testament religions contained moments of supernatural grace whose influence necessarily asserted itself in the external reality of these religions, and, in view of the fact that the real man can concretely live the proffered relationship with God only in a socially constituted manner, he must have had the right, indeed the duty, to live this relationship within the socio-religious reality offered him in his historical situation.

Thesis 3. If the second thesis is correct, then Christianity encounters the man of the extra-Christian religion not merely as a non-Christian pure and simple, but as one who, in one respect or another, can and must be considered already an anonymous Christian. It would be false to consider the pagan a man untouched by God's grace and truth.

If the pagan has already experienced God's grace and if in certain cases he has already accepted this grace as the unfathomable, final entelechy of his existence in the acceptance of the Incomprehensible and of the open horizon of his existence pressing on into the infinite, then truly revelation has already occurred in him, even before the missionary word encounters him from without. This is so because this grace, *qua* a priori horizon of all his intellectual activity, is not known objectively, but is concomitantly present in the subjective consciousness. Thus the external revelation is for him not just the proclamation of what before was completely unknown, as when one informs a Bavarian child for the first time in school that there is a continent called Australia, but is the objective-conceptual expression of what this individual, in the depth of his intellectual existence, has already attained or is capable of attaining.

Space does not permit a more detailed proof of the fact that this *fides implicita* is dogmatically possible for the so-called pagan. We offer nothing more than the thesis and an indication of the direction in which its proof could be found. But if it is true that the pagan, as the object of the Church's missionary activity, is or can be a man who, prior to this contact, searches for his salvation, and in certain cases finds it, and if at the same time it is true that this salvation is the salvation of Christ, because there is no other salvation, then such a one is necessarily able to be not only an anonymous theist, but also an anonymous Christian.

It is true, then, that in the last analysis the preaching of the gospel does not make a Christian of a man completely abandoned by God and Christ, but transforms an anonymous Christian into a man who within the grace-filled depths of his nature is conscious of his Christianity objectively and reflectively as well as in a socially constituted profession thereof, in the Church. This is not to deny but rather to affirm that his express awakening to his previously anonymous Christianity is a part of the growth of Christianity itself, a higher evolutionary phase demanded by the very nature of Christianity, and so has a place in the same divine order as all else connected with salvation.

But from the above conception one may not infer that the express preaching of Christianity is superfluous, since even without it a man can already be an anonymous Christian. Such a con-

clusion is just as false, and for the same reasons, as when someone would try to conclude that one could dispense with the two
sacraments of baptism and penance because one can be justified prior to receiving these two sacraments by his subjective acts
of faith and contrition alone. The reflex awakening to a previously anonymous Christianity is demanded (1) by the incarnational and social structure of grace and Christianity, and (2)
therefore, because a clearer, purer, more reflex acknowledgment
of Christianity offers a greater chance of salvation for the individual than if he remained simply an anonymous Christian.

If the message of the Church encounters a man who is a "non-
Christian" only in the sense of an anonymous, not yet awakened,
Christianity, then the Church must take account of this fact in
her missionary work and draw the necessary conclusions for her
missionary strategy. One surmises that this has not always been
the case. What this means more precisely cannot here be further
developed.

Thesis 4. If on the one hand there is little chance that religious pluralism in the Christian's concrete situation will vanish
in the foreseeable future, and if on the other hand non-Christian-
ity may be quite correctly understood by the Christian as an
anonymous type of Christianity which he always meets in a
missionary way as a world that needs to be brought to an express
awareness of that which it already possesses as the divine offer,
or even more, as the unreflex and unexpressed accepted gift of
divine grace, then the Church today will not be so prone to
consider herself as the exclusive community of those awaiting
salvation, but rather as the historically visible vanguard—the historically and socially constituted expression of that which the
Christian knows to exist as a hidden reality even outside the visibility of the Church.

But first: while it is necessary to work, suffer and pray continually and indefatigably for the union of all humanity in the one Church of Christ, still, for reasons of theology and not only of profane history, we must expect that the foreseeable future will not witness the disappearance of religious pluralism from our own historical, existential milieu. We know from the gospel that opposition to Christ and the Church will remain until the end of time. We even have to expect, as more probable, an intensification of Christianity's excruciating existence.

But if this opposition to the Church cannot be limited to the purely private realm of the individual, but rather must have a public-historical character, and if this opposition is to be present in a history which now, in contrast to earlier times, possesses a global unity, then the lasting opposition to the Church can no longer be localized to the exclusion of a defined and limited historical region, say that of the Western world. It must be with us, and everywhere. And this fact is part and parcel of what Christians must learn to anticipate and endure.

The Church which is at the same time the homogeneous characterization of a culture itself homogeneous (the Medieval Church) will exist no longer when history can no more turn her back on its present phase of global unity. In a unified world history where every situation is a moment of every other, the "inevitable," public opposition to Christianity exists as a moment in the existential milieu of all Christendom.

Yet, as long as Christendom, which always faces opposition and really cannot expect ever to be free from it, believes in God's general salvific will—believes therefore that God with his unseen grace can conquer even where the Church does not, where the Church meets nothing but contradiction—then this Church cannot consider herself as *one* dialectical moment within the totality of history. Rather she must consider herself as she who by her faith has already in hope and love overcome her opposition: the Church's opponents are simply those who have not yet recognized what they really are or can be, especially when their opposition is merely superficial. They are already anonymous Christians, and the Church is not the community of those who have, in distinction to those who lack, the grace of God. Rather she is the community of those who can expressly profess what they *and* the others hope to be.

To the non-Christian it may appear presumptuous that the Christian values all that is wholesome in a man and all that is healed in holiness in him as the fruit of the grace of his Christ, as anonymous Christianity, and considers the non-Christian a Christian who has not yet reflectively awakened to himself. But the Christian cannot forego such "presumption." Actually, it is the path of profoundest humility for himself and the Church. For it once again permits God to be greater than man and the Church.

The Church will approach the non-Christian of tomorrow with that attitude which Paul expressed when he said: "What therefore you worship [*worship!*] in ignorance, that I proclaim to you" (Acts 17:23). With such understanding one can be tolerant, forbearing, and yet inexorable toward all non-Christian religions.

The Redemption of the Universe

by STANISLAS LYONNET

REDEMPTION, as the term is used by St. Paul, implies above all
the redemption of man. As a matter of fact, it implies almost exclusively the redemption of man. At times, however, Paul's redemptive horizon broadens to embrace the whole of creation, the
classic instance of which is chapter eight of the epistle to the
Romans.

It is this passage which we would like to examine here, and
we are the first to admit the difficulties involved. The chief problem is the obscurity of the Apostle's expression, giving rise for
centuries now to variant exegetical interpretations. Even today
agreement is far from universal. Yet such difficulties should not
keep us from the truths which the Apostle clearly intended to
expound to the Romans, and which he would undoubtedly apply
to the twentieth century Christian—especially since Paul's teaching of a cosmic redemption is more pertinent today than at any
other moment in history.

Paul begins his eighth chapter in Romans with a reference to
the fifth. He restates his doctrine of the Christian life whose vital
principle is the working of the Holy Spirit in us: a life of peace
as befits those already reconciled with him and certain of a
definitive salvation already possessed in hope. Yet though reconciled, humanity is not exempt from suffering and death. Far from
establishing an obstacle to our hope, suffering and death are
rather, in the words of the Apostle, *"conditiones optimae"*
(5:3–4), and to such a degree that in chapter eight he draws from
them a new motive for hope (8:17ff).

Taking a closer look at the passage, we find that Paul says that if "we suffer with Christ we shall also be glorified with him." He continues: "For I think that the sufferings of the present time are not to be compared to the glory which is to be revealed in us. Indeed, creation, filled with expectation, awaits the revelation of the sons of God: if creation was made subject to vanity—and not by its own choice but because of him who made it subject—it is with the hope that creation itself be liberated from the servitude of corruption to enter into the freedom of the glory of the children of God. For we know that all creation groans in the pains of childbirth until today. And not only it; we ourselves who possess the first fruits of the Spirit, we groan within ourselves in the expectation of the redemption of our body." [1]

Confronted by language so profound, the hearer might protest that the Apostle's creative imagination has carried him away, that he has forsaken the solid ground of dogma and theology to indulge in exalted but illusory dreams of poetic fancy. In the case of Paul such a hypothesis is, a priori, hardly tenable. Rather, is not the hearer at fault? Possibly he lacks the insight to understand the metaphorical element of Paul's language.

We shall answer this question in the second section of our paper by examining the objective context of the Apostle's affirmation. But first it would be well to place Paul's statements in their proper context, the biblical context. And then it will remain for us to show briefly in a third section how the Christian future, far from turning Christians away from their present task, both justifies and transfigures it.

I

In refutation to the reproach of poetic flight, Paul could repeat what he previously had said to the procurator Portius Festus, who had been scandalized to hear a man of good judgment such as Paul preaching the resurrection of Christ in the presence of King Agrippa: "I am not mad, excellent Festus, but I speak words of truth and sound sense" (Acts 26:25).

Then Paul appealed to the King himself. Though strange and incomprehensible to the ears of a pagan like Festus, Paul's statements could not surprise a Jew like King Agrippa, who was at home with the Scriptures. "For the king knows about these things and to him I speak with complete confidence" (v. 26). "Do you believe the prophets, King Agrippa? I know that you do!" (v. 27). To modern readers the Apostle poses the same question: "Do you believe in the prophets?" If so: "Reread what they have proclaimed and my teaching will cease to seem an enigma to you."

In our specific problem, in fact in regard to all of Pauline theology, it is important never to lose sight of the fact that Paul was a Jew for whom the Old Testament was and remained the Book par excellence. The Apostle spoke excellent Greek, but he thought essentially in the categories of the Jews of his day.

A Jew brought up on the Scriptures would always be acutely aware of the unity of the redemptive plan. The history of salvation which the Bible recounts is not presented to the Jew as a series of distinct and separate episodes, but rather as the realization of a single plan of love. True, the plan unfolds itself in history and progressively so; but it is of one piece. The unity of this plan can be demonstrated by the fact that the Bible sums up its successive stages in a single word: alliance, *berit*, which the Greek Septuagint translates as *diatheke*, "the Testament"—undoubtedly to lay the accent upon the divine initiative.

In the Old Testament the alliance between God and Israel was not a treaty between two equals, but rather and above all the gift of God to a people whom he had freely singled out, not through any merit on their part, but as Deuteronomy recalls, "out of love for them and to keep the oath made to their fathers" (Deut. 7:8). More significant yet, the oath made to Abraham, which was the basis for the alliance of Sinai, was itself called an "alliance," a "testament." This alliance was irrevocable, as would be the messianic alliance made on behalf of David, according to Psalm 88: "Forever will I continue my kindness to him, and my alliance shall stand firm with him. . . . I will not violate my alliance nor change the utterance of my lips. Once have I sworn by my holiness: I will never lie to David" (vs. 29–36).

Finally, the definitive realization of God's salvific plan in the "last times" is also referred to as an "alliance," or a "testament." The book of Isaias in the second and third parts makes more than one allusion to it. Jeremias described it explicitly as a "new alliance" (31:33), and Christ was to use this term at the Last Supper to proclaim formally the continuity and the unity of the "Two Testaments."

Further, the Bible speaks of an alliance prior to Abraham—a universal alliance established by God with mankind in the person of Noah after the whole of humanity had been re-created in the cataclysm of the deluge. This alliance extended beyond the human world and in some way embraced the material universe as well.

We read in chapters eight and nine of Genesis: "I will no more curse the earth because of man . . . never again will I destroy living things as I have done. So long as the earth lasts, seedtime and harvest, cold and heat, summer and winter, night and day, shall not cease" (Gen. 8:21–22). "Behold I have established my alliance with you, and with your descendants; and with every living being among you, all that has come forth out of the ark, all the living things of the earth. I have established my alliance with you: never again will all flesh be destroyed by the waters of the flood, nor shall there be from henceforth a flood to lay waste to the earth" (Gen. 9:9–11).

The sign of this alliance was not inscribed in the flesh of man by circumcision, as was the case with Abraham, but rather in the universe, in the broad heavens, so as to signify that the alliance with Noah was not limited to any one part of the created world, but embraced its totality. "This is the sign of the alliance which I place between me and you and all living beings among you from generation unto generation: I set my bow in the cloud, and it shall be the sign of alliance between me and the earth" (Gen. 9:12–13).

Thus after the cataclysm of the deluge, the punishment for man's sin, the physical universe regained its equilibrium, its harmony, its rhythm—precisely that of which the creation narrative spoke. Certainly the solemn declaration of Gen. 8:22: "So long as the earth lasts . . . summer and winter, night and day, shall not cease" evokes the words of Gen. 1:3–5: "God divided the light and the darkness. And there was evening and there was morning . . ." Similarly the promise of Gen. 8:21: "I will no more curse the earth because of man" recalls the words of Gen. 3:17: "Cursed is the earth because of you."

Confronted by this spectacle of the harmony of the *kosmos*, the Greek was struck above all by a beauty which delighted his eyes as well as his mind, while the Israelite, "instructed by the Scriptures," first encountered the sign of a God faithful to his plan of love. Jeremias, for instance, expressly compared the alliance with David to the alliance with heaven and earth (Jer. 33:20, 25). Perhaps this was also what the Psalmist was thinking of when he proclaimed that "the heavens declare the glory of God" and devoted the second half of his psalm to praising the gift of the Law: "*Lex Domini immaculata.*" It is, in any event, the image Paul created for the pagan peasants of Lystra by reminding them that "God has not failed to give witness to himself by his kindnesses, giving you rains and fruitful seasons from heaven, filling your hearts with food and gladness" (Acts 14:16–17; cf. Ps. 103).

Moreover, for the Israelite, the history of salvation did not begin only with Abraham or Noah, nor even with Adam. It began with creation itself. This was its first act. Thus, to cite but one example, in Psalm 135, recounting this "history of salvation" in the form of "litanies" with the refrain "for his great love is without end," the Psalmist began with the work of creation: "He alone spread out the earth upon the waters . . . He made the great lights . . . the sun to rule over the day . . . the moon and the stars to rule over the night. . . ." Then, without any transition, follow the "historical" benefits on behalf of Israel which the Bible terms precisely the "unspeakable works" of God: "He smote Egypt in her first-born . . . brought forth Israel from her midst . . . He divided the sea of rushes into two parts . . ." (v. 4–13).

In this regard, the extra-canonical Jewish tradition outdid the biblical tradition itself, if one may so express it, and in its attempt to emphasize still more the unity of the history of salvation it intentionally fixed its various stages on the same calendar day. So, according to the book of Jubilees, the sacrifice of Isaac was set on the 15th of Nisan, the same day on which the Pasch would later be celebrated. I will cite only one particularly significant example of this typical process. It deals fittingly with the feast of the Pasch.

According to Exodus, the Pasch commemorates a single event: "the night during which Jahweh had watched over his people to bring them forth from the land of Egypt" (Exod. 12:42). The Palestinian Targum, the more or less paraphrastic translation of the Hebrew text into the current Aramaic, offers an extremely informative gloss on this section. It is not just a single night which this feast celebrates. Rather it is four nights which sum up, as we shall see, the whole history of salvation.

The first night is that on which the Word of God appeared in order to create the world. (For us Christians the anniversary of the creation of the world is Sunday, the first day of the week, that day on which Christ rose, as the breviary hymn has it: *Primo die quo Trinitas Beata mundum condidit, vel quo resurgens Conditor nos, morte victa, liberat.*) The second night commemorates the time when the Word of God made an alliance with Abraham and promised him the birth of a son in whom all the nations of the earth would be blessed; another tradition of the Targum even adds the commemoration of the sacrifice of Isaac, that is, his "spiritual birth," which, in fact, according to the book of Jubilees, took place on the 15th of Nisan. The third night is that during which the Word of the Lord, striking the first-born of the Egyptians, delivered Israel from bondage in order to constitute Israel the first-born son of God. The fourth night is not of the past, but of the future, when the messianic king will come on the clouds to preside at the definitive redemption of Israel.

Four nights, four births: birth of the universe, birth of Israel, birth of the new world, birth of the "new heavens" and the "new earth," according to the expression of Isaias (65:17) taken up again in the Apocalypse (21:1) and the second epistle of St. Peter (3:13).

One can readily see how, for a Jew "instructed in the Scriptures," the history of the universe was a part of the history of salvation. Created for man, the universe in some way shares his destiny. Just as the execution of the first alliance with Noah had cosmic implications so the eschatological alliance will necessarily have its impact on the whole of creation.

But what were as yet only more or less vague suggestions—differently interpreted by the Jewish doctors themselves—was to become in Paul a clearly defined doctrine. The resurrection of Christ would bring together bits of truth until then dispersed throughout the Old Testament. On the road to Damascus Saul the Jew, disciple of Gamaliel, encountered the risen Christ. His eyes opened under the guidance of the Spirit, the Apostle saw written, as it were, in the splendor of Christ's glorified body, the destiny to which God invited not only every human person but even the entire universe.

This we will now show by determining in as precise a manner as possible, the exact meaning of the Apostle's teachings in Rom. 8:17–23.

II

It seems possible to disengage from these verses at least a threefold doctrine, which, for clarity's sake, can be formulated in the following propositions: (1) The redemption of the universe is only a consequence of the redemption of man; (2) It is, more precisely, a consequence of the redemption of man's body; (3) Yet the universe is not simply an instrument of man's redemption—it is itself an object of redemption.

1. The redemption of the universe, a consequence of the redemption of man

Without a shadow of doubt this affirmation emerges from the whole of the Apostle's argumentation in the present passage: the redemption of the universe can only be conceived in connection with the redemption of man. The latter is primary from any point of view. Unlike some more or less gnostic representations of contemporaries who thought man would be freed from matter because God would transport him to a new universe, for Paul, as for the Bible, it is precisely because man is saved that he can draw the whole universe after him into this salvation. Already in the Old Testament man is at the center of the universe; all the more is this true of the New Testament since we know that God has deigned to take up residence among us.

The bold proclamation of this fundamental doctrine by the new religion was the more commendable since it directly contradicted some of the most profound tendencies of Greek philosophy. One recalls the jeers of Celsus which Origen has preserved for us in his *Contra Celsum*. Celsus compares Christians "to moths swarming about at night, to ants filing out from their hill, or to frogs leaving their pond and saying: 'We are those to whom God has foretold everything and revealed all things to come; and overlooking the whole cosmos and the course of the stars, neglecting even this immense earth, he communicates his designs for the world to us, and us alone. To us alone has he sent his heralds, and sends them even now, solicitous as he is of uniting us to him eternally.' "

"Truly," gibes Celsus, "we are like little grub worms who cry out: 'God exists, and of a sudden we have become completely like God. To us he has subjected everything—the earth, water, air, stars. Everything exists for us and has received the command to serve us. And, because some have sinned, God will come or will send his Son to consume the impious in flames, and to lead us, the others, into eternal life with him.' " "Such language," adds Celsus, "would be somewhat more tolerable on the part of worms or frogs than on the part of Jews and Christians" (Origen, *Contra Celsum*, 4, 23; P.G. 11, 1060).

Such words are not to be taken as said simply in jest. Rather we are here confronted by one of the most typical reactions of the Greek spirit to the central dogma of Christianity. One hundred and fifty years later, the philosopher Plotinus expressed himself with no less vigor, and a Plotinist like E. Bréhier does not hesitate to describe this declamation as "one of the most beautiful and haughty reactions of Hellenic rationalism to the religious individualism which was overrunning the Greco-Roman world during this epoch." Here Bréhier is certainly referring to Christianity, in particular to the central place it allots the human person. He continues: "Plotinus does not attack the details of Christian belief—this he leaves to two of his dearest disciples, Amelius and Porphyry; he himself goes straight to its principle, i.e., the exaltation of the believer who relates everything to his own salvation. In opposition to this Plotinus upholds the ancient Hellenic tradition according to which the true end of man consists in understanding his place in the system of realities and not in assigning the first place to himself." [2]

Bréhier has in mind here the treatise of Plotinus *Against the Gnostics* (II, ch. 9). It is clear enough that Plotinus is alluding to Christians: those "senseless men who let themselves be persuaded when they hear words such as these: You will be superior to all things, above men as well as gods (i.e., stellar deities). How great is presumption among men! Once they were humble, modest, and simple people of the world; now they give heed to the words: You are a son of God; the others whom you admired so much are not sons of God—not even the stars to whom tradition bids us offer homage. You have become without effort superior to heaven itself!" (II, 9, 9).

"These men pretend," says Plotinus elsewhere, "that Providence works uniquely in their favor . . . But Providence watches over the All rather than over the parts, and the soul of the All receives this guidance much more than the parts . . . Who of these senseless ones who think themselves to be above wisdom, enjoys the wondrous order and wisdom of the universe?" (II, 9, 16). Plotinus then invites them to contemplate "the beauties of the visible world, its proportions, its harmony and the spectacle which the stars offer in spite of their distance" (*ibid.*).

Yet, even at the risk of giving scandal to cultured Hellenistic minds, Paul makes no allowance for such a conception. If he speaks of a redemption of the universe, he conceives of it only in dependence on that of man.

2. The redemption of the universe as a consequence of the redemption of man's body

The redemption of the universe is in Paul's thought essentially a corollary of the resurrection of the body and consequently is based, like it, on the fact of the resurrection of Christ.

At the beginning of this chapter Paul explains that Christ, in virtue of his death and resurrection, communicates to human nature and to each Christian in particular a new principle which is none other than the Holy Spirit, the third person of the Holy Trinity. The Christian is defined as one animated by the Holy Spirit. Now in verse 11 the Apostle adds that this new principle not only exercises its influence on the soul, but is equally the source of life for the Christian's body, as it was for Christ's body: "If the Spirit of him who raised Jesus from the dead dwells in you . . . He will give life to your mortal bodies too, by his spirit who dwells in you."

Paul introduces our passage, in verses 17 and 18, by referring to the resurrection of the body: he speaks of the "glorification" which awaits those who are conjoined to the passion of Christ, and of the "glory" which, as a result, must be revealed in them. Here, as in the entire epistle, Paul has in mind salvation in its fullness which is completed only with the resurrection of the body at the Parousia.

Again, verse 23, concluding our passage, leaves no room for doubt: after referring to the expectation of the universe, Paul mentions the expectation of the Christian which he defines with unmistakable clarity as the expectation of "the redemption of our body"; certainly not in the sense that the Christian awaits an emancipation from the body! He awaits with firm hope the liberation of his body itself, as well as his soul, from the carnal condition. In other words, it will partake of the same condition as the risen body of Christ.

3. *The universe, object of the redemption*

The Christian expects, too, with an equally firm hope that this new condition will become—in a manner impossible for us to imagine—the lot of the entire universe.

Here (v. 19) Paul adds to the clear statements concerning the present and future of the world an allusion to the past whose exact meaning is not certain and upon which not all exegetes are in agreement. On this point the Apostle seems to be taking up—without going beyond—the affirmation of Genesis (3:17) in which God, speaking to our first parents after their sin, says to Adam: "Cursed be the earth because of you . . . thorns and thistles shall it bring forth for you." There are evidently several ways of understanding such an affirmation. For St. Thomas, for example, thorns and thistles would have grown on the earth even if man had not sinned; but in this case their growth would not have been *"in poenam hominis"* (II–II, q. 164, art. 2, ad 1).

We will not delay over this problem which St. Paul did not intend to treat *ex professo*. The past of the universe certainly interests him much less than its present and its future. In regard to the present and future his thought does not present the same obscurity. Whatever may have been the primitive state of the universe before sin, its present state is not the definitive one. Like the human universe, the material universe itself is in expectation of a future state.

Paul, in describing this expectation, does not hesitate to make use of imagery. He portrays the whole of creation awaiting its deliverance as a person who, head thrust forward (*apokaradokia*, v. 19), fixes his eyes on the horizon, whence, with the return of Christ, the new day will finally dawn for mankind in full possession of the glory destined for the children of God.

The universe will not be content merely to look on from the outside at this triumph of redeemed humanity, as an impressed spectator delighting in a magnificent panorama. The material universe is called to share in the future state of the children of God. "It will be freed," says Paul, from what in its present state is "vanity, servitude and corruption," in order to share in "the freedom of the glory of the children of God." It will leave, then, its present condition to enter this new one which the Apostle does not hesitate to call a "freedom"—in fact, a freedom that is quite the same as that belonging to the glory of the children of God: and not merely, as it is often translated, "the glorious freedom of the children of God," but "the freedom of the glory of the children of God."

In Paul's mind the term "glory," especially in this eschatological context, signifies a very precise reality—the active and visible presence of God himself which is communicated to the humanity of Christ glorified in his resurrection and ascension; it is through Christ's glorified humanity that this presence will be communicated to our humanity in its fullness at the general resurrection of the body.

According to the Apostle, this assertion itself rests on a certitude of faith. For "we know" from the Scriptures, continues Paul, that the present universe "is in labor" toward a better state —odinei, is in the pains of childbirth: the Apostle does not shrink from the deeply human and richly expressive biblical metaphor of the pains of childbirth (v. 22). From a purely human point of view that is incapable of going beyond appearances, the universe, true enough, seems at times to be floundering under the weight of torturing evil. Faith teaches us, however, that this is not the sign of agony, but rather the presage of birth.

Such an article of faith was most likely part of the very first Credo of the Church. St. Peter, from the start of his preaching on the day of Pentecost, referred to this "universal restoration" of which God had spoken through the mouth of his holy prophets (Acts 3:21). Moreover, Paul mentions it not only in this passage of the epistle to the Romans, but also in the epistles to the Colossians and Ephesians. The Apostle is careful not to limit his horizon to the human world alone. If he is thinking here above all of the angelic world (because of the adversaries he must combat, especially in the letter to the Colossians), he nevertheless affirms with particular emphasis that Christ—the Christ made flesh, according to what seems to me the correct opinion of a number of modern exegetes—is the very center of the entire creation.

The absolute dependence of the entire universe on Christ is mirrored in the use of the prepositions *en, eis,* and *dia.* "Everything was created by him and for him; everything subsists in him." As Huby clearly and precisely explains: "In him all things have been created as in the supreme center of unity, harmony and cohesion, which gives the world its meaning, its value and thereby its reality, or, to use another metaphor, the nucleus, the meeting point (Lightfoot) where all the threads, all the forces of the universe converge and are co-ordinated. Were one to have an instantaneous view of the whole universe, past, present and future, he would see every being as ontologically dependent on Christ and as definitively intelligible only through him" (*Épîtres de la captivité,* p. 40).

In its turn, the epistle to the Ephesians describes explicitly the salvific plan of God as the recapitulation of all things in Christ—not just all men, but all things; so much so that nothing that exists should escape the vital influence of Christ. Each, of course, comes under this influence in a way proper to its own condition, but nothing is deprived of its rebirth. In short, God has created nothing for death, but rather only for life.

Finally, this authentically biblical doctrine was taken into the entire Catholic tradition without exception. The Greek Fathers were not alone in taking delight in the unity of the creative and redemptive plan, the fact that the entire universe shares the destiny of the human nature assumed by the Son of God. The hymns of victory of a St. John Chrysostom found their Latin echo in a St. Ambrose, who saw in the resurrection of Christ the resurrection of the entire universe and not just that of man: "*Resurrexit in eo mundus, resurrexit in eo caelum, resurrexit in eo terra. Erat enim caelum novum et terra nova*" (*De fide resurrectionis.* Second Nocturn of the Fifth Sunday after Easter).

But even if we skip over all other examples, St. Thomas' magnificent conclusion to the *Summa Contra Gentiles* sums up this Latin tradition superbly. "Because all corporal beings," explains the Angelic Doctor, "exist in some way for man, it is fitting that at that time (after the last judgment) the state of the entire corporal universe will be transformed, so that it may be in harmony with what will then be the state of man. And since men will then be incorruptible, the present state of corruptibility will be removed from the corporal universe. This is what the Apostle teaches (Rom. 8:21). Thus, since the material universe will finally be adapted to the state of man, and since men will not only be freed from corruption, but clothed in glory, the material universe must also acquire in its way *quamdam claritatis gloriam.* This is the teaching of Apocalypse 21:1: '*Vidi caelum novum*'; and Isaias 65:17: 'Behold I create new heavens and a new earth and the former things shall not be in remembrance . . . But you will rejoice and be glad forever. Amen.'" With this citation and with this hymn of triumph the work of the Angelic Doctor ends.

In Paul's day Jewish thought, it seems, was divided. Certain doctors represented the end of the world as an annihilation, a sort of general conflagration, in the manner of the Stoic *ekpurosis*; others saw it as a transformation. For Paul and for Christianity, there is no possible doubt. The universe is not destined to be destroyed, but to be transformed, to be, as the human body, "glorified" in its own way.

Of course, revelation teaches us nothing about the "how" of this transformation—revelation does not furnish us with any information of a properly "cosmological" order. Its teaching is of the religious order, not the "scientific." But it teaches us with certitude, that however this transformation may come about, it will lead to life and not to death.

In the same way, the dogma of the resurrection of the body cannot supply the biologist with a new datum; yet it teaches the Christian a truth far more important, though of another order. It teaches him that, appearances to the contrary, this body, in which he may already detect the ravages of sickness, which he knows is going to decompose and turn to dust, is nevertheless promised a share in the glory of the risen Christ.

But by this very fact, i.e., precisely because we have to deal with an essentially religious doctrine and not one of a purely scientific nature, the dogma of the redemption of the universe has not been revealed to us only, nor even principally, to render our intellectual world-synthesis more sweeping and more unified. Before all else this doctrine is intended to direct our lives and shape our attitudes, or—in the words of St. Paul—it should permit us to "walk in a manner worthy of the Lord" (Col. 1:10). This is the point we wish to elaborate in our final section.

III

Three lessons—three important consequences—seem to flow directly from the Pauline doctrine we have just expounded.

1. From the fact that the goal of Christian hope is placed in the redemption of the body and of the universe, it follows that the Christian conception of "salvation" is essentially a collective conception. For the bodily resurrection is characterized by the

fact that, with the exception of Christ and his mother, it will take place for all at the same time, at the end of time, at that moment of "time" which the New Testament calls the Parousia.

Admittedly, this great hope has ceased little by little to be the true expectation of most Christians. We are accustomed to think only of what we call "the salvation of our soul," forgetting that this salvation is itself only a part of a whole. Moreover, a number of exegetes have thought it necessary to contrast in Paul two conceptions of salvation. They maintain that the first, whereby salvation is obtained by the resurrection of the body, is a relic of his Judaism which he later abandoned, replacing it by the Greek conception. In the Greek conception the resurrection no longer plays any real role and salvation is obtained immediately after death in the union of the soul, finally emancipated from the bonds of the body, with the divinity.

Nothing could be more inaccurate. To the end of his life, Paul never ceased to await the resurrection and the return of Christ at the Parousia—the redemption of the universe—all the while believing that at his death he would rejoin Christ in God. He never saw the slightest contradiction between these two aspects, as if it would be necessary to adopt the one and reject the other. However, the second aspect was basically individualistic; the first, on the contrary, was essentially collective and complemented the hope of Paul as well as of all early Christians.

For them, even if a Christian was definitively united to God in what was later termed the "beatific vision," his salvation was not yet complete. He would be fully "saved" only on taking possession of his glorious body, which means when all the elect were saved along with him or, to use a Pauline formula, when the body of Christ attained its perfect state. *"Irrequietum est cor meum donec requiescat in Te"*; or better yet, to avoid any ambiguity: *"Donec requiescamus omnes in Te!"*

2. From the fact that the redemption of the body extends to

the whole universe, it follows that the work of man—his efforts to master the material universe, to draw out its secrets, to domesticate and utilize it, to transform brute matter into instruments of greater and greater perfection right up to "electronic brains" capable of operations defying the intelligence even of the man who made them—all such human work acquires a value for eternity.

Of course, matter offers man a resistance which can only be overcome by painful efforts. This is the painful, "laborious" character of human work which the Bible affirms as a penalty of original sin. But it never insinuates that without sin man would not have had to work. It even says explicitly that Adam before his sin was placed in the earthly Paradise "to cultivate it."

For the sinner, work, by reasons of its inherent painfulness, is a means of expiation or purification, the means par excellence. "You shall eat your bread in the sweat of your brow" (Gen. 3:19). But let us be careful not to restrict the value of work to this single aspect or even to consider it simply as a means of earning a living. Work has another, perhaps less familiar, aspect which springs immediately from the dogma of the redemption of the universe.

God has not created this universe to destine it to death. He has placed in our hands an unfinished universe, entrusting to us the glorious mission of perfecting his work. Because of sin, man is incapable of fulfilling this mission without painful effort, but God, in deciding to redeem man and in promising him a Redeemer, has entrusted this task to him once again, so to speak, and has enabled him to bring it to completion.

For the God of the Bible is exactly the opposite of Zeus who was jealous of man's happiness and who reserved to himself the secrets of nature, condemning Prometheus for having loved men too much in bringing them fire. For us Christians every new advance in the harnessing of nature by man, every new conquest of itself enters into the divine plan. It continues creation. It enables material creation to tend toward the end for which it was created. Such advances prepare in a certain, though enigmatic, way for the future redemption of the universe. In similar fashion, each time the spirit takes a greater hold on the human body, rendering it a more docile servant of the soul, it prepares in a real, but nonetheless enigmatic, manner for the future resurrection of the body.

3. Finally, from this there comes a third, equally important lesson. We have seen that Paul and the Bible conceived the redemption of the universe only as dependent upon the redemption of man himself. Without the redemption of man there could be neither redemption of the body nor, consequently, redemption of the universe. It follows that any effort to prepare for a redemption of the universe through human labor alone, without regard for the redemption of man, is a total delusion. By the same token, every so-called asceticism that tends to submit the body to the soul without looking toward the redemption of this soul can lead only to tragic failure. The body would then rise only to imprison the soul completely. Believing that he was working toward his salvation, man would be working in fact toward the loss of his soul as well as his body.

Gnostics may consider matter itself evil. But for Paul, as for the Bible, evil exists only in man—more precisely in the spirit of the man who, instead of ordering himself to God and others, seeks to order others and even God to himself. It follows then of necessity that every conquest of the universe which is not ordered toward establishing in man the reign of love serves to strengthen in him the tyranny of egoism; far from preparing the redemption of the universe, it can only contribute to its ruin. On the other hand, each time that man strives by his work—even if without apparent success—to place the universe at the service of love, it must be said that he is mysteriously but efficaciously preparing the world for redemption.

In this way one may see how authentic Christian hope in a future world—far from luring the Christian from concern for the world, far from turning him aside from enriching the universe through dedicated labor—makes just such effort one of his most pressing duties. For, if what we have said is correct, if a "redeemed" universe can in the final analysis only be a universe placed entirely at the service of love, who then but the Christian—I mean the man authentically inspired by the love of Christ (for there is no other, whether he bears officially the name of Christian or whether he is one in fact without knowing it)—who then but such a man is capable of placing the universe at the service of love and thus contributing, modestly but efficaciously, to the redemption of the universe, the object of his hope?

NOTES

[1] Among the recent studies devoted to this passage of the epistle to the Romans, see in particular A. Viard, "Expectatio creaturae" in *Revue Biblique*, 69 (1952), pp. 337–54, and A. M. Dubarle, "Le gemissement des creatures dans l'ordre du Cosmos" in *Revue des Sciences phil. et theol.*, 38 (1954), pp. 445–65.

With regard to the timeliness and importance of the problem, permit us to cite this reflection of M. Blondel which is taken from the *Correspondance M. Blondel–A. Valensin*, vol. 1, p. 47: "The problem of the Incarnation seems to me . . . (perhaps antecedent to any other philosophical question) to be the touchstone for a true cosmology in an integral metaphysics . . . I share the ideas and sentiments of P. Teilhard de Chardin with regard to the problems of Christology. Before horizons enlarged by the natural and human sciences, one cannot, without a betrayal of Catholicism, be content with mediocre explanations and limited viewpoints which make a historical accident of Christ, which isolate him in the cosmos as an unrelated incident and which seem to make of him an intruder, not one at home, in the overwhelming and hostile immensity of the universe. Long before Loisyism . . . I recognized with intense clarity the alternative: either fall back on a dead symbolism, or advance toward an integral realism which would put Christian metaphysics in accord with the mysticism lived by the saints and the faithful themselves . . . We are drawn towards the *"instauratio tota in Christo"* . . . Let us advance then without hesitation, in that direction in which as we grow in our appreciation of man and the world, so much more will Christ grow in our minds and hearts." Blondel remarks further in the same work (p. 48) that it is indispensable "to indicate clearly and with increased force the absolute transcendence of the divine gift, the inevitably supernatural character of the deifying design, and as a consequence the moral transformation and the spiritual expansion which grace permits and which it must accomplish." On this *Correspondance,* see J. Levie in *Nouvelle revue theologique,* 91 (1959), pp. 1073–81.

² *Plotin-Ennéades,* texte établi et traduit par E. Bréhier, vol. II, pp. 107–10.

PART THREE

The Church
in Council

The Council and Liturgical Reform

by JOSEF JUNGMANN

On December 7, 1962, in the final assembly of its first session, the Second Vatican Council voted by a great majority to enact the first chapter of its schema—the improvement of the holy liturgy. At present this event changes nothing in our liturgical ceremonies; it merely determines a few principles as to how the coming liturgical reform should be carried out.

Actually the chapter itself does not become effective as Church law until autumn, 1963, after the concluding chapters of the schema (on the Mass, the sacraments, the breviary, the Church year, Church art, and so forth) have been discussed, approved, and receive papal proclamation. And even then we shall have to wait a year or two while the liturgical texts and rubrics involved are confirmed, edited, and finally published. Yet despite all this, December 7, 1962, will surely be recognized in coming centuries as a decisive date in the history of the Church and her life of worship.

Why? What has happened? Simply this: a centuries-old taboo has been destroyed. Theodore Klauser once designated post-Tridentine liturgy as the "age of dormancy" or "of the rubric." Most of us grew up in this age. At the turn of the century and long thereafter the word was, "Hands off the liturgy"; it was almost as immune to change as Holy Scripture. Even when the waves of the liturgical movement surged over the land and we were sincerely concerned with making the liturgy at hand meaningful to the faithful, even then no one really seriously thought that the liturgy itself could ever be tampered with. Indeed, the faithful were to be led to the Mass; but that the Mass should meet the people half-way was still a precarious opinion up to 1950. Yet this is the opinion the Council has now proclaimed and made law. The age of dormancy has come to an end. The first notable breakthrough came with the Easter liturgy reform in 1951. It was a far-reaching renovation proceeding from one significant change; with the decree of the Council this renovation became a sweeping reformation.

Since the official phrasing of the decree on liturgy is as yet unknown, the only source at our disposal is the semi-official résumé by Cyprian Vagaggini, O.S.B., in the December 8 issue of *Osservatore Romano*. Vagaggini is professor at the Collegium Anselmianum in Rome, and author of the book, *Theological Dimensions of the Liturgy* (Collegeville, 1959). In his résumé he presents the main ideas of the decree, and on basic points the exact phrasing; he complements this with a running commentary drawn from first-hand acquaintance with the matter as consultor of both the preparatory commission and the actual conciliar commission on the liturgy. Here we shall consider only those features which are of primary importance for the coming reform.

From the dawn of the Council the one desire and hope in the liturgical sphere, expressed in innumerable suggestions from both public and private sources, was a relaxation in the regulations on language; the Mass of the Catechumens, as it is still called today, or at least the readings were desired in the vernacular. This suggestion has actually been approved, even though the concrete application to the Mass is not expressly elaborated in the first chapter.

According to Article 36, Latin remains the proper language in the province of the Latin liturgy. Yet "in the Mass as well as in the administration of the sacraments, and in the other parts of the liturgy" a greater place is to be assigned to the vernacular, "especially in the readings, in addresses to the people, in many prayers and chants." From the course of the discussion on language in the Aula Concilii, adequately described by the Catholic Press Office, one may well conclude that what is to remain in Latin is primarily the sacred prayer of the Mass, Preface and Canon. It is noteworthy that all the discussions of possible reforms, especially in regard to the language, centered about the Mass celebrated with the congregation, Sunday Mass above all. Obviously, no essential change in language is required for private Masses.

Thus the Council has fulfilled the general expectation concerning the liturgical language, but in reality its action is far more decisive. The Council seeks a true reform of the liturgy. Already in the introduction there occurs the daring word *instauratio,* a word capable of jarring many an unsuspecting Council Father and yet deliberately retained. This reform is not intended in the purely historical sense so prominent in the liturgical restoration following the Council of Trent. Trent proposed to reform the liturgy "according to the order and manner of the Fathers," that is, of Christian antiquity. As far as was possible with the inadequate means of the age, those distracting accessories acquired in preceding centuries were to be eliminated, and the original structure brought to the fore.

However, the reform demanded by Vatican II, despite its stress on adherence to tradition, is to be entirely directed toward the faithful. Article 33 says so expressly, and Article 34 draws the momentous conclusion: in structure the ceremonies should be "simple and transparent, so that in general they do not require much explanation." Active participation of the faithful in divine worship is practically a foregone conclusion.

This article states a principle which was completely foreign not only to the liturgical reform following Trent, but even to the beginnings of the liturgical movement one hundred years ago; more than foreign, it was the exact opposite of the prevailing liturgical attitude. To Abbot Prosper Gueranger, the famed forerunner of the liturgical movement, the liturgy was meant to be obscure, not transparent. Liturgy was a sanctuary, off limits for the mere believer. Again and again the principle was stressed that mysterious ways and strange language express the symbol of *the holy,* and inspire reverence in the faithful. This approach scrupulously imitated Christian antiquity's practice of secrecy, but forgot that the wall of secrecy was erected between the Christian community and profane paganism, not between the altar and the faithful.

Today we have again become aware, and the Council heightens that awareness, that the faithful—those baptized in the mystery of Christ and continually confirmed anew in this mystery through participation in the sacraments—must receive life precisely from this mystery in order to persevere in the midst of a pagan world. Indicatively, Church architecture has already realized that today it is no longer the nave of the medieval cathedral but its choir that must be the model for church space: the faithful, gathered around the altar, have been called to take part in the reality of the altar.[1]

Here it already becomes evident that in the mind of the Council the liturgical reform must evolve from a more fundamental view of the Church. It is not mere chance that the final days of this same session were dedicated to the theme of the Church. The discussion was primarily directed to overcoming the concept of a juridical, authoritative Church, the Church of the clergy.

The program for reform of the liturgy was an advance application of this new viewpoint: If liturgy is the divine worship of the Church, then one must not conceive Church as the authority which prescribes determined rites, appoints officials, and in this way conducts divine worship "in the name of the Church"; no, Church must be conceived as the community of the faithful which itself truly accomplishes divine worship—certainly under the direction of the sacramentally ordained priest who receives his formal authorization from the bishop in union with the head of the universal Church. The ecclesial gathering is no longer viewed as an assembly demanded solely by Church law in which the faithful attend a mysterious procedure, as if looking on from a distance at a ceremony which has no meaning for them. Rather this gathering is itself the true realization of the concept of Church: the visible union of those called by God in Christ, the citizens of the holy place. The Council thus provided an unexpected confirmation and stimulation of the awareness of Church in the hearts of men.

A second important decision of the Council concerns the possible diversification of the Roman liturgy, so markedly unified since the reform of Trent.

Until the early Middle Ages the Roman liturgy embraced only Rome and its surroundings; even in the sixteenth century it was limited to Middle and Western Europe. Now it has become the liturgy of the greater part of a world Church extending to every continent, the liturgy of nations to whom Western culture, with its Greek and Latin foundation, is as foreign as Chinese or Indian culture is to the European.

No one would dare maintain that the bishops of mission countries unanimously demanded diversification and the greater liberty consequent to it; voices were also raised in favor of preserving the Roman forms of divine worship as faithfully as possible, and these were not exclusively the voices of native Europeans. But the desire for liberty in opposition to the obligatory continuation of the Roman system made such a deep impression that in the end the suggested formulas of the commission were accepted almost unanimously. As stated in Article 22, henceforth the competent ecclesiastical authority of the area (*competens auctoritas ecclesiastica territorialis*) is empowered to accommodate the liturgy to the particular needs of the land or nation; the right of administration belongs to the regional authorities, and only the approbation (*probare seu confirmare*) is reserved to Rome.

The Bishops' Conferences, still in the developing stage, are the authorities primarily intended here. True, in the original draft the broader expression, *auctoritas territorialis*, replaced the term Bishops' Conferences, but the concept had to be more precisely determined in the discussions of the Council, and there were also various administrative bodies to be considered, depending upon the situation—provincial synods as well as Bishops' Conferences representing an entire nation or continent.

By virtue of this decision, a Bishops' Conference in India or Japan could in preference to Latin instate the native tongue as the liturgical language. It could alter liturgical vestments or surround the Catechumenate, the introductory step to adult baptism, with a liturgy more expressive of national spirit and culture than are the Roman Ritual's traditional forms.

In reality this distribution of power is nothing more than the restoration and more precise formulation of the criteria which determined liturgical life prior to the Council of Trent. The basic principle at that time was that each church should follow the example set by its proper ecclesiastical province. Thus when Gabriel Biel (d. 1495) gave his explanation of the Mass in Tübingen, he based it upon the practice of the metropolitan in power, the Archbishop of Mainz. Churches in the North adhered to the custom of Drontheim or Lund, and the suffragans of Salzburg to the order of their see city. Yet prior to the printing press strict conformity was neither expected nor possible.

The astonishing thing is that the liturgy, inherited from the Roman church and received in the northern countries in the time

of the Carolingian empire, was so faithfully retained and preserved as the uncontested standard, even though there was no
written law to this effect. Naturally bishops everywhere allowed
various additions and accepted proven customs from other prov-
inces, but awareness of solidarity prevented them from radical
experimentation with the ancient foundations of the liturgy.
Thus despite certain liberty, the text of the Canon of the Mass
as well as that of the Mass propers of Sundays and holydays was
preserved intact from the time of Gregory the Great. We may
feel confident that something of this respectful attitude toward
tradition will influence future decisions as well.

A strictly uniform liturgy is not essential to the Church; like
the bride of the king of Psalm 44, the Church is arrayed in a
gown woven of many colors. This was emphasized in the Council
as pointedly as possible. Holy Mass, which opened every session
in the Aula Concilii, was celebrated in one of the non-Roman
rites of the universal Church once or twice a week. One could
witness a Byzantine Mass in Greek one day, a Mass in Arabic
the next, or even in the Old Slavic language, and witness the
words of consecration sung out loud by the celebrant. Or again
in the Ethiopian rite one could hear the passionate cries of
praise and greeting from the congregation in response to these
same words of consecration. There was also the Armenian Mass,
which as late as the end of the Middle Ages added Roman elements to its ancient institutions, and the Mass of the Chaldeans
with the poetic lilt of its fervent Communion prayers.

But the West had its surprises too. Not only the Mass in the
Ambrosian rite, celebrated by the Cardinal of Milan, but also
late medieval variations of the Roman Mass opened the session
at times: Mass in the rite of the Dominicans with their short
Confiteor, in the rite of Braga, Portugal, with its Marian beginning and ending, and its solemn bows of reverence, and what
proved most surprising for many, our own Roman Mass in the

Slavic language, a custom of long standing in several dioceses on the coast of Dalmatia.

All this was meant to show explicitly how open the ranking Church administration is to worthy traditions of individual churches, whether from East or West. But more than tolerance was involved. As the bishops pointed out in their speeches, this variety of rites is proper and valid not only for the culture of past centuries, but also for the future, which will have the right to demand the same variety in certain situations. It was likewise to be expected that the example of these liturgical experiences would be recalled in the discussion on whether or not silence need be observed throughout the entirety of the Canon of the Roman Mass.

Our increasing readiness to accept without hesitation a usage characteristic of another rite is the very attitude which, according to the history of the liturgy, Rome itself observed up to the late Middle Ages. Many of the feasts of our liturgical calendar, the prayers at the beginning or end of Mass and during the Offertory, the ceremonies of ordination of the priesthood, and so forth, which are prescribed by the Roman liturgy, were borrowed prior to Trent from practices developed in the northern countries. Rome even borrowed from the Eastern liturgies of Syria and Greece before the Schism. The Improperia and the Trisagion (the threefold refrain still sung in the Greek) on Good Friday, and the Agnus Dei of our daily Mass are prayers which Rome extracted from the Eastern liturgies during the seventh and eighth centuries. It was only after the Schism with its strife and enmity that such borrowing came to an end.

Should not we moderns, living in a period of global unity and striving for Christian unity, encourage such renovation, if not by a direct exchange of liturgical forms, at least on the basis of mutual stimulation? It would be unnatural to retain as our most basic principle the mere conservation of the ancient. This anxious preservation of what we already have is feasible only as a stage in our development.

Yet on the other hand, our broader knowledge of the manifold forms of divine worship, present and past, presents a great temptation to fall into an unhealthy eclecticism and to imprudently incorporate elements into our liturgical heritage which detract from the unity of the whole; our separated brothers are particularly exposed to this danger in their otherwise promising attempts at reform.

A third group of stipulations merits consideration as being significant for the future. It concerns the role of the individual bishop in liturgical legislation. Today Canon 1257 of canon law is still in effect; by it, the Apostolic See alone has the power to effect changes in the liturgy and to approve liturgical books. Article 22, quoted above, states: Competent for the administration of the liturgy are the Apostolic See and, in certain matters, the bishop.

The bishop's authority in liturgical matters is plainly limited to that sphere in which no precepts have been formulated for the entire Latin Church. This sphere includes a more detailed elaboration of the ceremonies of the Mass and the administration of the sacraments, the arrangements for processions and special functions—above all, evening devotions.

Basically, the bishop always had authority over these things. But up to the present his contribution was merely to insure the observance of liturgical laws, to prevent abuses in the spiritual life of the faithful, and further to watch over religious exercises conducted in churches and public chapels (Cn. 1259, 1261).

The Canon's rather negative terminology hardly expressed a very high estimation of the areas of spiritual life left to the care of the bishop. The Council speaks a different language altogether. It assigns to the bishop a positive role. In addition to the liturgy prescribed in the official books of the Roman Church, it stresses the "special dignity" of the religious services conducted in various dioceses upon injunction of the bishop; it explicitly recommends "services of the Word" (*celebrationes verbi*), above all as evening devotions on the vigils of holydays and in the seasons of Advent and Lent. The stimulus for this recommendation came, surprisingly enough, from the bishops of South America, the priest-poor land; they no doubt are especially interested in providing divine services conducted by laymen as a substitute for Sunday Mass in widely scattered village churches. The Bishop of Posadas, who made this suggestion in the name of the 25 bishops from Argentina, rightly envisions such services as an important stimulus to religious renewal.[2]

This is a limited change, but one of immense significance. It indicates a growing respect for the word of God, and so will meet the approval of our separated brothers. In general, it means a rebirth of that part of the hours of prayer outside of the Mass which traditionally belonged to the congregation.

Today these hours appear almost exclusively in the form of the breviary, and we scarcely realize that our present form of eight hours originated much later (in the fourth century)[3] when it was adapted to the schedule of monastic life; still later, in the Middle Ages, the entire clergy began to pray the hours. But according to early Church tradition only one morning hour and one evening hour were sung publicly in the cathedral or parish church, and these were prayed by clergy and laity together (though no formal obligation bound the faithful) just as various Christian communities (Maronites, Chaldeans) still observe these hours today in the Orient. The morning hour, Matins, was finally replaced by daily Mass in the West; the evening hour, Vespers, also lost its popularity with the passage of time. The chanting of psalms in Latin no longer appealed to the modern man.

In our time, evening devotions have gradually come to the

fore. But in many countries they are without direction and are exposed to neglect. By their very structure the many novenas, triduums, and the like seem to linger too much on the periphery of genuine piety; from the liturgical standpoint they scarcely deserve any guidance.[4]

The German diocesan hymn books have shown such a remarkable development that the bishops may well accept them as the basis for their official text of devotional liturgy. In these books it has become apparent that evening devotions must be adapted to the divine worship of the Church; their themes, necessarily derived from the history of the economy of salvation, must follow the development of the Church year; therefore, the structure of the devotions should correspond to the essence of both the Church and the ecclesial gathering. How? The word of Scripture must play a prominent role; the prayers and hymns of the congregation must attain their summary fulfillment in the prayer of the priest.

It is no wonder that the plan of the Second Vatican Council to conduct a sweeping reform of the liturgy evoked apprehension in many circles: Should not the liturgy remain essentially constant? In our restless world, should not peace and stability find at least one last refuge in the liturgy? Is it not for divine worship to preserve the sacred age-old formula which mirrors the eternity of God? Is it necessary that every service be reduced to the vulgar plane of common intelligibility?

Many point out—and not without reason—that in the history of religion even the earliest cultures attached great importance to ancient rites, even though they had completely lost their meaning. In their sacrifice ritual the Hethites utilized texts from tongues no longer spoken. Persian elements persisted in the Roman cult of Mithras. Even at the Council, facts of this kind were recounted, and examples drawn from present-day India. Nevertheless, the Council approved the plans for reform by an overwhelming majority, including the decree on language; this was evidently an expression of the conviction that the Church is subjected to a higher law than that of anxious adherence to the ancient and traditional.

Human institutions can become fixed in their ways, but the Church is aware that the Spirit of God lives and works in her without ceasing. And He it is who forces her to shed the crust of old age and to fulfill her mission in freshness of youth and newness of manner—and not least of all in regard to the liturgy. Did not our Lord himself explain to the Samaritan woman that the Father desires true adorers, who worship him, not in the stereotyped fashion of Garizim or the Temple of Jerusalem, but in spirit and truth (John 4:23ff)?

Of this we may be certain: in the Church—which is not only Catholic, heartily welcoming all races, but also apostolic, surpassing all time—reverence for tradition will prove strong enough to insure respect for our sacred heritage and deliver it unadulterated to future generations, even in divine worship.

NOTES

[1] Herbert Muck, "Die liturgische Neuordnung alter Dome und Pfarrkirchen," in: *Zeitschrift fuer katholische Theologie* 85 (1963), I.

[2] Cf. *Christlicher Sonntag,* December 24, 1962, p. 398ff, or, *Civita Cattolica,* December 1, 1962, p. 496.

[3] Cf. Jungmann, *Public Worship,* pp. 149–52.

[4] See G. Martimort's evaluation of the *pia exercitia* in his *La Priére de l'Église* (Paris: 1961), p. 9ff.

Theological Implications of Liturgical Discussion at the Council

by PIET FRANSEN

IN THE COURSE of a discussion it is always important to keep in mind, or at least to look for the underlying motives which determine the distinctive orientation, the particular perspective of the participant's thought. Generally the underlying motivation of thought does not rise to the surface of the discussion. Usually this is not because it cannot be expressed—though this may be the case—but quite simply because it rarely occurs to an individual to search out the very bedrock of his own thinking. One is for or against an issue almost by intuition.

These motives can differ widely in kind. There are the psychological incentives, education, habit, the personal advantages which one might gain from a given solution; there are also the spontaneous reactions of sympathy or antipathy. Again, there are motives of a speculative nature which—it must be admitted—are not always active stimuli to thought, but which one must discover in order to understand discussions between men of definite habits of thought. In brief, as the English say, "A man has many reasons for what he does, the good ones and the real one!" It is not our concern here to judge the personal attitudes of the bishops, to look for the "real reasons"; rather, we want to bring to light the fact that, among the "good ones," there are also certain systems of thought, or at least certain general points of view,

which determine in part the attitude and reaction of the bishops
to the schema on the liturgy.

One might wonder, indeed, why the bishops have held such
discussions over matters which are apparently so simple. The
schema of the sacred liturgy is in reality quite modest, even very
cautious. It explicitly declines to define any truths of the faith.
This is why it is not called a *"dogmatic* constitution." It proceeds from very general principles expressed in biblical and
patristic language. This is the reason it was entitled "The Constitution on the Sacred Liturgy." From these principles it draws
various practical, but general, conclusions which are not to be
imposed upon the entire Church, but whose elaboration is to be
left to a commission appointed by the Pope which would carry
out this work over a period of five years.

Certain more important applications, such as the introduction
of the vernacular, communion under two species, con-celebration,
the eventual remodeling of the breviary to meet the needs of
priests in the active apostolate, are confided to the initiative of
"episcopal conferences." And here we find already a debated text.
The preparatory commission had written, "Sit vero Conferentiae
episcopalis in singulis regionibus . . . limites et modum linguae
vernaculae in Liturgiam admittendae *statuere,* actis Sancta Sede
recognitis."

The text has been modified by the subcommittee for amend-
ments at the instigation of its president, Cardinal Confalonieri,
in such a way that the right of proposal falls to the bishops and
the right of decision to the Holy See. The Cardinal felt that the
clause was lacking in respect for the Holy See. Here we can
already see two attitudes confronting one another in regard to
the Holy See, both determined by habits of reverence and of
life, but also quite different theological opinions concerning the
role of pontifical Primacy and the relations between the Primacy
and the world episcopate.

Why were the discussions of the Fathers so prolonged? There is, first of all, a psychological reason. They had all freshly arrived in Rome. They had discovered that they could speak freely. Certain ones among them had a gift for speaking, and others an absolute appetite; still others had an accumulation of things in their heart which finally had to come out. Hence a flood of eloquence which, if freedom of speech was to be respected, could not be staunched save by a sense of tedium or of satiety that would force the Fathers to limit themselves. This is precisely what happened after All Saints' Day. It was noted early that, in order to carry out the suggestion of the Presidency that the major lines of thought be defined and formed before the discussions, several of the bishops had agreed to delegate only one of their number to represent their point of view.

On the sixth of November the saturation point had been reached. The Secretary General then announced that the Holy Father had empowered the Presidency to propose to the Fathers that it limit the debates as soon as it recognized that the discussions contained no new contribution. The Fathers were then to approve or reject the proposal of the Presidency by standing or remaining seated. The Syrian Cardinal Tappouni, who was President that day, immediately moved that the vote be taken, thereby arousing enthusiastic applause from the assembly. It could be added that Msgr. Felici had chosen his moment well. The last Father to speak on the Mass had wandered remarkably far from his subject to the great irritation of the whole body of bishops. Agreement was nearly unanimous. Without further ado the third chapter on sacraments and sacramentals was taken up.

In one of his writings the Australian humorist Northcote Parkinson pointed out a law according to which the length of the debates in administrative assemblies is in inverse proportion to their importance. Do not misunderstand me! I do not mean that the schema on the sacred liturgy is not important. On the contrary, although at times it may have seemed unimportant, it presupposes a conception of the Church and of the sacraments which is notably richer than anything we commonly find in the manuals. It is only that the discussions did not generally bear upon these fundamental questions; more frequently, it seemed to me, they lingered over points which were lacking in dogmatic importance, such as the introduction of the vernacular into the liturgy. Did Our Lord or the Apostles ever speak Latin? Nevertheless, there is no one who, in regard to Latin, does not have very decided opinions!

The situation, in fact, is more complex. I shall explain. It goes without saying that the Fathers of the Council did not always discuss theology and dogma, but at the same time it is evident that their positions were largely determined by theological views which were often quite divergent.

No one should be surprised at this; not if they remember the Holy Father's words at the opening of the Council. The English translation, based on the Italian text, reads as follows: "The substance of the ancient doctrine contained in the deposit of faith is one thing; another is the formulation in which it is clothed. This in turn is determined, with regard to its form and fitness of expression, by the needs of a given magisterium and by the requirements of a style which is, above all, pastoral."

The Latin text is less clear and less obvious, which proves once again that Latin, too, has its drawbacks as a vehicle for the expression of dogma. Very apt for scholastic theology, which was built on this language, Latin loses its advantages as soon as it comes into contact with more modern points of view. The Latin text says: "Est enim aliud ipsum depositum Fidei, seu veritates, quae veneranda doctrina nostra continentur, aliud modus, quo eaedem enuntiantur, eodem tamen sensu eademque sententia. Huic quippe modo plurimum tribuendum erit et patienter, si opus fuerit, in eo elaborandum; scilicet eae inducendae erunt rationes res exponendi, quae cum magisterio, cuius indoles praesertim pastoralis est, magis congruant." [1]

If it were a simple matter of terminology, as the Latin text would indicate, there would seem to be no reason why the Pope should have dwelt on such considerations, which, after all, were not called in question by anyone. The Pope certainly had in view different modes of thought, all convergent, but arising from different perspectives. He even goes further, in the passage which follows, when he recommends precisely that an effort be made above all to present these truths in terms which would be in keeping with the practical level of pastoral activity, that is, in consonance with the work of caring for souls and directing the Christian apostolate. We may affirm, then, that the translations have rendered the thought of the Holy Father more or less correctly, and have indeed expressed it more clearly than the very obscure Latin text. [2]

Too frequently we consider the liturgy a monkish hobby, a sort of ecclesiastical fashion which changes with the season; we think it is subject to undue influence from the prevailing democratic spirit, or that in the "young churches" it is a victim to the eddies of anti-colonialist reaction, etc. Such influences can arouse certain restless, fanatic or unbalanced minds which are, inevitably, to be found in this domain where religious questions, particularly liturgical ones, by their absolute character, exercise an undeniable attraction over neurotic personalities. But, by God's grace, the Church holds in her bosom a large majority of normal minds who, in spite of small neuroses from which no one is exempt according to certain psychologists, possess a sufficiently solid common sense and spirit of faith to direct their attention to more substantial and worthy matters.

Let us enlarge upon the theological concepts which underlie the discussions on the liturgy. We must limit ourselves to certain more important considerations. It is not a matter here of reviewing the whole of theology. That, however, would be desirable, since in theology everything is interconnected, and one aspect of a problem cannot be altered without calling into question all the other theological theses.

1. A Different Conception of the Church

There is, basically, a notion which is subject to differing opinions: the Church. At the risk of exaggeration, or of being a little too schematic, I shall underline two extreme positions which, in fact, in the teaching of theology and in the learned reviews are susceptible of many nuances and intermediate attitudes.

There is a conception of the Church which may be represented in the form of a pyramid, so to speak. At the summit is the pope through whom all the hierarchical powers pass, since he is the vicar of Christ. He alone possesses the plentitude of sacerdotal and juridical power. Under him are found the bishops. Although, in present-day Catholic theology, it is popular to emphasize the collegial character of the episcopate, this pyramidal theology of the Church is the one which current canon law has in great part retained (let us not forget that it was promulgated in 1918!), and it betokens, on the contrary, an atomistic view of the episcopate.

Each residential bishop in charge of a diocese is completely independent of the other bishops, his powers being limited by the pope alone, who acts in and governs the Church through the Roman Curia. Thus, canon law has not provided any juridical structure for the episcopal conferences referred to in the Constitution on the Liturgy, even though these conferences, such as exist in Germany and in Bavaria, were instituted as early as the end of the nineteenth century at the instigation of Leo XIII. The bishops assemble as equals, and, if they accept the decisions of the majority it is solely because they are in accord, or else, by a sort of implicit contract, they have confided the exercise of these powers under a very restricted form to the episcopal conference of their nation or of their continent. If they cannot accept the decisions of the majority of the bishops, they reserve full right to refuse to apply these decisions within the boundaries of their dioceses.

Below the bishops are the priests who differ from the former only in that their power of jurisdiction is limited and submitted to the approbation and control of the local bishops. The faithful come next. They are obedient to their pastors and attend with devotion the ecclesial prayers pronounced in their name by those consecrated for that purpose. This is their role above all at Mass and in the reception of the sacraments. Nothing is expected of them but obedience and a devout and religious attention to the prayer of the Church. They form the base of the pyramid.

The other conception of the Church—I repeat, I am obliged to simplify—begins with the faithful. We might describe it in terms of a series of concentric circles. All without exception—pope, bishops, priests, clerics and laity—are the faithful; that is, they are believers, consecrated by baptism and confirmation and gathered together by this fact into the people of God, the royal and priestly people whose internal cohesion is assured by grace, that is, by the presence and sanctifying indwelling of the Holy Trinity, the only true and vivifying source of all created grace.

This people of God is, then, at the same time the mystical body of Christ. Within this mystical body and this visible people, certain persons receive the sacrament of Orders, a consecration and so, also, a deputation by which they are vested with a function of authority, of witness through the Word and of sanctification.

This consecration is given in the sacrament of Orders, and its origin is fundamentally divine; it is not, therefore, communicated by the pope, but by Christ himself, acting within the sacraments, although its concrete and practical exercise may and even should be regulated by the jurisdictional powers within the Church.

Its practical application on the concrete and immediate level of canon law has taken different forms in the past and should assume still others in the future. In other words, if the fundamental aspect of the divine mission is unchangeable, its practical exercise should be allowed to find different forms of expression adapted to the conditions of time and place. When the Church was restricted to the Mediterranean basin, it was organized quite differently from now, when for the first time in its history it finds itself confronted with the fact of her world dimensions.

This special consecration to the priesthood does not render the ministers of the Church ontologically superior to the simple faithful; they remain in fact part of the faithful. But it gives them a true mission in the name of Christ, in the power of his Spirit; it gives them a real and efficacious ecclesial function, particularly in the domain of the sacraments. These ministers are, above all, the bishops, assembled as successors to the apostles in an episcopal college.

We are speaking here of ecclesial structures. This aspect of collegiality is within a structural element, given in ordination, and unites the bishops, by the will of Christ and through the institution of Orders, in one single body which represents the head of the mystical body, the risen Christ. Note that it is no longer a question of independent atoms indirectly related to one another through their common bond with the Holy See, or through a casual agreement of pastoral collaboration within a given country. It is a question of a real and living collegiality, forming part of the very constitution of the Church.

On the positive, juridical plane, this collegiality may assume different forms of expression which can change and adapt themselves to the changing needs of the hour. In this perspective, an episcopal conference is the positive, juridical expression, within the frontiers of a single country or of a group of nations, of the profound, organic and structural collegiality which we have been discussing. In other words, canon law must find a practical solution within and a viable synthesis for two areas of truth: from the one springs the collegial mission of the episcopate; from the other the practical possibilities and necessities of a given time.

The episcopal conferences, then, should not receive their power from the Holy Father, though on the practical level of the life of the Church he may have a perfect right to govern the exercise of this collegiality. Neither should the conferences suppose a tacit or implicit contract of the bishops among themselves. The basis for their existence is rooted more deeply still in the very nature of the Church. It is only because we are accustomed to speak in an almost exclusively juridical language, and because we are emerging from an epoch which has been individualistic and "atomistic" in the extreme, that we find ourselves constrained to insist so heavily on this matter. This idea was perfectly evident in the first centuries and was expressed by the multiple forms of "communion" between the churches and between the bishops, the visible heads of these churches.

The bishops are assisted by their priests, who are ordained for this purpose, that is, as *cooperatores ordinis nostri,* collaborators with the episcopacy whether the latter is individual, collective, or pontifical.

Within the episcopal college is the pope, successor of St. Peter, assisted by his Curia which has been appointed to fulfill this function, but appointed to serve only on the juridical level. The Curia is not involved in the essential structure of the Church, but is only a practical agency of a juridical nature, so it is always subject to the necessities of reform and re-adaptation. Quite simply, the pope is faced with the practical impossibility of exercising the manifold duties of the Primacy, as it exists in our days, without an effective and specialized corps of assistants.

The first title of the pope is that of bishop of Rome. When he addresses himself to the other bishops he gives them the traditional title of "brothers in the episcopacy." He has received a special mission of unity, which is not a new consecration, but a mission of universal jurisdiction, which also has been expressed and will be expressed in diverse, positive, juridical forms.

It is quite understandable why by taking this other view of the Church as a point of departure, one would necessarily react differently to the concrete, pastoral problems of liturgy as these were proposed for the approval of the Council in the schema on the liturgy.

Everyone, evidently, accepts the need for an active participation by the laity in the sacred mysteries, but such participation does not always have the same meaning, the same urgency, and above all, it does not carry the same nuances for everyone. Some will fall into facile contentment with any form of participation, even if it is reduced to the simple role of a devout and sincere attendance, and, particularly in regard to the sacraments, a fruitful attendance. One can still hear such remarks as: Why forbid the praying of the rosary during Mass? It is the self-styled missal of the poor and simple. Why abolish certain hymns merely because they have no relation to the mystery being celebrated (as in Italy, the "Ave Maria" of Schubert which is sung during the Canon)? Why not be content with translations of the missal, since these allow educated persons to join themselves more consciously and intelligently to the prayers which only the celebrant says validly and in a priestly manner in their name?

For others, again, it is a question here of a fundamental need, and even, on the pastoral level, a matter of life or death. It is in the mystery of the Eucharist, the third sacrament of initiation, that the Church, the temple of the Holy Spirit, is daily constituted, made new, as it were, and built up by God. The symbolic form of this mystery, that is, its liturgical realization, should, then, give expression to the fundamental fact that in the Mass, and *mutatis mutandis,* similarly in the sacraments, the Father is gathering to himself a people in Christ through the power of his Spirit, and by so doing is saving us. The laity, consecrated by baptism and confirmation, forms thus a part of the priestly and royal people of God, and participates with full right in the liturgical action which is their action also.

Only the function of sanctification (the sacral function), sacerdotal in the strict sense, is reserved to the bishops and to their collaborators, the priests. The bishop alone, or his priests and clerics, each according to his order, presides, preaches the Word, pronounces the prayers in the name of all, and represents precisely the *per Dominum nostrum Jesum Christum* which forms the essential law of ecclesial and liturgical prayer. In so far as he is a representative of the same risen Christ, the bishop unites mystically and sacramentally the sacrifice of the faithful and of the entire Church to the eternal sacrifice of Christ. This he does in the prayers of the Canon which culminate in the Anamnesis, the commemoration of the words of Christ at the Last Supper, which we call the Consecration. This is also valid for the other sacraments, each according to its nature and ecclesial structure.

In this view of the Church, the participation of the faithful is a central, structural, organic element. Because the sacraments by their nature are the visible expression of the invisible and divine mystery of grace which they make present in the midst of the community assembled by God in God's name, the liturgy, whose role it is to express in visible and concrete rites the content of our faith, must absolutely be reformed along these lines each time that historical or local conditions, as in the case of the "young churches," have diminished, impoverished or distorted its symbolic meaning. It is not, therefore, a matter of archaeologizing —may I be forgiven the term—much less of creating a work of art, or of indulging in aestheticism. It is simply a matter of rediscovering the clarity of symbols and liturgical rites, their immediate and basic transparency.

Nevertheless, the liturgy carries within its essential symbolism the indispensable and living reference to tradition. It will be useful and indeed necessary not only to avoid a break with tradition, even in the rites not instituted by Christ, but to express through new symbols, or through ancient formulas which will have been stripped of their numberless excrescences, *quod semper, quod ubique, quod ab omnibus*—what has always been believed, at all times, in all places by all the faithful. It goes without saying that this principle also has a profound pastoral value.

This said, one can easily understand the difference of opinions which became evident in the heart of the Council in regard to the episcopal conferences. For those who held to the first conception of the Church, to ask that the power to make decisions be granted to these conferences would be tantamount to a lack of deference to the Roman pontiff. In their mind such an exorbitant request is not possible except at the cost of a concession on the part of the Holy See, or in virtue of an agreement between the bishops of a single country made in order to work together more efficaciously in the future on urgent pastoral questions. This is the view of episcopal authority contained implicitly in canon law, which refused to accord juridical recognition to the above-mentioned conferences.

For others, the episcopal conferences, possessing a limited but real competency, are, at the concrete level of jurisdiction, an expression of the power which inheres in the episcopacy. This episcopal jurisdiction is not completely absorbed by the pope's power of universal jurisdiction; it is exercised (in union, obviously, with the Holy See) within the perspective of the collegial episcopate. As we have seen, this union with the Holy See is above all another facet of the collegial episcopate, the Holy

Father belonging like all the other bishops to the episcopal college. In the case of the pope, it is true, the collegiality is reinforced by the fact that the Primacy, bearing as it does an essential witness to unity, manifests itself, among other ways, in terms of its universal jurisdiction.

2. A Different View of the Sacraments

While speaking of the theology of the Church, it has been necessary to have recourse at the same time to certain principles of sacramental theology. In this field there are also two quite different views which must be taken into account in order to understand the conciliar discussions.

There is a doctrine of the sacraments which dates from the sixteenth century and which was introduced by nominalism, a philosophy roughly similar to the logical analysis so widespread in Anglo-Saxon countries. From the theological point of view, this school refused to construct an organic doctrine of the Christian mysteries, but made the diverse elements which constituted a dogmatic whole (for example the different dogmatic aspects of a sacrament), depend upon divine decrees, thereby leaving the way open for a certain extrinsicism which lingers in numerous theological manuals. The traces of nominalism are far from total extinction if only because of the fact that certain facets of this theological tradition were retained by the Council of Trent, the majority of whose members were nominalists.

But today it would be well to recall, especially when contemplating the formulation of certain constitutions established by the Preparatory Commission of Theology, that the Council of Trent categorically and systematically refused to align itself with any of the theological schools of thought existing within the Catholic Church. If Trent, particularly in sacramental matters, took on certain aspects of nominalist theology in its canons, we must look for the explanation of this above all in the fact that this current of thought presented a minimalist answer to the problems of sacramental theology. Trent, then, often chose the formula which was acceptable to all as the minimum requirement of faith (as in the case of the explanation of the notion of *opus operatum*), which meant a return to the nominalist formula.

In reality, Trent had no other aim than to condemn the Lutheran position on the matter. It did not intend, by any means, to present an exhaustive and complete instruction on Catholic dogma. After the Council, given the heat of the controversy with the Protestants and the fact that we had to wait four centuries before the Acts of the Council were published, its canons on the sacraments generally were invested with an absolute and exhaustive value; and this is wrong.

In the above theology of the sacraments, stress is placed upon the validity of the sacramental act. A liturgical and sacramental act carried out by a person ordained to that end, who has moreover the intention of doing what the Church wills and who pronounces correctly—remember the unfortunate and, at bottom, unwholesome casuistry concerning the forms of the sacraments—the formulas established by the Church as the sacramental form—such an act is, quite simply, valid; that is, the sacrament gives the sacramental grace attached by Christ to this ecclesial act. The priest is the instrument of Christ, an instrument whose proper efficacy is principally rooted in the correct and (juridically) qualified execution of the sacramental sign.

Since Duns Scotus, of the believer who receives the sacrament nothing more is asked than the intention to receive it and the absence of any positive impediment to the infusion of grace. Practically speaking, this means, in the case of the sacraments of the living, the absence of all conscious mortal sin, and in the case of the other sacraments, the beginning of conversion and a sincere desire for pardon.

It must be remembered further that grace had lost betimes its living meaning of a personal relationship with the Persons of the Holy Trinity. Detached from the mystery of the Trinity it had become in preaching and in catechetics a vague, I would say almost neuter, divine power, a supernatural power, a sort of divine fluid which illumined our intelligence and fortified our will.

Despite the risk of presenting a caricature of this theology, I will be a little schematic in order to bring out its dangers yet more clearly. It is understood that the good theologians of this school have never formally defended what I am about to present, but experience proves that this caricature has more or less infected even the use of the sacraments. Neverthless, this use was frequently better than the theology which inspired it.

An overemphasis, then, has been placed on the correct execution of the sacramental sign, because, correctly administered, the sacrament obtains its effect of itself, *ex opere operato*. The devotion of the priest in no wise affects the efficacy of the sacramental sign, nor for that matter does the personal devotion of the believer who receives the sacrament.

But the question is precisely how to view this efficacy, thus detached from its reference to a personal act of the priest or of the worshiper. So long as there is no intention of expressing anything other than the undeniable fact of the fundamental pre-eminence of the grace which saves us in Christ, these formulas hold no particular danger. But the moment one separates this efficacy, even slightly, from the primacy of the divine within the sacrament, and clings too strongly to the correct execution of the sign, of the *opus sacramenti*, one can fall into magic.

By this devotion and this living faith the believer who receives the sacrament is able to receive another kind of grace, not sacramental, and that *ex opere operantis*, by which God rewards his openness of heart and his personal effort. Hence, once again, one stands but one step away from excusing and even admitting as proper (and I read this in an American review treating of the introduction of the vernacular into the Mass) the pronunciation of the Latin prayers at a speed which is unintelligible even to one who knows Latin: One need not understand! It is a mystery! —the eternal excuse so easily subject to abuse.

Thus the primary fact that the liturgy is essentially a prayer is forgotten, and we come very quickly, in the practice of the sacraments, to a liturgical form in which no normal person, educated outside the Catholic fold, can recognize any longer a sacred act. It is regrettable that in present-day Catholicism, one cannot find a religious recitation of the liturgical prayers except in those countries where the presence of Protestants has obliged the priests to correct such unfortunate and scandalous habits.

In this way one comes dangerously close to magic, not to black magic, obviously, which is practiced against the will of God, but, even so, to what specialists in comparative religion call white magic, which pretends to be performed with divine approbation. Christ has indeed instituted the sacramental acts; we have therefore the right to carry them out in his name. Since it is Christ who acts through the instrumentality of these rites, it would seem that we have eschewed all danger of magic and assured the rites of their character as religious acts.

This is correct, but it is not sufficient, especially in consideration of the dangerous simplification which obtains on the level of preaching and catechesis. A magic act is not, in effect, any longer a religious act, but is the very negation of religion. It is a human act by which man pretends to wield a divine power conferred upon him by certain words and gestures believed to be especially potent and efficacious. This danger is strengthened by the "fetishism" of Latin. It is said that Latin is more orthodox, more sane, more traditional, but the fear which certain minds experience at the suggestion that it be dropped for the sacramental form could at times border on fetishism, and so also on a magical conception of the sacraments, which is all the more dangerous since it remains unconscious.

But leaving aside the caricature (which unhappily seems only too real on the level of popularized theology), let us retain of this tendency only the theological expressions which remain conscious of the divine mystery. To the theologians and bishops who were formed in this school of theology it is evident that the introduction of the vernacular has only a very relative importance, and the participation of the faithful, in this conception, is reduced to the strict minimum required for what would be called, in terms rather too close to nominalist theology, a "fruitful" reception of the sacraments: If we are without mortal sin, sacramental grace is "infused" into us, and we are sure to possess it even if we have not resolved to change our way of life.

According to this theological view, the sacraments would become an easier way to reach God. Drawn out to its logical conclusion, and here again we are bordering on caricature, such a conception would present the sacraments as dispensing us from our obligation of sincere and total conversion of heart in the spirit of faith and charity.

From the standpoint of such a theology, there is no necessity, or at any rate no urgency to reform or to rethink from the very bottom the present situation of the liturgy, though certain adaptations and simplifications of detail might be accepted without difficulty. There is no objection to changing certain rites or to simplifying them, or even, if some bishops insist in countries where the situation is more difficult, to granting special and particular indults, secretly perhaps, more or less as the Congregation of Rites has done these past years.

There is, nevertheless, another theology of the sacraments which takes its authority from a much more ancient and venerable tradition and coincides with the thinking of St. Thomas, who himself struggled to express in the (modern) language of his epoch the sacramental theology of the Fathers, as has been very well demonstrated by Father Schillebeeckx, O.P., Professor at the University of Nijmegen, in his study on the curious evolution of the words "matter and form" in scholastic theology.

St. Thomas insists on the fact that the divine economy of grace has not changed, and that for the Church, as for our Old Testament forebears, there is no salvation without faith and charity. In other words, the sacraments cannot in any manner be an excuse to love God less; they cannot be an "ersatz" which would dispense us from offering to God the good and true "merchandise" which he expects from us, that is, our heart, a capital which is gently and almost unknowingly accumulated and upon which we may draw for heaven.

Once again—it is necessary to repeat, because so many stupid things have been said on the subject—on the plane of a personal conversion of heart *there is no difference* between the one who must find God outside the Church and without the sacraments, and ourselves. If the sacraments can and should be called "easier" means for finding God, this "easiness" does not lie with us, but comes from the side of the divine mercy which, adapting itself to our nature, has deigned to come down among us and to remain *present and active* under the visibility and humanity of the sacred rites.

This personal faith, then, should be assumed into the liturgical action as a structural element, organically *indispensable,* since the liturgy must, by its very nature, express visibly what is taking place invisibly between God and ourselves. God does not save us *automatically,* but saves us as responsible and free persons, or rather as persons freed by his grace, which is present in the sacraments.

Do not bring up the baptism of infants as an objection. In this sacramental rite the Church receives the infants into her fold, consecrates them as members of the people of God and truly separates them from solidarity with the sin of the world which they had at birth. Thus this sacrament already has very real fruits and so a true meaning from the moment it is administered. But, it is evident that to obtain their full effect this consecration and this association with the people of God must be ratified by the infant once he has become an adult. In other words, the renewal of the promises of baptism is not merely a touching ceremony; it does not have simply a pastoral import in our dechristianized societies, but possesses in reality a profound dogmatic meaning. In this renewal of baptismal promises, baptism attains, at last, its full meaning and its human and divine significance.

The *opus operatum* and the *opus operantis* are two connected notions, inseparable from one another, which express two necessary facets of a single dialectic movement. The *opus operantis*—and this was the opinion of St. Thomas—is nothing other than the personal aspect, we would say the "existential" aspect of our Christian commitment, determined and supported in us, let us not forget, by the very power of the *opus operatum* of the sacrament. The pre-eminence of the *opus operatum* over the *opus operantis* is only the expression, in technical language and on the level of theological speculation, of the divine primacy in every sanctifying action.

St. Thomas used a terminology which unfortunately is no longer found in our manuals, where as always juridical terminology has been preferred by speaking almost exclusively of the validity of the sacraments and of their fruit (*sacramentum validum et fructuosum*). St. Thomas' vocabulary, however, coincides quite well with the terminology introduced by Karl Rahner in his study on grace in which he attempts to restore its personal character.

Rahner distinguishes in all grace, both habitual and actual, the aspect of "offered" grace—the German word *die vorgegebene*

Gnade is more expressive—a grace which is truly *given* to me, but as an existential a priori of my engagement as a Christian; and the aspect of "accepted" grace, *die angenommene Gnade,* which is the same grace, let us not forget, but in so far as it is efficaciously realized in my Christian commitment. St. Thomas uses a similar terminology. The sacraments enacted authentically within the Church—I am avoiding the juridical terms of validity —have their own verity, the *veritas sacramenti.* That is, they express in their truly liturgical symbolism what they give us in fact. As the catechisms say, "They signify what they give us," and so in this sense are true. Their signs do not lie to us or deceive us.

But in the personal act of faith by which the subject has accepted the grace (obviously always *in virtue* of the divine primacy, and *so* in virtue of the *opus operatum*) these signs obtain their *veritas simpliciter.* In other words, they bring into full reality, on the personal level of our commitment, what they signify and present in their sacred symbolism. This truth of the sacraments attains, then, its full purpose and its meaning in our engagement of faith; it terminates the dialogue, begun by God, with the liturgical "Amen" which stands at the very foundation of our Christian life.

Within such a theological perspective, it is understandable that there can be no question of a few changes in rites. It is a matter of rethinking the liturgical fact as such, of restoring to the liturgical symbols their transparence, of reinstating or of restoring those liturgical structures which, over the course of centuries, under the influence of an impoverished sacramental theology and through the addition of less useful structures, have lost their authentic meaning.

One encounters here an objection which is ceaselessly abused: We must respect the mystery! This was repeated at the Council and even in the press conferences. In the press's German Center

the Abbot of Beuron took up this fallacious argument once again.
Cardinal Garcias of Bombay quite rightly objected to this reasoning, indicating it as pagan. The pagans "hide" everything that
appertains to their god. After the incarnation, the mystery of the
divine epiphany, the Christian economy does not hide its God,
but manifests him. For St. Augustine *mysterium* had almost the
same meaning as *sacramentum,* and signified "the *manifestation*
of what is hidden, because divine and invisible." St. John con-
firms this: "No one has at any time seen God. The only-begotten
Son, who is in the bosom of the Father, he has revealed him"
(John 1:18).

The liturgy should not, then, hide its God, but in and through
Christ must *manifest* what is of itself invisible and imperceptible
to our senses and to our intelligence. The Christian attitude is,
therefore, totally different from the pagan. During the first centuries of the Church the divine mysteries were only hidden from
the uninitiated, and even the famous *lex arcani,* also much
abused, was only applied during a determined era and even then
not by the universal Church. But for the faithful it was impera-
tive to make manifest, to show, to express the divine and eternal
reality of the God who saves us in Christ through his Spirit.

For these theologians, again, the active participation of the
faithful is a matter of life and death, since it turns upon the very
essence of the sacramental act, inseparable from our Christian
commitment, inseparable from our complete submission to God
in faith and in charity. Moreover, it is impossible to restore the
divine dialogue expressed in liturgical action if, on the level of
symbolism, the dialogue has become nonexistent. The liturgical
dialogue only expresses or reveals on the plane of ritual and symbolic action, the truth of the divine dialogue in which God addresses himself to us, calls us by our name and asks for our faith,
our personal and liturgical "Amen."

Finally, we must remember—and this is still more important—

the true trinitarian nature of the sacraments. Grace is founded principally upon the fact of the divine and creative presence within our souls, a presence at once inviting and alluring if we are in the state of mortal sin, a full and loving indwelling if we are in a state of grace. Created grace is nothing other than the fruit of this indwelling and the bond which joins us to the Divine Persons. This is but a facet of the movement which, springing from the depths of the Father, reconciles us to the Son in the power of his Spirit and leads us again *ut servi in Servo et filii in Filio,* in faith and in charity to the Father, remade in the image of the Son under the creative impulse of the Spirit.

Sacramental grace is no different. It, too, and likewise the sacraments (above all Holy Mass) contain and visibly manifest the invisible mystery of the Holy Trinity dwelling in us. Sacramental efficacy should not be considered so much from the too physical and material viewpoint of an instrumental cause (which "infuses," so to speak, a certain quantity of grace) as from the perspective of the very efficacy of God, Three and One, as this expresses itself through sacramental and ecclesial symbolism.

The liturgy is, then, the true "celebration" of the highest mysteries of our faith, a celebration which contains a commemoration of the mysteries of the incarnation, the manifestation of the mystery of our present sanctification, and the solemn announcement of its final and eschatological realization. "O sacrum convivium, in quo Christus sumitur, recolitur memoria Passionis ejus, mens impletur gratia, et futurae gloriae nobis pignus datur." "O sacred banquet in which Christ becomes our food, the memory of his Passion is renewed, the soul is filled with grace, and a pledge of future glory is bestowed."

In this manner alone will we be able to speak again a language which will be understood by our Eastern brothers and by our separated brothers. We shall be able thus to give to the sacraments, and particularly to the celebration of the Eucharist, a richness of meaning and a plenitude which we now lack. For theologians of this mind what is needed is a true reformation of the liturgy from within, a rethinking in terms of the fullness of our faith.

NOTES

[1] *Acta Apostolicae Sedis,* November 26, 1962, p. 792.

[2] In his address to the cardinals on December 23, the Pope confirmed in Italian the above interpretation of his words.

Free Expression and Obedience in the Church

by JOSEF RATZINGER

FORTY-ODD YEARS have passed since Romano Guardini spoke of an awakening of the Church in souls. Strictly speaking such awakening continues in our day, but the attitude with which we approach the Church has changed immensely. At the time of Guardini's remark liberalism's decline had fostered a fresh appreciation for the idea of community. And over the Church, once rejected as outmoded, swept a wave of yearning, hope and joy, so memorably summarized in Gertrude von Le Fort's *Hymns to the Church*.

But in 1945 came the capitulation, and with it a different atmosphere altogether. The German Reich had not failed to exploit the era with its esteem for community and authority, nostalgia for the past, and anti-liberal sentiment; the Reich brutally betrayed these ideals, and the war, the days of disillusionment, soon put an end to them.

Gradually there emerged a different attitude in regard to the Church. It was no longer a time for hymns. The new mood, that of the wary man, the man freed from delusions, was set by Ida Friederike Görres' *Letter to the Church*. With her *Letter* she almost singlehandedly initiated a new literary trend: ecclesial criticism.

It must be admitted that, once confronted with this predicament, the Church displayed a certain perplexity. This is hardly surprising since, naturally, it is more pleasant to receive praise than come to terms with criticism. The period prior to the Council only served to increase such perplexity. For on the one hand we were urged to submit suggestions concerning renovation, that is, to indicate what needed reform and investigation; while on the other hand, incidents such as the measures taken against Fr. Lombardi gave the impression that "free speech in the Church" was to be confined, in the main, to acceptance of the status quo. Furthermore, the only topics seemingly open to criticism were "created" ones already existing within areas officially sanctioned by the Church as "targets of criticism." All of which posed a serious predicament for the Council, for how can there be a Council without responsible exchange of views, without frank discussions? And how can there be frank discussion without freedom? Now in the early stages of Vaticanum II, we should earnestly inquire as to precisely in what sense debate, criticism, protest, and the right of dissent can be said to arise legitimately from the Church's very nature, and where the line is to be drawn in such matters.[1]

1. Our Basis: Holiness and Sin in the Church

We can best reach the heart of the matter by contrasting salvation in the Old Testament to that in the New. The Old Testament was God's covenant rooted in his promise and his election. Its temples, its priesthood, its form of worship were of divine institution. Its Law was divine law, and its kingship bore the promise of unending permanency. Could such a form of worship instituted by God himself be tampered with? Could anyone oppose a priesthood divinely founded? Could anyone foretell the end of an institution whose permanancy was guaranteed by God? Yes, Christ could and did. He not only prophesied the temple's destruction, but illustrated it by a symbolic act: for surely this was the meaning behind the cleansing of the temple, linked as it was to the proclamation of a "new temple not built by the hand of man." (Mark 11:11-19; 14:58; 15, 29ff; John 2:19).[2] Christians seldom appreciate the magnitude of such an event. For them the Old Covenant is precisely that, an "old" covenant, doomed to replacement by the new.

However, the matter is hardly so elementary. This covenant, for its entire duration, was *the* Covenant, not an "old" covenant. It was the *one* Covenant that God had contracted in this world. Certainly there was no clear indication that it would—or even should—one day become "old." And the fact was corroborated by the prophetic promises of a new covenant, which understandably were of scant significance to the Israelitic mind (Jer. 31:31ff). These prophecies had been made wholly in terms of the *last* Time, that eschatological time of a divine world of peace (Isa. 11). Yet, in Old Testament times the Torah was God's word and temple worship was God's command. Thus for the Israelitic conscience an attack upon the Old Covenant must have been the equivalent of an attack upon the sacramental order for a Christian in New Testament times.

And yet the following considerations reveal to us the very real difference. Besides the temple and its official, hereditary priesthood there existed, from the beginning, the prophets whom God himself freely chose. And beyond the institution, worship, and the law, there was, from the beginning, the "free word" which God had claimed for his own in Israel—the word of these prophets. The tragic figure of the prophet Jeremiah, who was repeatedly arrested as an heretic, who was chastised, persecuted and condemned to death as an enemy of God's word and law, and who finally ended his days in bleak oblivion, an anonymous exile —this tragic figure traces most vividly for posterity the essence and frightening demands of the prophetic mission.

Indeed, the office of prophecy consisted not so much in some type of prognostication as in prophetic protest itself—a protest against the self-sufficiency of those institutions that had substituted rituals for morality and ceremonies for conversion (cf. Isa. 58).[3] The prophet was God's witness who summoned the authority of God himself against arbitrary human interpretation of his word, against the abuse of the divine vocation—be it openly or underhandedly—for selfish ends. It was the prophet who safeguarded God's word against men.

This prophetic criticism in the Old Testament, although defied and persecuted by those in power, was recognized nonetheless, time and again, as the true voice of God. This was criticism that could reach such a degree of asperity as to designate the ravager of the temple, the godless King of Babel, as "servant of God" (Jer. 25:9), a criticism whereby even the destruction of the temple, the very heart of Israel, emerged as an act of divine worship in comparison with the all too pharisaical homage which had become customary within that sanctuary.

The first great attempt at a Christian theology, the preaching of Stephen the Deacon (Acts 7:1–53) continued in this critical vein. His discourses bear out the historical truth that God has always sided with the suffering and persecuted rather than with the "institution." Furthermore, Stephen established Christ's legitimacy precisely by placing him as one with the family of the persecuted, i.e., in the family of the prophets. According to Stephen, the very fact that the rulers rejected Christ and that he became the sufferer for the sake of the word indicated that he was a prophet and the fulfillment of the prophets.

And it is true that history inclines us to consider Jesus the fulfillment of the prophecies not because several prophecies were fulfilled by him, but rather because, following the prophets' example, he suffered and endured all to the end and thus joined himself with them in their traditional repudiation of the self-glorification carried on within the levitical institutions. Furthermore, he truly abolished the temple once and for all (John 2:19) by establishing his own body as a "self-offering" in place of the temple sacrifice (Heb. 10:5ff in connection with Ps. 40 which was inspired by the "spirit of the prophets").

This prophetic theme in theology as found in Stephen's sermon has received far too little attention. However, one finds a trace of it, faint though this may be, in the Fathers of the Church when they discern in the words of Malachias 1:10f a prophecy of the sacrifice of the Mass. These words, which foretell a pure food-offering from "the rising of the sun to its setting," appear at the termination of the prophetic period in Israel, the last glimmer of the grand prophetic criticism of worship in previous centuries, and they incorporate this tradition of criticism.

Thus the true meaning of this passage cannot be understood properly unless one takes into account the prophetic stream from which it flows. It belongs to the prophetic style which in reaction to temple sacrifices introduces as a sort of counterpoint in the great double fugue of the Old Testament, the demand for man himself, his obedience, and his heart in contrast to mere ritual and ceremonial form. This is the category in which the Old Testament surpasses itself and opens itself to the acceptance of something new and greater.

We say that Malachias 1:10f found its fulfillment in the sacrifice of the Church based on Christ's sacrifice. By this we mean that Christ's death does not merely signify a fulfillment of the true meaning of the temple sacrifice, but that also and above all it signifies completion of the prophetic message.

This brings us to the New Testament and the question: is the situation here similar? Is Truth still on the side of the suffering, on the side of those branded and cast out by the authorities? Heinrich Hermelink believed that the nature of the Reformation and Counter-Reformation was to be understood by looking at them from such a point of view. He asserted that on the one hand, there existed the historical fact of the incarnation of the

Word. The Word, however, by becoming flesh, exposed himself to shortsightedness and misunderstanding. Thus God would see to it that his Word should be kept pure through prophetic repudiation "which the Lord of history himself awakens and arouses to combat the tenacious bonds that bind his Word to worldly powers and worldly existence." [4]

And Hermelink adds: "In the dialogue between ourselves and our Catholic brothers our real responsibility is to lead them to an understanding—and not just an intellectual understanding but a religious one—of the active attitude of protest which since Luther has not ceased to prod us and drive us on." [5]

At first glance such reasoning seems logical enough. However, to use the idea of prophetic protest to justify the right of a Christian existence outside the Church, ignores two facts. First of all, a misunderstanding is indicated by the truth that the prophets of Israel, to whom Hermelink alludes, remained prophets *in* Israel, where they suffered their lot to the end, and as sufferers thus became witnesses to God and "martyrs." Jesus himself accomplished his mission as mission *in* Israel: "Do not go among the heathen, or to any Samaritan town, but proceed instead to the lost sheep of Israel's house" (Matt. 10:5f).[6] He acknowledged the authority of the teachers of Israel to the very end: "The Scribes and Pharisees have taken Moses' seat. So do everything they tell you, and observe it all, but do not do as they do, for they talk but do not act" (Matt. 23:2f).

The earliest apostolic preaching as well as the preaching of the Apostle Paul also originated as preaching *to* and *in* Israel. It was only after a painful struggle that the apostles as a whole, acting in the name of the Church (Acts 15:6–29), ventured to extend their mission to the heathens and thus effected that turning point in the history of salvation which marks the end of the Old Testament and the beginning of the New, the Church.[7] Nevertheless, there remained the conviction that no man could have dared to make such a move on his own. Only God's new approach through Jesus Christ justified it. How painfully the first Christian generation smarted under their separation from Judaism can best be gathered from Romans 9–11.

The second omission is contained within the first. As a result of the separation of the believers in Christ from the community of Israel, the Christians came to realize that God's covenant, until that time, was the "Old Covenant." Consequently from that moment on, it was so designated. Simultaneously the way was opened for the realization that, now in the midst of this world and contrary to all expectation, the eschatological covenant of God promised by the prophets already had become reality in the community of Jesus Christ: the final and incontestable alliance of God with men that was never again to become "old."

But once again the question arose: How could the "Old Covenant" become old, and what constituted the "new" of the New Covenant, that is, the final and irrevocable alliance? Until that time the answer had been obvious: The "Old Covenant" was the covenant of the present world; the New Covenant was that of the next eon. But with the commencement of the second covenant within temporal history the question took on entirely new implications.

In the fourth chapter of his epistle to the Romans, Paul clearly outlines the basic elements for a solution. According to him we may say that the alliance with Israel became "old" because it was conditional only. The New Covenant is absolute, *un*conditional, and this is what makes it "new." In other words, Israel was accepted on the condition "that you fulfill the Law"; "that you do all that is written down in the works of Moses" (ev., e.g., Deut. 11:22–31; chap. 28).

In this contract both parties committed themselves to a pledge: Jahweh would bring salvation to Israel *if* Israel for its part kept the law. The alliance, then, was made dependent on the condition of human morality. From this came the function of the prophets in its deepest sense. It was their duty insistently to remind their people of this condition, and to point out that all splendor of worship was to no avail if the *whole* condition was not fulfilled—the *entire* Law must be kept. Obviously, this was never done and never will be done because no man is *entirely* good.

Therefore if salvation had depended exclusively on human morality as a strict condition, then there *was* no salvation for mankind (Rom. 4:14). In this sense the Old Testament drama of man remained undetermined—there existed no assurance that it would not simply end with the repudiation of all men in a shrilly dissonant tragedy.

On the contrary, with the New Testament God himself became man and God accepted those men who believed in Jesus Christ for the sake of the man Jesus Christ. Consequently the drama of world history resolved into a definite "yes" because this time God entered into a new, an unconditioned alliance.

The Church, the new people of God, is not bound by a proviso as Israel was, but is accepted by God unconditionally. Her acceptability hinges no longer on the unreliable condition of human morality, but rests firm on the absolute of Christ's grace and saving deed (Rom. 4:16). The Church is not founded (as was Israel) on the morality of man, but rather on the grace issued against the amorality of man, on the incarnation of God. She is founded on an obstinacy [8]—the obstinacy of a divine grace which refuses the chains of condition and has decided once and for all to save mankind. For this reason the Church differs from the community of the Old Covenant precisely because she is no longer conditioned but absolute, based upon the absolute God. In so far as she is final and irreproachable because rooted in Jesus Christ, she is forever the holy Church—holy because of the irrevocable obstinacy of divine grace.

Seen in this light, prophetic criticism in the old sense of the word has spent itself; i.e., criticism that might proclaim the end of the Church, the transformation of the same into invalid "old" testament. The prophetic criticism in this extremely radical sense can never again exist because the proviso on which it was based no longer prevails. The Church now possesses this absolute obstinacy of divine grace, God's final salvific will as its essential element. She herself is thereby as absolute and holy as the concrete presence of this divine obstinacy in the world, and her essence will not allow succession.[9] She is the authentic receptacle of God's saving actions and to find one preferable to her is an impossibility.

At this point the answer to our initial question suggests itself. We can say: the Church is the final, unsurpassable placement of the divine salvific operation within man. This being true, man can create for himself no other place outside of or beyond the Church. He must bear his witness to God within the Church, an essential part of which witness is the *credo Ecclesiam:* I believe that through this Church God effects the salvation of the world. Now, this final and unsurpassable character of the Church is rooted in the incarnation of the divine Word which is the concrete realization of the obstinacy of divine grace. In other words, the Church is the perpetual witness to God's salvation of man the sinner. Subsequently, it is proper to the Church that the men who form her be sinners, because she is born from grace.

The Fathers illustrated this last fact with the bold imagery of *casta meretrix.* Seen from her historical origin, the Church is the "whore"; she stems from the Babylon of this world, but Christ cleansed her and transformed her into a "bride." Urs von Balthasar has pointed out with penetrating insight that this is no mere historical statement (as would be, for instance: "She was once unclean—now she is clean"); rather it denotes the tension inherent in the life of the Church. The Church draws her life from the forgiveness that transforms her from whore to bride. God is calling the Church continuously unto himself out of Babylon, man's natural abode. In every generation he calls his Church which is "Church" precisely because of his grace.[10]

This fact becomes clear if we carefully examine the basic mystery of the incarnation, the Word become flesh. We have come to look upon the incarnation as the foundation of and justification for the institutional aspect of the Church, for there the incarnation, God's taking up of earthly form, finds its continuation. This is undeniable, but it remains one-sided and inadequate if uncomplemented by a fact equally true, namely, that the incarnation represents in no way the ultimate of Christianity. The mystery of Christ is the mystery of the cross; the incarnation is only the beginning of that journey which reaches its culmination at Calvary. The theology of the cross necessarily belongs to the theology of the incarnation—the one without the other would be bereft of meaning. This then means that all earthly institutions must suffer a "crucifixion" in order to attain true fulfillment, for all earthly form is contingent.

Doubtless it is a mistake arbitrarily to reduce the Church to the level of an "Old Testament" by withdrawing into the "superiority" of protest, i.e., by attempting to appeal against the Church to an authority which actually cannot and does not exist outside the Church. Yet it is equally wrong to consider the incarnation the whole, the total quintessence, and therefore the end, thus decreeing the Church to be the perfected kingdom promised by God, which in effect would be a denial of her great eschatological future, her transformation into judgment and end, as well as an attempt to foist her off as spotless and unimpeachable in this present world. Such action would be false, for her divine mystery is a mystery administered by men and these, men who have not yet attained their goal, *are* the Church.

The obstinacy of divine grace, an obstinacy pregnant with the precious mystery of finality, has not yet ripened into full bloom, but is still bound to the sign of the cross, bound to men who are in need of the cross if they are to reach their glory. There would be no point to God's obstinacy unless these men, for whom it is expressed and in whom it is realized, are also sinners in need of the criticism and the *crisis* of the cross. Grace, being absolute, implies of itself human inadequacy, and such human inadequacy justifies criticism of those in the Church. To repeat then, these men *are* the Church and that Church cannot be considered as pure abstraction, independent of and divorced from these her human members. Rather this Church lives in these men even though she transcends mankind by the divine grace which she transmits to them. Thus within her earthly existence, the Church though holy remains a sinful Church that *as* Church never ceases to pray "Forgive us our sins as we forgive those who sin against us."

St. Augustine instructed his faithful in similar manner: "Even the saints are tainted by daily sin. The whole Church cries: 'Forgive us our sins!' She is, therefore, blemished and wrinkled (Eph. 5:27). But through contrition these blemishes are removed, these wrinkles smoothed away. The Church's unceasing prayer is one of contrition that she may be made pure. And so it will remain until the end of time." [11]

2. "Dark am I, and yet comely" (Cant. 1:5)

Here an example will aid further reflection on the existence of the Church in this world, a reflection necessary before deciding the Christian's proper attitude in regard to the Church. Consider the figure of Peter to whom the Lord entrusted the same fullness of power in Matthew 16:19 that he supplied to the entire apostolic college in Matthew 18:18. Peter, there, was the symbolic embodiment of the Church's essence.

As to whether or not the promise of Primacy in Matthew 16:17ff was recorded by the Evangelist in its proper place, contemporary exegetes generally argue that just a few verses later the Lord illogically called Peter Satan to his face (16:23) for attempting to restrain him from the Passion. Furthermore, according to the chronology of Mark, the denunciation scene took place in Caesarea Philippi (Mark 8:33); thus the promise of Primacy could hardly have occurred at the same time as his denunciation: Christ could hardly have called Simon "rock of the Church" and "Satan" within so short a time. Therefore each event demanded its separate setting.[12]

Here we shall not attempt to resolve this exegetical difficulty. We can, however, apart from the problem of locating historically the promise of Primacy, establish that the synchronism of "rock" and "Satan" (and *skandalon,* meaning "stumbling block") contains no impossibility *per se,* at least for the biblical mentality. On the contrary, such a paradox is quite in keeping with and characteristic of the man who truly understands God's "folly," the victory of God's might through man's weakness, God's triumph through the failure of the cross. As we saw above, it was just such a mentality that could designate the King of Babel "God's servant" (Jer. 25:9): this King, although thoroughly corrupt, received the honored name of the Messiah because Jahweh had seen fit to use him as an instrument in his history of salvation. Such a mentality is a far cry from the sophistication of mere human reasoning.

In the present case, the image that the Bible wishes to convey is more like the following: Were everything to depend solely on Peter, were "flesh and blood" the source of his authority, then he *could* become a "Satan" and a "stumbling block." But if he is not dependent on mere humanity, if it is God who takes him into his service, then he could become, as God's instrument, truly the "cosmic rock."[13]

This name refers not to Peter's own virtue and character, but is rather a *nomen officii*, not a name merited but a call to serve. This is a name denoting divine election and delegation of which no man in himself is worthy—least of all Peter, whose character suggests anything but rock-bound stability! That he of all people should be declared the "rock" is precisely and primarily that basic paradox of the divine power operating through weakness. Peter is of himself irresolute; he is lacking in faith (Matt. 14:30). Nevertheless, by the grace of God he is the rock upon which the Church stands. Peter's entire being is determined by this dialectic that becomes particularly noticeable whenever his office is mentioned expressly in the New Testament.

The investiture of primacy in John 21:15–17 is made with reference to his previous denial. In Luke (22:31ff) the promise is followed immediately by the prophecy of the denial while the promise in Matthew stands in glaring contrast to Peter's renunciation as "Satan" and "stumbling block." As always, here is the promise of the imposition of divine power upon human frailty whereby not man but God clearly is redeemer. As always, the obstinacy of grace does not permit itself to be disarmed by man's inability: rather the victory of God's love surmounts this inability; it prevails, refusing to be overwhelmed by the sin of man.

An additional remark must be injected here. We have relapsed into the sophistries of purely human reasoning, which refuses to admit the power of grace, and today we are careful to dismiss the dualism within Peter by distinguishing between the rock and the stumbling block. We, preferring the triumph of man to God, have lost the biblical mentality. We argue that the Peter of the denial is the Peter prior to Easter. The Peter after Pentecost is the rock and subsequently we create for ourselves an idealized image. Yet in both instances, it is the identical Peter. Peter, prior to Easter, was capable of uttering amid mass apostasy those words of unsurpassed beauty: "Lord, to whom shall we go?

Thou hast words of everlasting life, and we have come to believe and to know that thou art the Christ, the Son of God" (John 6:68f). On the other hand, after Pentecost, is it not Peter—ever stumbling block and rock in one—who compromises Christian freedom (Gal. 2:11ff) for fear of the Jews?

And does not this situation remain true throughout history? Has not the pope, the successor of Peter, always been *petra* and *skandalon*, simultaneously God's rock and stumbling stone? Has not heroic perseverance always been demanded of the faithful in the face of this divine paradox so humbling to their pride? It will always be a matter of enduring this tension between rock and Satan, this mysterious mixture of extreme opposites. Luther discerned the satanical element with devastating clarity, and his judgment was no mere exaggeration. His mistake, rather, lay in his inability to tolerate the biblical paradox arising from the basic tension of a faith that lives not from merit but grace. Actually, no one should have understood such a paradox better than the man who formulated *"simul justus et peccator"* referring to man at once justified yet sinful.

It was the Donatist Tyconius who perhaps best expressed the tension within the Church between *kepha* and Satan. He spoke of the Church as possessing a right side and a left side and said that she is at once Christ and Antichrist, Jerusalem and Babylon, so that the words of the Canticle stand true: "Dark am I, and [despite that fact] comely" (Cant. 1:5). Actually Origen was the first to recognize in this passage an expression of the Church's paradoxical tension.[14] Tyconius merely summarized a line of thought that is to be found throughout the entire patristic tradition, and which Augustine himself adopted to a certain degree.[15]

The simple fact which emerges from this tradition is that it is impossible to contemplate the Church independently of the men who make up the Church; the idealization of a Church divorced from the human element corresponds to no historical reality. The

Church lives through men in a temporal world; she lives in a truly human manner despite the divine mystery she bears within herself. The institution as institution also bears its burden of humanity; it too shares the human vanity of the stumbling block. And who is not perfectly aware of the fact? Yet, the Church remains the holy-sinful Church, both witness to and realization of God's unconquerable grace, of his gracious favor whereby he loves us in our very unworthiness. It is on account of such frailty that the Church is and remains God's "good news," the glad tidings of a salvation that far surpasses all hope and comprehension.

Finally, we could draw a lesson from the Middle Ages, that period when, at least according to our own rather naïve idealization of the era, Christianity enjoyed a pristine splendor. Two characteristic texts reveal that it was an age when Christianity was highly aware of the Church's dark and paradoxical mystery and possessed the courage to give it utterance.

Guillaume d'Auvergne, the great theologian and Bishop of Paris, wrote the following, frightening as it may sound: ". . . who would not shudder to see the Church with a donkey's head or the believing soul with fangs of a wolf, a piggish snout, pale, sunken cheeks, the neck of a bull, and with an appearance so monstrously hideous that all upon beholding it stiffen in horror? Who would not brand such frightful disfigurement 'Babylon' rather than take it to be the Church of Christ; who would not call it wilderness rather than City of God? Because of such brute bestiality on the part of the Church's wicked members with whom the Church is teeming and whose deeds obliterate those of her other members, heretics condemn the Church as 'whore' and 'Babylon.' No doubt degenerate and nominal Christians deserve such criticism and yet this condemnation is extended by their accusers to all Christians. The Church is no longer a bride but becomes a monster of frightful deformity and savagery . . . and it is clear that, under such conditions, it can no longer be said of her: 'Thou art all fair, in thee is no blemish.' " [16]

Gerhoh von Reichersberg, the Bavarian reform-theologian, paints a picture equally disparaging: "that in thy midst, O Jerusalem, should live a people all but completely Babylonian" [17] he writes, and continues in the name of the Church: "I, the Church, do not claim for myself spotlessness as did Novatians and Catharists. I am aware of the number of sinners within my fold and spurn not penance, but rather pray: 'Forgive us our sins.' " [18]

We should ask ourselves, then, if our present-day theologians no longer venture to use such drastic language, whether this of itself is an indication of a higher moral standard or rather of a mitigated love that no longer enflames our heart with a holy jealousy for God's cause in this world (2 Cor. 11:2); is it not a sign of a love grown cold, a love that no longer has the courage to suffer for and because of the beloved? He who no longer is shocked when a friend fails, who no longer suffers from it and struggles for his friend's recovery, he no longer loves. Should not this hold true as well in our relationship with the Church?

3. The Witness of the Christian

How, then, is the Christian to conduct himself with regard to the historically living Church? Critically (for the sake of the Church's integrity)?; or how? We are tempted to state simply: He must love her, the Church, and all else will ensue from the "logic of love." *Dilige et quod vis, fac,* applies here as well. In practice, this rule is impossible to overstep and the choice of the best course of action—speaking out or remaining silent, quiet submission or a zealous persistence to secure a place for the Church in contemporary society—all depends ultimately on the unshakable foundation of love for the Church.

Nevertheless, the theologian does wish for something more

definite. He wants to investigate the structure of this *sentire Ecclesiam,* this "empathy towards the Church." He needs this in order to obtain a more precise indication of the proper direction to follow even though, when it comes to the actual decision, one is forced to rely on oneself, on subjective faith, hope and love, and cannot depend simply on an objective rule.

To summarize, then: the Church has assumed the mantle of the prophets, the heritage of those who suffered for truth's sake. She herself entered into history as the Church of martyrs. She, as a whole, has borne the prophetic burden of suffering for truth. Therefore the "prophetic" in her cannot be dead. On the contrary, it makes its true abode in her. However, one may object that the "prophetic" has won its victory in the Church and subsequently has lost its critical function. But to do so would be to misconstrue the essence of human history as well as the particular mode by which the New Covenant, indeed the Spirit and the divine, exist in the world.

For, as we saw above, the recall of the Church from Babylon, the transformation from "whore" to "bride," from "stumbling block" to "cornerstone" is not a distant event that occurred once and for all at the dawn of her history. There is much more to it than that. She is summoned ever anew. She stands, as it were, ever upon the threshold. And the *pascha,* the "passing-over" from this world's existence into newness of spirit, remains first and last her vital primary principle. In this sense, the Easter mystery is the abiding form of the Church's existence in this world.

The Church lives and thrives on the call of the spirit, in the "crisis," that tension aroused by the transition from the old to the new. Was it by chance alone that the great saints had to struggle not only with the world but also within the Church as well; that they wrestled with the temptation of the Church to become "world" and suffered within the Church and at the hand of the Church? A Francis of Assisi, for example, or an Ignatius of Loyola who, arrested for the third time during the Inquisition, rotted in a Salamanca prison, chained for twenty-two days to his companion Calisto. And yet Ignatius retained enough courage and cheerful faith to say: "In all of Salamanca there are not so many shackles and chains that I would not put up with more for the love of God." [19] Thus he renounced no part of his mission and none of his obedience to the Church.

A summary of what thus far has been established shows the Christian median between freedom of speech and submissive obedience to lie within two fundamental polarities.

1. The Christian enjoys the knowledge that the voice of the prophets has so triumphed in the Church that it wondrously surpasses and transfigures the prophetic mission. How? Not through final fulfillment of the covenant by men, but though the gratuitous goodness of God who, despite human failures, remains gracious toward them and demands nothing more than their trusting acceptance of his graciousness. The Christian realizes that the definitive character of God's new people in the Church has its foundation not in human achievements, but in that divine favor whose revocation no human failure can effect.

Thus in the Church the Christian discerns the finality of God's mercy as well as his own obligation to acquiesce. This sets a limit to his critical protest, a limit which should not be exceeded. Yet he realizes as well that this Church, precisely because she exists through the obstinacy of God's grace, also stands amid ceaseless temptation and failure. He knows that she is constantly in the throes of the chasmic strain between rock and stumbling stone, between *"petra"* and "Satan." Only faith can surmount this existential tension to which the Christian is destined in his obedience to the Church.

It stands to reason, then, that in this way obedience *as* obedience takes on a new aspect: the obligation of "bearing witness," the duty to strive for the integrity of the Church, to battle against the "Babylon" within her that raises its head not only among the laity, not only among individual Christians, but even higher up within the very core of the Church's structure. Not only does it appear but it does so necessarily in that mysterious "must" through which the Church originated: "Did not the Christ *have to* suffer thus before entering into his glory?" (Luke 24:26). Therefore it is evident that even within the Church such bearing of witness will now as ever prove painful, open as it is to misunderstanding, suspicion, even condemnation.

Meanwhile, the servility of the sycophants (branded by the genuine prophets of the Old Testament as "false prophets"), of those who shy from and shun every collision, who prize above all their calm complacency, is not true obedience. The true obedience is that which remains obedient even while bearing witness in suffering; it is that obedience which is forthright truthfulness and which is animated by the persistent power of love. It is this obedience that has fructified the Church throughout the centuries and has drawn her away from the temptations of "Babylon" to the side of her crucified Lord.

A schooling in *sentire Ecclesiam* should lead us to none other than just such an obedience which is born of truth and leads to truth. What the Church needs today, as always, are not adulators to extol the status quo, but men whose humility and obedience are no less than their passion for truth; men who brave every misunderstanding and attack as they bear witness; men who, in a word, love the Church more than ease and the unruffled course of their personal destiny.

2. We can also look at the matter from the moral point of view. He who feels himself impelled to give critical witness ought to consider various aspects of the question. He must inquire of himself whether or not he has the necessary assurance to justify such a course of action. Secondly, his earnestness in the matter

should be determined by the importance his protest can claim according to the scale of theological value. This scale indicates the degree to which the Church *qua* Church agrees with an assertion or movement, and consequently the degree to which this movement or assertion may or may not be criticized. Obviously, when one confronts the deposit of faith as such, criticism must cease.

Further, since criticism never enjoys the invulnerability of a doctrine of the faith, it is clear that of itself criticism is open to reassessment and the criticism of others. Therefore, one should subject his own opinion to thorough and relentless inspection before attempting to criticize another. In an age of relativism, skepticism, and doctrinaire independence, it is a relief to find in the midst of intellectual chaos one last refuge demanding of one a respectful, obedient attitude rather than summoning one to debate. That is one restriction which must be kept in mind.

There is another and of equal importance: we must take into consideration the brother weak in faith, the unbelieving world surrounding us, and, too, the infirmity of our own faith, so capable of withering once we retreat behind the barrier of criticism and of deteriorating into the self-pitying rancor of one misunderstood.

On the other hand, however, there exists in contrast to discretion, another factor which must be taken into consideration. Truth, as well as love, possesses a right of its own and over sheer utility it takes precedence—truth from which stems that strict necessity for prophetic charisma, and which can demand of one the duty of bearing public witness. For were it necessary to wait for the day when the truth would no longer be misinterpreted and taken advantage of, we might well find that it had lost all effect.

Therefore the restrictions listed above are not meant to muzzle the prophetic element within the Church. Such restrictions are worthwhile only in so far as they serve to integrate this element into the organism of Christ's body where the law of truth is equal to that of love: But again in these matters, all things taken into consideration, there is no absolute norm except for the necessity of an obedient decision made in the light of the faith.

At present we must waive specific questions in regard to the nature of "free speech in the Church"—for example, what part does the layman play in it, and what is its significance to the relationship between layman and clergy, etc.—in order to establish a final and fundamental point. Until now we have been considering the individual in relation to the whole. Now we can say something concerning the "whole," concerning the role of the institution and of office as such. The Church needs the spirit of freedom and of sincere forthrightness because she is bound by the command, "Do not stifle the Spirit" (1 Thess. 5:19), which is valid for all time.

Upon hearing such words, who can help but recall Paul's account of his collision with Peter: "But when Cephas came to Antioch, I rebuked him to his face, for his own conduct condemned him. . . . But when I say they were not straightforward about the truths of the good news, I said to Cephas, right before them all, 'If you live like a heathen and not like a Jew, though you are a Jew yourself, why should you try to make the heathen live like Jews?' " (Gal. 2:11–14).

Yet, if it was a weakness in Peter to have compromised the freedom of the gospel for fear of James' supporters, it was his greatness which enabled him to accept the liberty of Paul, who "rebuked him to his face." And today the Church owes her life to this liberty which paved the way for her entry to the heathen world.

But where could the like of it occur today? In our day and age, one would not dare reproach the Church as did Guillaume d'Auvergne the Church of his time. Naturally today the Church cannot be accused of being so degenerate and monstrous that "all who behold her stiffen in horror." And it can hardly be claimed, "that nowadays the chariot of the Church" runs "not forward but backward since the horses run backward pushing her in reverse." [20] But might she not be taken to task for holding the reins a bit too tightly, for the creation of too many norms, so that not a few of these helped abandon the century to disbelief rather than save it? In other words, might she not be rebuked for trusting too little that power of truth which lives and triumphs in the faith, for entrenching herself behind exterior safeguards instead of relying on the truth, which is inherent in liberty and shuns such defenses?

Perhaps we of today need a reminder that boldness is one of the basic Christian attitudes referred to most frequently in the New Testament. Boldness it was that made Peter step forward and preach to the Jews (Acts 2:29; 4:13, 29, 31). What would it not mean for the Church in the world of today—in a century that thirsts after freedom, in an era which walked out of the Church for the sake of freedom, illusory though it may have been—if the words of Paul could ring with the force of old, could actually mature until veritably visible: those magnificent words into which Paul poured the full expression of his faith: "But wherever the spirit of the Lord is, there is freedom" (2 Cor. 3:17).

NOTES

[1] Cf., in reference to the entire question, K. Rahner, *Das Freie Wort in der Kirche* (2nd ed.; Einsiedeln: 1953); K. Rahner, *Gefahren im heutigen Katholizismus* (3rd ed.; Einsiedeln: 1950).

[2] Cf. Y. Congar, *Le mystère du temple* (Paris: 1958); a résumé by J. Ratzinger, "Haus Gottes" in *LThK²*, V, 32f.

³ Cf. the comprehensive article "προφητής" by Krämer-Rendtorff-Meyer-Friedrich in the *ThWNT*, VI, pp. 781–863; also instructive is the chapter "Jesus der Prophet" in O. Cullmann's *Die Christologie des Neuen Testamentes* (Tübingen: 1957), pp. 11–49.

⁴ H. Hermelink, *Katholizismus und Protestantismus im Gespräch um die Una Sancta* (Stuttgart: 1949), p. 49.

⁵ *Idem*, p. 51.

⁶ J. Jeremias, *Jesu Verheissung für die Völker* (2nd ed.; Stuttgart: 1959), pp. 16–33.

⁷ Cf. E. Peterson, "Die Kirche," in: *Theologische Traktate* (München: 1951), pp. 409–29; H. Schlier, "Die Entscheidung für die Heidenmission in der Urchristenheit" in: *Die Zeit der Kirche* (2nd ed.; Freiburg: 1958), pp. 90–107.

⁸ German: *Dennoch*—literally, "nevertheless."

⁹ Cf. for the concept "absolute" as employed here, the excellent article by H. Fries, "Absolutheitsanspruch des Christentums," in *LThK²*, I, pp. 71–74.

¹⁰ H. U. v. Balthasar, "Casta meretrix," in: *Sponsa Verbi* (Einsiedeln: 1961), pp. 203–305, especially 218ff, 238f, 276; cf. K. Rahner, *Die Kirche der Sünder* (Wien: 1948).

¹¹ *Sermo* 181, 5, 7: PL 38, 982; cited from Balthasar *op. cit.*, p. 300.

¹² Cf. the compilation of literature in J. Betz, "Die Gründung der Kirche durch den historischen Jesus," in: *Theol. Quartalschrift* 138 (1958), pp. 152–83; O. Cullmann, *Petrus* (2nd ed.; Zürich: 1960); A. Lang, *Der Auftrag der Kirche* (3rd ed.; München: 1962), pp. 58–99.

¹³ On the idea of the cosmic rock: J. Jeremias, *Golgotha* (Leipzig: 1926).

¹⁴ *In Cant. hom.* 2, 4 (Baehrens 8, 47), quoted according to Balthasar, p. 298; on Tyconius: J. Ratzinger, "Beobachtungen zum Kirchenbegriff des Tyconius im 'Liber regularum,'" in: *Revue des Etudes Augustiniennes* 2 (1956), pp. 173–85.

¹⁵ Cf. Balthasar, p. 300f.

¹⁶ From the commentary to the Canticle, quoted according to Balthasar, p. 207; cf. the fundamental work by H. Riedlinger, *Die Makellosigkeit der Kirche in den lateinischen Hoheliedkommentaren des Mittelalters*

(Münster: 1958), where the text, pp. 243–54, is edited; see also the other texts of Guillaume used by Balthasar in p. 205ff and Dante's presentation treated in p. 203f, portraying the whore of Babylon herself sitting, instead of Beatrice, in the Chariot of the Church and making love to a giant (the king of France).

[17] PL 194, 40 A; cited from Balthasar, p. 293.

[18] PL 193, 1135 AD; Balthasar, p. 296.

[19] L.v. Matt–H. Rahner, *Ignatius von Loyola* (Würzburg: 1955), p. 187.

[20] Cited in Balthasar, p. 205.

Appendix

The Human Existence of Christ

Basis for a Christocentric Ecclesiology

by FELIX MALMBERG

IN GOD MADE MAN, Jesus Christ, the second person of the blessed Trinity, took on an individual human nature which he still possesses. So teaches the Catholic faith. This union is so intimate and personal that Jesus is a single person in two really distinct natures, so that the divine person of the Word is also truly and fully man.

Such is the so-called hypostatic union, a union in the person and by the person. The third General Council, that of Ephesus, called it, in the words of St. Cyril of Alexandria, "a union which is to us mysterious and ineffable." [1] Theologians unanimously agree with St. Thomas that this union stands on a higher level than any other union of God with creatures, [2] that it is quite unique, and that it surpasses any kind of union known to us. [3]

Although no example taken from the world of creatures [4] can fully explain this union, [5] a comparison will help to make it clearer: I am a person and possess a true human nature through which I am a man. In the same way, as a consequence of the hypostatic union, the second person of the blessed Trinity possesses a human nature through which he is really man. Now this concrete, individual, complete human nature belongs as a whole, together with everything it is and has, to God the Son, as to the only person who holds and possesses this nature as his own. Hence the man Jesus of Nazareth is really the Son of God. God has truly become man, and this man is truly God.

Truly man: he has a true human nature, just as we all have, like ours in all but sin. Therefore God made man has also a formally human existence. If Jesus had no formally human existence, then he would not exist according to his formally human nature: his human nature would not be formally a human nature. To be truly man, to exist truly as man, to lead a truly human existence without having a formally human existence, is no less impossible than to think without having an intellect. This truth seems to us to impose itself with such force, to be so obvious, that we would spend no more time on it, did not a considerable number of respected Thomists still defend the thesis that there is no created human existence in Christ. Hence it is not out of place to enlarge upon the theme.

We need not look far before finding the reasons which have led these theologians to deny a created human existence in Christ. Faith tells us that God made man is a single person, the divine person of the Word. Now a single person possesses only a single being. So there is in Christ only a single being, the divine being of the Word. If there were also in Christ a created, human being, a being distinct from the divine essence, then this consequence would no longer hold—there would be in Christ two distinct existences, and this would contradict the unity of the person.

At the end of the argument a question immediately springs to mind: then how do you salvage the truth, equally stressed by Christian doctrine, that there are two real natures in Christ? These theologians answer by an appeal to the real distinction in all things except God between essence and existence, a distinction held by all followers of St. Thomas. In every creature the real principle by virtue of which it is this limited and finite being (its essence) is objectively different from the real principle by virtue of which it is (its existence). Only in God, who is unlimited and infinite, are essence and existence fully identical.

God's essence is precisely to exist. Now in Christ, they claim, a human essence is actuated into existence, not by the connatural human existence, but, in a mysterious and supernatural way, by the divine existence of the Word. God's infinite power enables him to make a true and real man without inserting a created human existence, by directly imparting his divine existence to Christ's human essence.

Actually there is no single historical argument, so far as we know, to show that the documents of the Church understand the expression "human nature of Christ" to mean either implicitly or explicitly Christ's human essence, in the technical sense which the word has in Thomist metaphysics, with reference to those innermost components of all basic realities, essence and existence.[6] We hope to be able to show later that the distinction between essence and existence need play no part here. Further, far from arising as a sort of theological consequence of the mystery, the distinction can play no part except when theology is engaged in harmonizing the data of faith in the matter of the hypostatic union with the justifiable claims of philosophical reasoning.

But, leaving that question aside, we maintain that the denial of a formally human principle of existence in Christ is just as untenable as the correlative assertion that it is replaced (in a supernatural and mysterious way) by the existence of the Word. For, to repeat, if Christ is truly man, then he also exists truly as man, and consequently has a human principle of existence as well. No one, not even God omnipotent, can make a formally human act of understanding without having a formally human intellect. Similarly, no one, not even God omnipotent, can lead a formally human existence without having a human, and so created, principle of existence. How could the formally divine existence play the part of a formally human existence? Even if this were possible, Christ's human nature would exist, not *as a* human nature, but as God.[7] It is, then, hardly surprising that many theologians accuse the above-mentioned Thomists of "monophysite leanings"—an unconscious monophysite tendency.[8]

On the other hand, if we accept a created human existence, a formally human principle of existence in Christ, do we not endanger the unity of the person? How can one reconcile this human existence, really distinct from the divine existence, with the strict unity of existence which belongs to Jesus Christ? In other words, how do we keep intact the Catholic doctrine that this man is really the Son of God?

In his highly stimulating works [9] Maurice de la Taille, S.J., tries to give a satisfactory answer to this question. The Word of God, in its character of divine act of being (*acte incréé*), imparts itself wholly and directly to the human essence of Christ, and in this way actuates this human unit into formally human existence in the person of the Word. The human principle of existence is therefore the created activation (*actuation créée*) through which Christ's human essence is activated into substantial human existence but into substantial human existence *in the Word of God*. The created activation which arises out of the activation of the human essence of Christ by the divine act of being is the formally human principle of existence with respect to this human essence. But by its very nature it is a principle of existence which unites to the Word's divine act of being. It is the grace of union for this human essence.

God the Son is not altered by uniting himself to a human essence, and by taking it up into his divine existence. The alteration occurs in the human essence, which keeps indeed a created existence by which it exists as the human essence of the divine Word, but keeps it in the manner of a *dispositio consequens*. By this is meant a last, necessary, disposition to the divine act of being, arising precisely from the activating causality on Christ's human essence of the divine act of being. There is in Christ, then, a single divine act of being, which activates Christ's humanity into human existence in the person of the Word. The strict unity of existence which belongs to Christ is hereby fully ensured. And, because this activation into human existence by the divine Word implies at the same time a formally human existence (as *actuation créée par acte incréé*), the reality of Christ's human nature is fully given its due.

However ingenious De la Taille's construction may be otherwise, it cannot satisfy us as a theological explanation of the hypostatic union. Further, he has the hypostatic union occur in the last resort between the Word and Christ's human *essence*. In this scheme the human essence has the function only of a *dispositio consequens*, an "adaptation and accommodation to the Word" [10] lent to the human essence by the activation by the Word, through which this essence is adapted to be the humanity of the Word.

Now the first objection here comes from our faith in the Christological doctrine. Existing as a man, leading a human existence, is the primary concern of the doctrine of the incarnation. But in this explanation it is relegated to a secondary position. The human existence is represented as a sort of subordinate connective by which the human essence cannot be united with anything but the Word. Further, De la Taille is perfectly right to stress that the human essence cannot, as such, exist in a state of union with the Word without a human existence. But as a result this human existence is far more for the human essence than a *dispositio consequens*, adapting it to be the humanity of the Word. For the human existence of Christ is an essential condition for Christ's human essence to enable it to be a human essence. "Human essence" is naturally and transcendentally connected with "human existence" in such a way that the former cannot exist, is nothing at all, without the latter.

Hence it is that Christ's human essence cannot be united to

the Word without a human existence, for Christ's human essence would then not be a human essence. It would be non-existent. Or, to look at it from another point of view, the creative causality of God in regard to Christ's human nature touches the whole of his humanity existing in the Word, and not only his human essence as distinct from his human existence. Now that causality of the Word which directly activates, which unites with itself, must stretch as far beyond Christ's human nature as does the creative causality of God. Accordingly, the Word directly activates the whole of Christ's existing human nature, and the distinction between human essence and human existence has no direct connection with our problem.

In our opinion, Père de la Taille was correct in seeing that the strict unity of the God made man, Jesus Christ, can be explained only through the divine act of being of the Word, and that the incarnation of the Son (as opposed to that of the Father or the Holy Spirit) demands the activating (as distinct from merely creative) causality of the Word. But unfortunately he has the hypostatic union occur between Christ's human essence and the divine Word. Hence the hypostatic union becomes not only unfounded, from the point of view of a mystery of faith, but also impossible.

On the one hand, then, one is forced by the reality of both natures of the God made man to grant him, besides his formally divine existence, also a created, formally human existence. On the other hand, one is forced by the strict unity of his person to allow him only one existence. This apparent contradiction is, as we have seen, only apparently solved if one allows the hypostatic union to occur between Christ's human essence and God the Son. The only solution to this difficulty which seems to us to be correct, to give due scope to all aspects of this central mystery of faith, is that of Augustine, Leo the Great and many others. This consists in putting the whole emphasis on the real identity between the creation and the assumption of Christ's human nature: *ipsa assumptione creatur,* it is created precisely through being assumed.[11]

So much we assert of the concrete, individual, existing human nature of Christ: it is wholly and completely, in all its reality, created. It is raised to existence out of nothing through the tripersonal fullness of being which is God, imparting itself as efficient cause. So much has Christ's humanity in common with that of every man. But in addition we must assert also of the same human nature of Christ: it is wholly and completely, in all its reality, assumed. It is hypostatically united to the Word, from being nothing, by the personal fullness of being which is God the Son, imparting himself as immediate activating cause. In this it differs from every other creature. Everything which is creature in Christ is united to the Word. This creature is wholly constituted by its relationship of union to the Word. So in this case a unique creation has taken place, resulting in a hypostatic union to the Word. And at the same time a unique assumption has taken place through the Word, a hypostatic appropriation, creative by its very nature. Let us consider Augustine's expression: created through being assumed.

Our human intellect staggers before these "secrets of God," but finds no contradiction. Far from it, as we shall see, the concept of creation, so obscure to our minds, receives some light from this highest relationship of a creature to his creator. But first we must briefly consider a claim which we have put forward as obvious, namely, that the hypostatic assumption of Christ's human nature to the divine Word presupposes an immediate activating causality on the part of the divine Word.

Jesus Christ, God made man, is a single person. But all the same, there are two really distinct natures in him. There is of course no question of two "parts" which somehow make up the single person. Also excluded in this sense is that the person of

Christ should be "composed." Nevertheless, the human nature exists in the single person as united with the godhead, and in this sense one can and must speak of a *"theandre compositum."* [12] Now the strict unity of divine and human natures within the one person Jesus Christ, within the God made man, compels one to posit a principle which unites the two natures. From the first it is clear that this can only be the divine nature, and not the human nature, and indeed the divine nature in so far as it is proper to the Son, since the direct effect of the hypostatic union is the incarnate *Word.* While the three divine persons together constitute the efficient cause of the union of the human nature with the Word, it is the Word alone which becomes man, the Word alone which takes on human nature. [13]

In this hypostatic uniting of the human nature to the Word, with the Word alone, the Word cannot conceivably remain wholly passive. As regards the Word, any causality of the blessed Trinity is unthinkable, let alone a causality on the part of the human nature. How, then, can it come about, unless the Word plays a very special part of its own in this hypostatic uniting, that this human nature (a human nature not metaphorical, but vitally real) should become the humanity of the Word, rather than that of the Father or of the Holy Spirit? It is said that the Word is only the terminus, without any causality proper to itself, the terminus with which the blessed Trinity, acting as a single cause, unites a human nature. But then all special influence on his own human nature is denied to the Word, and the most real and intimate unity between the human nature and God the Son is watered down into mere "terminism."

In Jesus a human nature has entered the Word of God. But this statement can only mean that the Word of God actively draws this human nature into himself. The traditional expression *assumpsit* is pregnant with meaning. He "took on" human nature, took it to himself, took it into himself. To what kind of causality, then, must we reduce this influence of the Word on Christ's human nature, whereby he makes it into his own humanity?

St. Thomas somewhere makes the remark: "Two things can form one unconditionally only if one stands as act and the other as potency." [14] Elsewhere he states: "In whatever thing are found two elements, one of which is complementary to the other, the relation of the one to the other is that of potency to act." [15]

The human nature can combine with the divine nature of the Word to make up Jesus Christ, the God made man, only if the relation of the divine nature of the Word to the human nature is that of an activating principle. The divine nature of the Word can complete the human nature to form God made man only if the relation of the human nature to the Word is that of potency to act. In the light of what has been said it will be clear that this activation by the Word must be a creative activation, different from that of any created activating principle, and that through it the potential principle which is activated is, by the very fact, created: "created through being assumed," says Augustine.

But is it not clearly nonsense to say that the uncreated Word, God himself, immediately activated a created potency? One modern author, for example, holds: "Transferred to the physical order the immediate activation of a created potency by uncreated being would be an absurdity." [16] In addition, is it not opposed to the concept of activating causality, understood in the literal sense, that this activation by the Word should simultaneously create the potency which it activates? The confrontation with philosophical concepts, to which these questions force us, will be of the greatest service in reaching a clear theological concept of the hypostatic union.

When we ascribe efficient causality to God we must purify the notion of all the imperfections which created, efficient causality necessarily includes. This leads us to a so-called "negativo-positive" notion (in the sense in which all our notions of God are negativo-positive)—a notion which continuously evades our imagination. Indeed we can never imagine an efficient causality which is not at the same time dependent on an already existent subject in which it effects something. But God's efficient causality is not dependent on anything. If he effects some perfection in a subject, at the same time he creates it, or at least holds it in existence (a continuous creation). So God's efficient causality is at the same time creative causality, pure giving and imparting, free of any outside influence whatsoever. But one can impart only what one has, and God *is* what he has. Hence God's efficient causality creates by imparting himself.

Once again, this is unimaginable to us, for in ourselves "impart" presupposes an already existing subject to which it is imparted. But in its purest, highest, divine form efficient causality must, of its nature, be creative, an imparting of self without any presuppositions, resulting in an effect different from the cause. Our idea of distinction must, however, be further clarified. God's creative activity is really identical with his being, and remains therefore totally in him—"formally immanent," as the scholastics say.[17]

But the effect, the creature distinct from God, cannot be so distinct from him that it should not remain also in him, and accordingly with him. All creation is in God. He carries it all in himself. St. Thomas teaches that he is in a certain sense the place in which all creation is situated.[18] In theology one calls God's creative activity "God's activity *ad extra.*" This is quite irreproachable, so long as one keeps in view that there is really no *extra* to God.[19] The property in the creature of being *extra* with relation to God signifies an opposition of creature to creator only by reason of the imperfection of the creature. It by no means implies that the creature is not in God, or that God is not in the creature.[20]

In short, if we want to describe philosophically the creative activity of God, then the following elements are essential to the description: An imparting of self, presupposing nothing and so immediate, by which an effect really distinct from God by reason of its imperfection comes to be in God, and so really in union with God. Clearly, even the correct philosophical concept of creation is full of obscurity, and teaches our intellects the prudent virtue of modesty. Who would dare, without contradicting what we have said, to maintain that God can not create a man who, as man (in his concrete, existent human nature) is truly distinct from God, and yet so intimately united with him that one must speak of a "hypostatic union"? That reason can not show this to be impossible will be yet clearer to us if we analyze our philosophical concept of "immediate efficient causality."

We derive this concept, as all our philosophical concepts, from the consideration of ourselves in the world. From the limitedness of things, from the imperfection of their being (it is, but it is only this and not that), we conclude their inner composition from a principle of essence and a principle of being. We see that the latter imparts itself completely and directly to the former, so that a limited entity arises. From the multiplicity of similar things (all these many particulars possess "this being," but all in limited and various ways) we conclude the inner composition of their being from a material principle (principle of limitation and the inherent possibility of indefinite multiplication of the units) and a formal principle (principle of the specifically identical perfection of being).

We see, again, that the latter imparts itself completely and directly to the former, so that a limited entity, endowed with a limited, individual, specific perfection of being, arises. Scholastic philosophy calls such complete and direct imparting of self (by the principle of being and the formal principle of the essence respectively) to the correlative receptive and limiting principle (the principle of essence and the material principle, respectively) "formal causality" or "activating causality in the strict sense." What strikes one immediately is that formal causality so conceived is essentially a very imperfect causality. The principle of being is limited by the correlative essence to which it imparts itself. The formal principle is limited by the correlative material principle to which it imparts itself.[21]

However, in the formal causes discovered by our intellect's natural powers we perceive different levels of perfection. As we climb from lifeless things, via plants and animals, to man, we find that, the higher we climb, the less is the essence imprisoned by matter. The less dependent that essence is on matter, the less it sinks into matter and becomes submerged in it, the more it controls and endows matter, drawing matter up with itself. Nevertheless, the union becomes ever more intimate, since a higher being possesses a greater degree of unity.

In the case of men, in our own case, we find a spiritual essence, which, as spirit, stands so far above matter that its existence is essentially independent of matter. This does not prevent it, in so far as it is essence, from being at the same time limited by matter. It is precisely through its spiritual perfection, according to St. Thomas, that it has the strength to impart to matter everything which the lower essences can impart, and more.[22] In our humanity the spirit has the primacy, although it remains true that we are essentially material. But matter does not submerge the human essence. On the contrary, matter is drawn upwards, and taken up into the being of the soul.[23] With regard to that wonder which is the spirit of man, let us content ourselves with drawing the following conclusion:

The created, immediately activating capacity which our spiritual human soul exercises on our human *compositum*, goes essentially hand in hand with an inner independence of, and dominating elevation above, matter, with a capacity to draw up matter and assume it into the spiritual perfection of the soul.[24] It is precisely on this account that our human *compositum* possesses a higher inner unity than do any lower natures.[25] This it is which shows the impossibility in philosophy of an immediately activating, uncreated causality in which the activating principle is totally independent of the subject activated. It shows the impossibility of a pure activation in which the subsistent act is merely received and in no way imprisoned (i.e. in no way limited), in which it only draws up to itself the subject activated, without itself being correspondingly lowered; in other words, an activation in which the activating cause is supposed to dominate the subject united to itself in the way of creation, an activation in which the most intimate conceivable unity of a creature with God is supposed to be realized.

Philosophy realizes that the so-called "reciprocity of good service," [26] which occurs in the relationships between matter and form and between act and potency, does not pertain to the essence of causality.[27] Philosophy realizes also that, when it is a question of the relations possible between creation and God, more than usual modesty is required of her. We can go so far as to ask whether our metaphysical concept of God's creative causality is not critically untenable, if the possibility, absolutely speaking, of the activating causality of God described above is excluded. For have we not seen that, according to our philosophical concept of creation, God immediately imparts himself to the creature which so comes into being? And even if every creative act need not necessarily cause a hypostatic union of creature to creator, nevertheless we cannot see how the concept of creation can be critically accounted for except by at least the metaphysical possibility of a hypostatic union. Thus the hypostatic union throws some light on the darkness which shrouds our concept of God's creative causality.

But is not the concept of a hypostatic union as such in conflict with the claims of reason? Let us boldly state the problem of the hypostatic union, as taught us by faith, between Christ's human nature and God the Son: how can the uncreated, formally divine being of the Word be the act of being of a created human nature? It is St. Thomas who shows us the road we must tread in our critical reflection on this problem, by drawing to our attention the infinity of God.[28]

God is infinite, the unlimited fullness of being. God's being comports no single limitation or exclusion. It is the exclusion of all exclusion. Being man comports as such the lack of other perfections. "To be," in the way a man is, excludes, for example, the perfection of being proper to an angel. Limitations pertain to the very being of every creature. Where being ends, nothingness begins. But God's being knows neither measure nor limit. When we say, "God is not a creature," we mean: "The imperfection of creation has nothing in common with the perfection of God." God is distinguished from creation by his absolute perfection.

So, if God is the unqualified affirmation, the negation of all negation, what a priori grounds can reason bring against the possibility of the incarnation? God's Word of affirmation (and faith tells us that God's Word was made man) imparts itself in all its absoluteness to a concrete, individual, existing human nature.[29] He rejects neither the human limitation of being nor the human perfection of being of this human nature, for Jesus is as fully human as we are, and his human nature is truly distinct from his divine nature. Only God's Word of affirmation also acts positively: he gives himself to the human nature. In consequence there is now a God made man, who is man and human, as God alone can be formally man and human, namely in a divine, absolute, unlimited way, in the way of being.

Immediately a difficulty springs up: are not these two concepts—"limited human perfection of being" and "in the unlimited way of being"—mutually exclusive? To which we answer: certainly a limited perfection of being can never *be* the unlimited perfection of being, nor vice versa. But there is no question here of that. The question is: can the unlimited perfection of being formally possess the limited perfection of being which is really distinct from it, and possess it in such a way that we must truly say: "God has taken on a human nature, God is now also man"? Why could not perfect being, which excludes nothing, possess the formally human perfection of being, in so far as the latter is distinct from the being of the Word by reason of its imperfection? Why could not the formally human perfection of being be taken on by the perfect being, and remain at the same time formally human and imperfect perfection of being?

For, once again, it is precisely by reason of the infinite perfection of being that one cannot see how even the highest conceivable union of a creature with this being can bring about anything else but that this creature should remain itself, yet in a divine way. According to the penetrating insight of St. Thomas, every creature naturally, according to what it is, belongs to God.[30] This appertaining to God determines the essence proper to each creature; and the more intimately the creature is united to God, the more, and more intensely, it becomes "that which it is." In short, when God the Son takes on a human nature in the hypostatic union—a mysterious truth put before us by the Christian faith, wholly surpassing our human understanding, which is not therefore justified in stigmatizing it as an impossibility—then the God made man must be formally man and human, and that in a supernatural, superhuman, divine way, or, to use a favorite expression of Emile Mersch, *divinement humain,* "divinely human."

The germ of the explanation we have given of the metaphysical possibility of the hypostatic union can be summed up in the magnificent exposition of St. Augustine: "No creature can be the contrary to God. For if he really is, and of God alone can this word properly be used (for what truly is remains unchangeable, since whatever changes was once what it no longer is, and is what one day it will no longer be) then God has no contrary. For, if we were asked what the contrary of white is, we should answer black, of hot, cold, of swift, slow, and so on. But when one asks what the contrary is of that which is, the correct answer is 'that which is not.' " [31]

Hence philosophy may not dismiss as senseless the possibility of a creative causality in God which at the same time unites its effect to himself in hypostatic union. Nor has it any more right to claim that an immediate causality, which at the same time brings what is activated into being out of nothing, contradicts reason: Hence neither creative assumption nor assumptive creation of Christ's human nature by the Word can be rejected.

Now it seems that, unless one thinks of the mystery of the incarnation in these supra-philosophical (though not therefore contra-philosophical) categories, one does it violence. God the Son, in whom, through whom, and for whom all was created (cf. Col. 1:15–16), creates for himself a human nature (through him), which is so intimately united with himself (in him), and so totally at his service (for him), that it must be called his own human nature, and this man must be truly Son of God.

All the rest of creation, which has its origin also in, through, and for the Word, finds its ultimate meaning both logically (or, to exclude all possibility of misunderstanding, theologically) and ontologically in the God made man (cf. Col. 1:17). However, his humanity, created and thereby called into existence, has,

alone of all creation, the privilege of being hypostatically one
with him in the whole of its formally human essence and existence. Hence there is no human person. Instead, the divine person of the Word has, in the act of creating it, appropriated to
himself a humanity. Creation by the Word was, for this humanity, identical with assumption by the Word: *creatione
assumitur.*

In our view, the formula of Augustine and Pope Leo deserves,
in a certain sense, to be preferred: in its assumption it was
created: *assumptione creatur.* The creation as such is common
to the three divine persons, while the assumption is strictly proper
to the Word. When we say that Christ's human nature was
created by the Word, we do not yet sufficiently express the
grounds for the quite unique hypostatic union of this humanity
with the Word, for "all things were made through him [the
Word], and without him was made nothing that has been made"
(John 1:3). However, when we say that Christ's human nature
was assumed by the Word, then it is expressly shown why this
creature is hypostatically united to the Word.

To be sure, Christ's human nature was not first created and
then assumed. In this case the creation was really identical with
the assumption. But this is not true of every creation, since
creation does not imply assumption. On the other hand, assumption does formally imply creation. "The Word of God creates"
does not, of itself, imply that what is created is united to the
Word in hypostatic union. On the other hand "the Word of
God assumes (hypostatically) into himself" does mean that
what is assumed is created. Hence the formulation, "Christ's
humanity is created by being assumed," expresses the full reality
of this unique creation far more precisely and profoundly than
the formulation, "Christ's humanity was assumed by being
created."

The unity of divinity and humanity in the one Christ is traditionally compared to the union of body and soul in a single man. "For as the rational soul and the flesh form one man, so God and man form one Christ," teaches the Creed *Quicumque*.[32] Thomas Aquinas also says in various passages that he knows no better comparison drawn from the created order than the union of body and soul.[33] We have followed his warning not to conceive Christ's divine nature as the form of his human nature, or as a part of that theandric *compositum* which is Christ. More than St. Thomas—or at any rate more expressly—we have tried to make full use of the comparison in order to reach a better conception of the immediately activating, quasi-formal causality of the Word, for nothing but this causality can explain the strict unity of the God made man.

In man the spiritual soul is the form of matter, yet at the same time is not dependent on matter, but rather dominates it and takes it up into substantial unity with its spiritual being (and this is the only way in which the inner unity of the *compositum* of matter and spirit which is man can be explained). Similarly in Christ, the divine Word is the immediately activating cause of the human nature, yet at the same time is in no way dependent on it. Rather, the Word created the humanity by activating it, and hence takes it up into hypostatic union with itself (and this is the only way, in our opinion, in which the inner unity of the God-man *compositum* which is Christ can be explained).

God's supernatural activity is characterized, is made precisely supernatural, as Maurice de la Taille rightly says, by the connection with unification implied in it.[34] Or, to use Karl Rahner's words, not so much "by issuing from the cause" as "by being taken into the basic ground form." [35] Or, as Emile Mersch likes to express it, it is not God's activity *ad extra,* but God's activity *ab extra ad intra*.[36]

Christ's human nature, being the human nature of God made man, is through and through theandric, through and through supernatural, through and through pure grace. It is the "being of union" (*"etre d'union"*—Mersch) in which all other supernatural realities participate. It is *the* grace of union. Can this be expressed more beautifully, with greater theological precision or in more conformity to tradition, than in St. Augustine's formula: *ipsa assumptione creatur?*

NOTES

[1] Denz. 111a: "Secreta quadam ineffabilique conjunctione."

[2] *Comp. Theol.*, c. 211: "excedens omnem aliam unionem Dei ad creaturam."

[3] *De Unione Verbi*, a. 1: "Haec est quaedam unio singularis supra omnes modos nobis notos."

[4] *De Unione Verbi*, a. 1: "in creaturis nullum sufficiens exemplum inveni(a)tur."

[5] S.c.G., IV, 41: "haec unio perfecte ab homine non vale(a)t explicari."

[6] By "components" we do not, of course, mean any quantitative parts, *partes extra partes*, but rather metaphysical *principia quibus*, which, though objectively distinct, are all the same wholly intermingled—a *distinctio totalis in totali identitate.*

[7] Compare the critical remarks of Dom H. Diepen on "la théorie de l'exstase" in *Revue Thomiste* 50 (1950), p. 296ff, and in the *Jaarboek van het Werkgenootschap van katholieke Theologen in Nederland* (1953), pp. 15ff.

[8] For example, Karl Adam: "Jesu menschliches Wesen im Licht der unchristlichen Verkündigung" in *Wissenshaft und Weisheit* 6 (1939), p. 114.

[9] "Actuation créée par acte incréé" in *Recherches de Science religieuse* 18 (1928), pp. 253–68. "Entretien amical d'Eudoxe et de Palamède sur la grâce d'union" in *Revue apologétique* 48 (1929), pp. 5–26, 129–45. *Mysterium Fidei* (Parisiis[3]: 1931), p. 514ff.

¹⁰ "Adaptation et habilitation au Verbe," "Actuation créée . . ." p. 260.

¹¹ Augustine, *contra sermonem Arianorum*, 8, 6 (P.L. 42, 688): "nec sic assumptus est ut prius creatus post assumeretur, sed ut ipsa assumptione crearetur."

Leo the Great, Ep. 35, 3 (P.L. 54, 807): "Natura quippe nostra non sic assumpta est ut prius creata post assumeretur, sed ut ipsa assumptione crearetur."

For the same doctrine in other words: Facundus of Hermiane, *Pro defensione trium capitulorum*, 11, 7 (P.L. 67, 818): "cui (humanitati) causa oriendi totumque quod orta est, ipsa fuit assumptio."

¹² Compare the dogmatic letter *"Omnium bonorum spes"* of Pope Agatho and the Synod of Rome (680), Denz. 288: "ex quibus (adunatis in eo naturis) inconfuse, inseparabiliter, et incommutabiliter est compositus." Hence St. Thomas too, in spite of his expressly different doctrine ("neque est possibile Deum aliquo modo in compositionem alicuius venire, nec sicut principium formale, nec sicut principium materiale" [S.T. I, 3, 8]), still says of Christ's person: "dicitur persona composita, in quantum unum duobus subsistit [S.T. III, 2, 4], non ratione partium, sed . . . sicut omne illud in quo duo conveniunt potest dici ex eis compositum" (III, 2, 4 ad 2).

¹³ S.T. III, 3, 4: "tres enim personae fecerunt ut humana natura uniretur uni personae Filii." III, 3, 2 ad 1: "non potest dici proprie quod Pater assumat naturam humanam."

¹⁴ S.c.G., I, 18: "Non enim plura possunt simpliciter unum fieri nisi aliquid sit ibi actus et aliud potentia."

¹⁵ S.c.G., II, 53: "In quocumque enim inveniuntur aliqua duo quorum unum est complementum alterius, proportio unius ad alterum est sicut proportio potentiae ad actum."

¹⁶ Dom H. Diepen, "La critique du baslisme selon S. Thomas d'Aquin" in *Revue Thomiste* 50 (1950), p. 302.

¹⁷ Cf., e.g., *De Pot.*, 3. 15.

¹⁸ *In 1 Sent.*, d. 37, q. 3, a. 3, sol.: "omnes angeli, immo omnia entia, sunt in loco (metaphorice sumpta) scil. in Deo qui omnia continet."

¹⁹ L. B. Geiger, O.P., *La participation dans la philosophie de S. Thomas d'Aquin* (Paris: 1942), p. 381: "Il n'y a point d'en dehors de Dieu."

²⁰ S.T. I, 8, 2 ad 3: "nihil est distans ab eo, quasi in se illud Deum

non habeat. Dicuntur tamen res distare a Deo, per dissimilitudinem naturae vel gratiae, sicut et ipse est super omnia per excellentiam suae naturae."

[21] Cf. note 7.

[22] S.T. I, 76, 4: "anima intellectiva . . . sicut virtute continet animam sensitivam et nutritivam, ita virtute continet omnes inferiores formas" (cf. ad 3). I, 76, 5 ad 3: "anima(e) intellectiva(e), quae quamvis sit una secundum essentiam, tamen propter sui perfectionem est multiplex in virtute." III, 2, 2 ad 2: "Sensitivam nobilius est in homine propter conjunctionem ad nobiliorem formam completivam quam . . . in bruto animali." III, 2, 5 ad 1: "anima sensitiva in animalibus constituit speciem, non autem in hominibus, quamvis in nobis sit virtuosior et nobilior: et hoc propter adjunctionem ulterioris et nobilioris perfectionis, scil. animae rationalis." III, 5, 4 ad 3: "corpus melius dispositum respondet animae humanae utpote intelligenti."

[23] *De Spirit. Creat.*, 2 ad 8: "corpus trahitur ad esse animae." S.T. III, 2, 6 ad 2: "in resurrectione corpus adveniet animae praeexistenti, non tamen accidentaliter, quia ad idem esse assumetur, ut scil. corpus habeat esse vitale per animam."

[24] S.T. I, 76, 1: "quanto forma est nobilior, tanto magis dominatur materiae corporali et minus ei immergitur, et magis sua operatione et virtute excedit eam . . . Anima autem humana est ultima in nobilitate formarum. Unde in tantum sua virtute excedit materiam corporalem, quod habet aliquam operationem et virtutem in qua nullo modo communicat materia corporalis, et haec virtus dicitur intellectus."

[25] St. Thomas teaches most emphatically: "quod anima illud esse in quo subsistit communicat materiae corporali, ex qua et anima intellectiva fit unum, ita quod illud esse quod est totius compositi est etiam ipsius animae, quod non accidit in aliis formis" (S.T. I, 76, 1 ad 5).

[26] "La réciprocité de bons services"—the expression comes originally from De la Taille, "*Actuation créée* . . ." p. 254.

[27] "L'échange causal n'appartien pas à la raison formelle de la causalité": H. Diepen in *Revue Thomiste* 50 (1950), p. 300.

[28] S.T. III, 3, 1 ad 2: "Hoc autem est proprium divinae personae propter eius infinitatem, ut fiat in ea concursus naturarum . . . secundum subsistentiam."

[29] S.T. III, 3, 1 obj 2: "illud ad quod aliquid assumitur communicatur

quodammodo ei quod in ipsum assumitur." But one should remember what we have already said: the imparting is creative: *ipsa assumptione creatur.*

[30] S.T. I, 60, 5: "omnis creatura naturaliter secundum id quod est. Dei est."

[31] Augustine, *de fide et symbolo*, 7 (P.L. 40, 185): "ex quo jam spiritualibus animis patere confido nullam creaturam Deo posse esse contrariam. Si enim ille est, et de solo Deo proprie dici potest hic verbum (quod enim vere est incommutabiliter manet, quoniam quod mutatur fuit aliquid quod jam non est, et erit quod nondum est) nihil ergo habet Deus contrariam. Si enim quaereretur a nobis quid est albo contrarium responderemus nigrum, si quaereretur quid sit calido contrarium responderemus frigidum, si quaereretur quid sit veloci contrarium responderemus tardum, et quaecumque similia. Cum autem quaeritur quid sit contrarium ei quod est, recte respondetur quod non est."

[32] Denz. 40: "Nam sicut anima rationalis et caro unus est homo, ita Deus et homo unus est Christus." Cf. Eug. Schiltz, C.I.C.M., "La comparaison du Symbole Quicumque vult" in *Ephemerides Theologicae Lovanienses* 24 (1948), pp. 440–54.

[33] S.c.G., IV, 41: "In omnibus autem rebus creatis nihil invenitur huic unioni tam simile sicut unio animae ad corpus." *De Unione Verbi*, a.1: "Huius autem unionis exemplum in rebus creatis nullum est propinquius quam unio animae rationalis ad corpus." *De rationibus fidei*, c.6: "Huius autem admirabilis unionis nullum convenientius exemplum inveniri potest quam unio corporis et animae rationalis."

[34] "C'est le rapport d'union qui se trouve impliqué": "Actuation créée . . ." p. 263.

[35] Not so much "das Aus-der-Ursache-Herausstellen" as "das In-den-Grund (forma)–Hineinnehmen": Karl Rahner, "Zur scholastischen Begrifflichkeit der ungeschaffenen Gnade" in *Zeitschrift für katholische Theologie* 63 (1939), p. 146, included in *Schriften zur Theologie* I (Einsiedeln: 1954), p. 358.

[36] "Filii in Filio" in *NRTh* 65 (1938), p. 826.